—·— ·THE· —·—
WRITER'S MIND

Making Writing Make Sense

—— · Michael Adams · ——

University of Texas at Austin

Scott, Foresman and Company
Glenview, Illinois
Dallas, Texas
Oakland, New Jersey
Palo Alto, California
Tucker, Georgia
London, England

—————— • FOR MOTHER • ——————

An Instructor's Manual is available. It may be obtained through your local Scott, Foresman representative or by writing to the English Editor, College Division, Scott, Foresman and Company, 1900 E. Lake Avenue, Glenview, IL 60025.

Acknowledgments
Literary credits appear on pp. 313–320.

Copyright © 1984 Scott, Foresman and Company.
All Rights Reserved.
Printed in the United States of America.

Library of Congress Cataloging in Publication Data
Adams, Michael, 1945–
    The writer's mind.
    Includes index.
    1. English language—Rhetoric. I. Title.
PE1408.A316 1984 808'.042 83–17195
ISBN 0–673–15810–1 (pbk.)

1 2 3 4 5 6 KPF 88 87 86 85 84 83

To Students

As a writer who has lovingly labored over essays and novels, I know what all writers know, but, like fortune-cookie wisdom, it's almost embarrassingly too succinct to be true: Desire Is Writing's Best Teacher. Not mechanics, not principles, not rules, not books. Simply, the desire to get it right—perfectly right. The desire to make the sound and rhythm of your words coincide with their sense leads to the discipline necessary to make prose exact and effective.

I begin with this rather sober paragraph because as a teacher of writing for over a decade, I know you'd much rather take a pill, inject a serum, or endure a brain transplant than summon the discipline and spend the time required to write effective prose. But I also know, and empathetically I might add, that there never will be a quick way to learn to write any more than there can be shortcuts to learning to play the violin. No magic wand. No TWENTIETH CENTURY PREPACK-AGED FREEZE-DRIED DROP-IN-BOILING-WATER AND PRESTO! ALL YOU NEED TO KNOW ABOUT WRITING IN THREE MINUTES! And yet, if you do not possess this desire, if you are not consumed with passion for words as Galileo was for his stars, are you doomed to the dungeon of Frustration and Insecurity? Not necessarily. For although without genuine desire you probably won't ever be ac-cepting the Pulitzer Prize, you still can somewhat painlessly learn to write competently—and competence is no meager accomplishment in an age of general indifference to the rightness of the written word.

Learning to write efficient and effective prose is difficult because you need to know two things at once: what it is you wish to say and how to say it. It does you no good to have a good thought in mind if you do not know how to effectively put it into words; and just because you are clever with words doesn't mean you have anything worthwhile to say. To overcome this obstacle, you need to acquire the right mental habits, the ones that help you find what it is you want to say and how you should go about saying it. I suggest three steps.

I. LEARN THE PRINCIPLES THAT GOVERN CLARITY, GRACE, AND FRESHNESS

By writing, you are transferring your information or ideas to another person via the medium of the written word. And if that transfer of information or ideas into prose is not *clear,* precisely clear, then you are not fully communicating with your reader, only partially communicating. If your transfer of ideas or information is not *graceful,* then you detract from the clarity of your thought by calling attention to the medium of the message instead of the message itself, the way gaps and pops and scratches on records pull your attention away from the music *to* the poor quality of the record. If you transfer your information or ideas to another in such a way that you lull him to sleep or bore him, then you are not taking advantage of the opportunities language offers to enhance your communication by keeping the reader alert and pleased with his reading.

Part 1 of the book guides you through the principles that govern each of these qualities in effective prose. As you move through my information and advice, you will discover that I ask you not to write but to edit as you go. I do this because a good way to quickly master these writing principles (as well as to see the composition process in all its parts) is to practice looking for them as you edit someone else's prose. By doing so, you begin to acquire what I call the Editor's Mind—the mental habit of the writer consciously applying the seven principles of clarity, the seven principles of grace, and the eight principles of freshness. By becoming a better editor, you become a better writer.

II. READ CAREFULLY

If you write often, then you will have plenty of occasions to sharpen your writing, but if you don't write daily or at least weekly, then you, like musicians and athletes (people equally concerned with discipline, movement, execution), will become rusty. As in other endeavors, in writing there are mental exercises you can do to keep your mind warmed up and limber. By reading carefully, always searching for the principles of clarity, grace, and freshness, you will discover the whetstone of the prose writer. Thus, the second part of the book guides you through a reading exercise—The Reader's Mind.

III. LEARN TO WRITE FEELING, WRITE SEEING, WRITE REASONING

Most of the prose you will be composing in freshman composition will be expository—from the Latin *expositio* meaning to expound—and a wide range of writing purposes can be included under that heading. Textbooks, newspapers, magazines, college essays, business reports, science and engineering project proposals, formal letters, all expound. Since expository writing—informing, evaluating, interpreting, persuading, predicting, analyzing—is so varied, an English teacher can't give you what you want—the ONE way to write well, the One Platonic style, once mastered, owned forever. There is no such perfect expository prose piece any more than there is the one perfect musical composition. To master every kind of writing, you would have to practice every kind of writing and, as you might imagine, that could take years. I can simplify this problem for you. An effective way to master all the skills and insights needed for effective expository prose is to do three things: write feeling, write seeing, write reasoning. Writing feeling (expressing your emotions) will make you more sensitive to sentence rhythm, to tone of voice, and will make you more comfortable with punctuation, for like a composer with his various notes and symbols, you will use punctuation to regulate the rhythm of your prose. Writing seeing (description and narration) will make you sensitive to detail and to precision, and will give you practice in creating mental pictures that make reading a vividly pleasant experience for the reader. And writing reasoning (a couple of arguments in this case) will give you practice in keeping your prose well organized, logical, and exact. It will sharpen your eye for ambiguity, help you understand the logic of punctuation and grammar, and even help you find what it is you wish to say. By writing feeling, seeing, and reasoning, you will afford yourself plenty of practice in applying the principles of clarity, grace, and freshness.

The arrangement of this text, the placing of my information and advice, is a movement from the outsight of the editor to the insight of the writer. I arranged the book this way because years of teaching and being taught by my students has convinced me this is the most efficient and effective way to learn to write efficiently and effectively. You will gain confidence in your writing ability because, at last, you will understand what you are doing. By combining the outsight of the editor objectively applying the principles with the insight that practice alone affords, you will have acquired the Writer's Mind.

Acknowledgments

I am grateful to the following reviewers for the advice and insight they offered during several drafts of the text: Jeff Rackham, University of North Carolina at Asheville; David Skwire, Cuyahoga Community College; and Joseph F. Trimmer, Ball State University. I would also like to thank Harriett Prentiss, who first believed in this book and then conscientiously guided it into publication, Lydia Webster, who not only diligently edited my prose, but also took care of countless details that spared my sanity, and Dorothea Adams, who, as editor, friend, and consoler, worked with me at every stage of this endeavor.

◆ OVERVIEW ◆

• CONTENTS •

PART • ONE
The Editor's Mind

Chapter 1 Clarity

2

Chapter 2 Grace

39

Chapter 3 Freshness

93

PART·TWO
The Reader's Mind

PART •THREE
The Writer's Mind

Chapter 4 Writing Feeling

173

Chapter 5 Writing Seeing

197

Chapter 6 Writing Reasoning

Appendix

Index

PART • ONE

THE
— • EDITOR'S • —
MIND

1. Clarity

In language clarity is everything.

—CONFUCIUS

Clarity is the supreme politeness of him who wields a pen.

—JEAN HENRI FABRE

I don't care how incorrect language may be if it only has fitness of epithet, energy, and clearness.

—WILLIAM JAMES

The scientist trying to explain his discovery, the accountant preparing his annual report, the student struggling with that first college essay, even the lover needing a silent messenger for his emotion, all know the importance of clarity. And they know, as well, how difficult it is to achieve.

To write clearly you must have control of your mind. And the sad fact is most people don't. Something else is in control: a language that is unwieldy, cumbersome, and difficult to make precise—and one peppered with the bad writing habits of writers who have preceded us. The seven principles of clarity are an antidote for the difficult language and bad habits you have inherited. Following these principles will put *you* in control.

1. REMOVE REDUNDANCY

A fine watch has no unnecessary gears; a fine prose passage has no unnecessary words. Writing is movement—the writer moving the mind of the reader with his words. Just as needless gears would make a watch unnecessarily large and cumbersome, throwing off the precision of movement, so needless words can make a paragraph unnecessarily long and cumbersome, throwing off the precision of thought. Yet we use unnecessary words all the time, usually without thinking. Have you heard someone exclaim, "What an unexpected surprise!"? What other kind of surprise could it be? An expected surprise? Think for a moment. A sensational tabloid assures us we are getting the *true* facts; a general testifying before a congressional committee warns that we are in *real* danger; a father advises his son with an *old* adage. Is there such a thing as an *untrue* fact? Are we ever in *unreal* danger? Are there any *young* adages? How many times have you heard these: consequent results, usual habit, grateful thanks, integral part, proper care, grave crisis, past history, advance planning, close proximity, good benefit? Such pairs of words are needlessly repetitive and do nothing but clutter the movement of thought. If you listen carefully, you'll hear these and other needless words all around you.

young teenager	proposed plan
total annihilation	mutual cooperation
join together	and moreover
near future	as to whether
end result	dates back from
consensus of opinion	descended down
repeat again	biography of his life
adequate enough	graceful in appearance
but nevertheless	carpenter by trade
necessary requisite	8:00 A.M. in the morning
viable alternative	classified into groups
final conclusion	each and every
completely surround	separate apart
total extinction	continue on
surrounding circumstances	made up of*

Some argue that this linguistic habit began in part in the eleventh century when the French-speaking Norman conquer-

---

*On occasion (and I stress "on occasion"), some of these pairs will not be needlessly redundant. In some experiments, for example, we get preliminary results and then *final results*. In a room of several teenagers, we may have some *young teenagers* and some old teenagers.

ors of England attempted to change the official language from Latin to French. Through the decades, both the conquerors and the conquered began using synonymous pairs of words that eventually found their way into legal documents and oft-read books such as the *Book of Common Prayer.* Today we still hear the redundant results: safe and sound, hearth and home, acknowledge and confess, dissemble nor cloak, assemble and meet, pray and beseech, perceive and know, power and might, aid and abet, cease and desist, null and void. Perhaps you are hearing a nine-hundred-year-old echo when our politicians tell us they will fulfill the "hopes and aspirations" of the American people.

Regardless of its origin, you, as a speaker and writer of English, have inherited a habit that careful writers learn to kick. Each year I have a student use a *new* beginning, and every week I see a newspaper columnist allude to that mysterious *original* source, and at least once a month I read a business report or letter that gives the reader the *consequent* results. I've even seen a billboard advertising a funeral home: PERPETUAL Care: FOREVER! The redundancy didn't make me feel any more secure.

To write clearly, you must begin by removing the deadwood of the language. When you are redundant you are not taking advantage of the full meaning of a word (for example, calligraphy means the art of beautiful writing, so there is no need to say "beautiful calligraphy") and you are cluttering your prose with unnecessary words that contribute nothing and often obscure meaning. And even if redundancy doesn't obscure meaning, it still fatigues the reader, who is forced to read twenty words instead of ten. Remember that the English language leans toward redundancy. Simply remove it.

Pay special attention to adverbs. Many writers have the habit of providing a sidekick for their verbs. Thus they write, the man *slowly* crawled, the woman *quickly* jerked the cloth, the boy shouted *loudly,* and the girl *carefully* eased out the door, when each verb ("crawled," "jerked," "shouted," and "eased") has the element of its sidekick adverb embedded within it.

Remember Alexander Pope's lines:

Words are like leaves; and where they most abound,
Much fruit of sense beneath is rarely found.

FOR PRACTICE

Remove the redundancy in the following:

1. His usual habit of complaining will eventually get him fired in the near future.

2. A necessary requisite for employment with us is an individual willingness to mutually cooperate with all other employees.

3. My school was completely annihilated by the fire.

4. We have no viable alternative except to continue on our present course of action.

5. My two twin sisters will be returning again next month.

6. Surrounding circumstances will force the mandatory closing of our offices at 4:00 P.M. in the afternoon.

7. I had to consider each individual alternative the judge gave me.

8. The city council has announced its proposed plan to, in the near future, authorize a full study of the city's auditing procedures.

9. The reason why I don't have any future plans for college is because my parents are broke.

10. The end result of all this writing will be better evaluative grades.

2. REMOVE WORDINESS

A man who uses a great many words to express his meaning is like a bad marksman who instead of aiming a single stone at an object takes up a handful and throws at it in hopes he may hit. **—SAMUEL JOHNSON**

Redundancy is the use of needlessly repetitive words, usually in pairs. Closely related, wordiness is the use of more words than you need to convey your meaning. "Senator Smith, as I personally see it, I don't believe that at this point in time my committee is ready to make a decision." How else could the speaker "see it"? Can the speaker impersonally see it? Doesn't "at this point" have to be "in time"? And can't we reduce "make a decision" to a simple "decide"? Do we even need "at this point"? If we get rid of the unnecessary baggage, we're left with this: "Senator Smith, I don't think my committee is ready to decide." It's quicker reading isn't it? Here is part of a student's paragraph.

> When my parents made the statement that they were in the process of deciding which college I could attend, I all of a sudden felt hollow. I was afraid they wouldn't take into consideration the fact that I already had my preferences.

Without the clutter it reads more quickly.

> When my parents said that they were deciding which college I could attend, I suddenly felt hollow. I feared they wouldn't consider my own preferences.

Clarity is sharp, precise, lean—something impossible with such unnecessary wordiness. Take a look at some of the most common clutterers of prose:

proved to be valuable	proved valuable
made the proposal	proposed
for the purpose of educating	to educate
during the course of the discussion	during the discussion
for the price of $100	for $100
during that time	while
arrived at an estimate	estimated
enclosed herewith	enclosed
the reason why	because
the question as to whether	whether
at an early date	soon
had occasion to be	was
take into consideration	consider
at the present time	now

the fact that	that
met with the approval of Smith	Smith approved
is in the process of being	is being
make a decision	decide
in order to	to
exhibits a tendency	tends
make a change	change
all of a sudden	suddenly
of the opinion	believes
during the time that	while
in this day and age	today
made a statement	stated
resembling in nature	like

By comparing the columns above you can see how removing clutter would considerably reduce a ten-page paper. Removing wordiness makes the reading quicker and the meaning of your words more immediate. The reader doesn't have to ponder at the end of your sentence. Take a look at this.

> Herewith you will find, in accordance with your request, a copy of the contract we took under advisement.

This sentence has to "soak in" a little before the meaning is clear. The following sentence gives us the meaning *immediately.*

> Enclosed is your requested copy of the contract we reviewed.

By removing the clutter of the language, you can say precisely what you wish to say—no more and no less. Follow Robert Southey's advice: "Be brief; for it is with words as with sunbeams, the more they are condensed the deeper they burn."

FOR PRACTICE

Remove the wordiness from the following:

1. ~~I have a tendency to~~ get nervous when I have to ~~make a decision~~ whether ~~or not~~ to ~~make another investment~~ in the stock market.

2. I would like to meet with you in connection with a cur-

rent decision that is in the process of being made by your accountants.

3. The fact that our team has been failing to successfully overcome a bad press is why their morale is not as high as it should be.

4. With regard to your advice that we extend our market on a national basis, I would like to express a contrary opinion.

5. I was lucky because I had occasion to be the president pro tem of the Senate for one day.

6. The fact that this particular decision is pending at the moment means that our department cannot take definite action at the present time.

7. His hat resembled in nature the kind of hat we call a Panama.

8. Enclosed you will find a copy of my resumé, which you requested.

9. He was in the process of asking me for a date when all of a sudden the phone went dead.

10. Despite the fact that the road tests didn't conclusively prove that very high speed creates a tendency for the wheels to vibrate, we still believe that there is a possible connection.

3. REMOVE AMBIGUITY

> English is, indeed, almost embarrassingly rich in words; and although this richness affords us a remarkable flexibility of expression, it presents us with real problems of choice of speech and writing.
> —G. H. VALLINS

You see it all around you. A billboard on a busy street: ATLAS HEALTH REDUCING SPA. You go there, I guess, if you're too wholesome and need to reduce your health a little. A tombstone in a quaint cemetery:

Erected to the memory of
William Burns
Accidently shot,
As a gesture of love by his brother

Not the kind of man you want to like you. The want ads in the local newspaper:

For Sale: Three-year-old mare by transferred lady with a long tail.

No wonder they transferred her. A line in a letter from a friend I was considering visiting:

Today we plastered our walls with some friends from Brazil.

I think I'll change my vacation plans. A sentence from a steamy, soap-opera novel:

William hid the letter that confirmed he was leaving his wife in a brown suitcase.

It's now a murder mystery.

In English it is easy to say what you don't mean. If you do not scrutinize your paper for ambiguous words, phrases, or sentences, you might find yourself and your teacher or employer reenacting a scene from *Alice's Adventures in Wonderland:*

"Then you should say what you mean," the Mad Hatter went on.
"I do," Alice hastily replied; "at least—at least I mean what I say—that's the same thing, you know."
"Not the same thing a bit!"

Just because you mean what you say doesn't mean you say what you mean. Often a writer, lost in the movement of his own words, doesn't step back from the paper and examine it closely for any word, phrase, or clause that offers the reader more than one meaning. The easiest way to ferret out ambiguity is to learn the most common causes of it.

Look for Words with More Than One Meaning

Since many English words have more than one meaning, it's easy to create ambiguity unintentionally. Sometimes the ambiguity is obvious: "The woman said the material couldn't be *felt.*" But just as often the two-meaning word is not so apparent: "My mother says that I need to find some more suitable friends." Think a minute. Does the writer mean that his mother wants him to find some *more* friends who are as suitable as the ones he already has, or does she want him to find some new friends who are suitable? It's not up to the reader to decide. Make sure that no word in your paper can be read any other way. A few more examples:

> There are certain ways to capture a wounded giraffe.

> The editors told me they would waste no time in reading my proposal.

> He is an Indian philosopher.

> Gang arrested in record heist.

FOR PRACTICE

Identify the ambiguous words in the following:

1. We have a report stating that one of our secretaries was turned into a security guard last Saturday night.

2. A disciplined worker with a questionable mind will more likely than not get the job.

3. The swimsuit looked as if it had been painted on.

4. Since Mr. Miller is such an important banker, interest rises every time he enters the stock exchange.

5. The firefighter told him he was foolish to dash back into the burning house just to save his records.

Properly Place All Modifying Words, Phrases, and Clauses

In the heat and speed of writing some writers fail to notice that they have placed their adverbs, phrases, or clauses in the wrong place. "My teacher has almost read every poem written in the nineteenth century." Unintentionally, the writer has said the teacher has not completely read any poem of the nineteenth century. "My mother promised before she died to give me her collection of first editions." The writer meant, "Before she died, my mother promised to give me her collection of first editions." If you do not place modifying words, phrases, and clauses next to the word or words they modify, you might say what you don't mean. A few examples:

The student who can't write clearly needs our writing lab.

I studied the history of women at Harvard.

The report will help our employees more completely to understand our procedures.

According to our charter, no rules can be applied to members that are ten or more years old.

FOR PRACTICE

Identify the misplaced modifying words, phrases, or clauses in the following:

1. I almost slept 30 hours over the weekend.
2. John told him immediately to leave the house.
3. He placed the wood next to the house that he would burn the next day.
4. The Perryton Company signed a bid for the Marvel estate, which we haven't evaluated yet.
5. I only wanted you to know how I felt.

Make Sure Each Pronoun Refers to Only One Noun

Forgetting that the reader is not reading with his mind, the writer often forgets that a pronoun might refer to another noun within the sentence—as this sentence clearly demonstrates. Avoid confusion by double-checking pronouns and their antecedents.

_____

Identify the ambiguous pronouns in the following:

   1. Betsy carefully removed the beautiful cover from the book before taking it home.
   2. We warned her about the dog, but for some reason it didn't bother her.
   3. The numbers confused the accountants until we ran them through the computer.
   4. The students didn't read the last ten pages, so I excluded them from the discussion.
   5. After the advisors from Cronox Company talked with our committee members, they decided that the plan was not feasible.

Make Sure Each Sentence Is Properly Punctuated

   Consider this sentence: After the flood, some witness said the police quickly left with the national guard and the Red Cross and the Emergency Medical Service unit stayed behind. Who stayed behind? A comma after "national guard" says one thing; a comma after "Red Cross" says another. In the sentence, "The man is a dirty book burner," is the man "dirty" or is he a "dirty-book burner?" It's not up to the reader to decide. You learn the rules of punctuation not to placate some dusty grammarian, but to ensure that your prose is clear, that it will be read exactly as you intend.

_____

How does lack of punctuation create ambiguity in the following?

   1. He said he wanted to see no one but Peter went in anyway.
   2. However you reacted to her painting and that is precisely what the artist wanted.

3. However you interpret these figures and tell me you don't arrive at the same conclusion.

4. Above the clouds were drifting like wood down a slow stream.

5. Just as my eyes opened the door creaked and moved just a little.

The best way to guard against ambiguity is to always anticipate your readers' reaction to your words. Remember that, in general, if there's any possibility for readers to misunderstand, they will; if there's any possibility for readers to get lost, they will; if there's any possibility for readers to get confused, they will. Writing with the readers in mind means that you search through your sentences for anything that might confuse, mislead, or distract *not you,* but your readers. The student who writes, "I am going to compare Joyce's prose style to Hemingway" is not thinking what he is saying. To show you just how easy it is to *not* say what you mean, consider the following statements motorists submitted immediately following their accidents.

In my attempt to kill a fly, I drove into the telephone pole.

I had been driving my car for 40 years when I fell asleep at the wheel and had the accident.

The other car attempted to cut in front of me, so I, with my right front bumper, removed his left rear taillight.

I collided with a stationary truck coming the other way.

A pedestrian hit me and went under my car.

The guy was all over the road. I had to swerve a number of times before I hit him.

To avoid hitting the bumper of the car in front, I struck the pedestrian.

The pedestrian had no idea which direction to go, so I ran over him.

Obviously, these writers were not writing with the reader in mind. Few writing habits are more important than scrutinizing your own prose for the reader's sake. By doing so, you are not only being considerate, but also avoiding any embarrassing reflection upon yourself.

> I had been learning to drive with power steering. I turned the wheel to what I thought was enough and found myself in a different direction going the opposite way.

4. USE PRECISE WORDS

The politician who tells us we should vote for him because he "remembers the past, understands the present, and has a vision for the future" has told us nothing. Does he mean that he remembers the floods of the past twenty years, knows the present dam is not adequate, and will raise our taxes to see that a new one is built?

The reason our politicians can get away with all this nonsense is that the language permits it. English is full of *general* words (aspects, things, circumstances, situations, attitudes, relationships), *vague, meaningless* words—those a friend uses when getting you a blind date (nice, interesting, fine, great, good personality), and *abstract* words—words for concepts and ideas (justice, freedom, love, democracy, value, trust). The easiest way to say absolutely nothing is to sprinkle your prose with several of these kinds of words.

Remember that words refer to reality. If I say, "The cow is black," I am referring to a specific object and a specific color. The words *cow* and *black* have what Stuart Chase calls a referent. But what if I say, "Freedom is truth." To what in reality do the words refer? Can you show me a freedom or point to a truth? Prose that is full of words without referents becomes so vague that often the writer himself can't explain what he means.

Many students write sentences like this: "There was one nice aspect to our relationship: We enjoyed doing things together." The writer knows what he means, but he has left behind in his mind all the details necessary to give the words any meaning. Readers are not mind readers, and it is not their job to supply all the details (or referents) behind words like "nice," "aspect," "things." You are not writing to make yourself *gener-*

ally understood; you are writing to say *precisely* what you mean. Take a look at the following paragraph:

> When boys and girls are born, they are the same. They do not have any of the male-role/female-role characteristics they will adopt in later life. Genes do not determine what is manly and what is feminine. Aspects in society do that. But from birth, girls and boys are put into separate categories. Almost immediately boys are treated as boys and girls as girls even though they are both just babies without any notion of what a male or female role is.

We know what this paragraph means, but not what it *precisely* means. The writer has left behind all the detail that led up to such general words as "characteristics," "manly," "feminine," "aspects," "categories," "treated." Here is the paragraph with the detail added.

> Girls are not born with dishpan hands and boys are not born with calluses. The biological differences are obvious, but no gene determines that boys shall throw a football and girls wave pom-poms. Society's norms do that. Society places labels on our sexes as if they were products in a supermarket. Virtually from the moment of birth, boys are roughly wrapped in bright blue while girls are softly cuddled in baby pink.
>
> —Susan Jucker

In the second version the reader doesn't have to attempt to supply the details for the author.

Vagueness occurs in business prose as well.

A job application letter:	I believe my leadership qualities and self-discipline would make me an asset to the company.
A sales letter:	We offer the finest work shoe on the market today.
A collection letter:	If Hauser Company cannot or does not fulfill the obligation of the contract, our legal department will be forced to take such action as is permitted by law. I will contact you in a few days about this matter.

By substituting concrete words for the vague and general words we can make the prose precisely and immediately clear.

> My experience as a submarine captain in World War II, as president of the American Legion for five years, and as vice-president of Stans Management Systems has given me the leadership skills required in all upper-management positions.

> Our work shoes, made from the highest-grade Argentine leather, are the only hand-stitched, hand-dyed, custom-made work shoes on the market today.

> If the Hauser Company does not send the payment by August 13, we will immediately begin legal action to collect the balance owed plus all legal fees. I will phone you next Tuesday to discuss this further.

Always write with specific words. Don't make your reader try to read your mind. Imagine your frustration if your teacher gave assignments like the following:

> Write a nice two-page essay on certain aspects of democracy you think valuable to the world.

FOR PRACTICE

Identify the vague or abstract words in the following:

1. Since we didn't receive your request within an appropriate amount of time, your order will result in some inconvenience.

2. I have made adequate progress in my Spanish course.

3. Because of some technical problems we are not on schedule.

4. In difficult situations we need an administrator who can take the heat.

5. We are losing many of our good people because our competitors' facilities are better.

6. Without state regulation we should improve our financial posture.

7. Communicating was the most interesting aspect of our relationship.

8. From my grandfather I learned the value of freedom.

9. We encourage all our customers to improve the morale of their employees by offering them financial incentive.

10. Mark Twain creates circumstances and situations that we can easily identify with.

5. AVOID JARGON

Once upon a point in time a small person named Little Red Riding Hood initiated plans for the preparation, delivery and transportation of foodstuffs to her grandmother, a senior citizen residing at a place of residence in a wooded area of indeterminate dimension.
—RUSSELL BAKER

I take my new toaster back to Howard's Hardware. The manager tells me, "Before you can get a refund we must make sure the defect occurred at the factory." Later that week I receive a letter from the same man. He wants to remind me about the conditions of the warranty. "In order to initiate a refund pursuant to your request we must ascertain that the product defect occurred prior to your purchase." Why does he write like that? Does he assume that when communication moves from mouth to paper the words must automatically become pompous and stilted? I feel as if I'm no longer talking to a person, but a machine—robot talk.

The same thing happens in my office. A student tells me he wants to write a paper on Shakespeare's use of imagery in Sonnet 73. "I noticed that Shakespeare uses a dying fire and falling leaves and fading twilight to suggest his own passing years." And yet, when the student writes his paper he talks like this:

A careful reader of Shakespeare's Sonnet 73 will perceive that the poet carefully articulates his fundamental metaphor by manipulating the integration of images concerning death or dying with his own emotional and intellectual state that is projected onto nature and natural phenomenon.

Such prose impresses no one but the author. Too many people write not to communicate, but to impress—to sound intelligent and well educated. They end up, however, sounding stuffy, pompous, and mechanical. Write simply. English is difficult enough as it is to make clear. There's no need to make it more difficult by resorting to jargon, or at the other extreme, by using substandard English; write as you naturally speak. You would not say "I am fully cognizant that I must interface with the committee if we are to effectuate our policy," so don't write it. Instead, write: "I know I must meet with the committee if we are to carry out the policy." Write to communicate clearly—not to impress. Avoid robot prose, what writers call jargon: the unnecessary use of multisyllabic, pretentious, often technical, words when simple, familiar words would do just as well.

FOR PRACTICE

Remove the jargon from the following:

1. Daily muscular activity will help remove the possibility of cardiovascular problems leading to coronary thrombosis.

2. Subsequent to interfacing with the employees, the president of the company offered an affirmative response to the viable proposal they had submitted.

3. I want to pursue a career in higher education as an imparter of knowledge to students.

4. As per the invoice dated December 22, I am enclosing the balance of said debt.

5. I had an unfavorable reaction to his personality within seconds of our first interaction.

6. Herewith enclosed is the plan to maximize our market potential in accordance with federal regulations.

7. By implementing an aerial attack strategy in the second half, we facilitated our movement of the football down the field.

8. The Smith firm will finalize their audit and offer responsive input pursuant to our agreement.

9. I am a consumer information specialist who utilizes feedback procedures to advise our clients about the uses and techniques of wallpaper hanging.

10. We will implement optimal management procedures after worker-management interaction.

6. USE ACTIVE VOICE

In English we have active and passive sentences. In an active sentence, the subject does the acting: *The thief stole the vase.* In a passive sentence, the subject receives the action: *The vase was stolen by the thief.* Although the passive sentence has its uses, especially in scientific and business prose, in general you should prefer active sentences. Active sentences not only make your prose more forceful, they also reduce the number of words needed. Look at part of a long report brought to me for editing:

> Applications were reviewed and judged against criteria established by the Texas Education Agency. The review was conducted by persons from throughout the state who had expertise in programs for gifted and talented students.

Simply by substituting active verbs for the "were" and "was," I reduced the sentences to this:

> Experts in programs for gifted and talented students reviewed and judged the applications against criteria established by the Texas Education Agency.

Using the active voice rather than the passive does not always add immediate clarity, but after twenty pages of passive sentences, a writer has used twice as many words as needed and thus has slowed the quick, energetic movement of thought that makes for stimulating and clear reading. The reader's mind moves faster if the sentences are free of clutter.

The active voice also makes your prose more vigorous and forceful. Compare the following sentences.

Passive: The crystal bowl was shattered by the thunder, and the room was lit up by the lightning.

Active: The thunder shattered the crystal bowl, and the lightning lit up the room.

Note two legitimate uses of the passive voice:

1. When the receiver of the action is more significant than the actor:

General Harold Smith was given the Medal of Honor for bravery in Viet Nam.

The dog's ears were clipped last week.

2. When the actor is not known.

Aaron's arm was bruised in the wreck.

The road was paved last Friday.

FOR PRACTICE

Remove the passive voice from the following:

1. The class was irritated by his rasping voice.
2. An agreement to merge with Philco was made by the executive committee. This was on March 21.
3. The rope was released by the climber.
4. It has been proved by our experiments with plastic and paper that we can manufacture a faster skate.
5. The cards were shuffled by the dealer before she asked for bets.
6. Your impatience with the order is understood by us. New efforts will be made to improve service.
7. The national anthem was sung with sincere emotion by Margaret Mann.
8. After the contract was reviewed by our legal staff, it was signed by Mr. Dark.
9. You will be expected to hand in the assignments on time.
10. The procedures taken by our staff were suggested by Ms. Kelly Stevens. They have been reviewed by Mr. Carter.

7. USE THE RIGHT WORD

An accountant who suggests that you *continuously* review the books over the next six months is asking the impossible. He means *continually.* The car salesman who claims that the back seat of the Rolls is *luxuriant* has implied that it is covered with lush leaves and flowers. He means *luxurious.* By restricting words to specific meaning, we, in effect, keep the language precise and, thus, assure clear communication. Always make certain that you are using the proper word. Following is a short glossary of some of the most commonly confused words.

Accept/Except *Accept* is a verb that means "to receive (something) gladly." *Except* can be a verb or a preposition. As a preposition, it means "but." As a verb, it means "to leave out, to exclude, to exempt."

I *accepted* the package for my ill mother.
All the invited guests came *except* Tom.
The teacher *excepts* certain students before the exam.

All right/Alright The proper spelling is *all right;* at present, *alright* is unacceptable.

All together/Altogether A choir *all together* (at the same time, in a group) sings the melody. The same choir can sing *altogether* (in total) twenty songs. Last night they sang an *altogether* (wholly, completely) different rendition of the hymn than they usually perform.

Allusion/Illusion If you *allude* to something, you indirectly refer to it. An *illusion* is something that doesn't exist—except in the mind.

He *alluded* to Hawthorne in his poem. His *allusion* is significant.
The magician created an *illusion* with the tiger and the cage.

Amount/Number You can count marbles. You can't count flour. The marbles are a *number;* the flour is an *amount.*

There are a *number* of marbles on the floor.
There is an *amount* of flour on the floor.

It is not logical to write, "A large amount of football fans dislike Howard Cosell."

does not mean more

Another/More Another does not mean *more* or *additional.* It is not accurate to write, "We have shipped sixteen tons this month and will ship another two tons next week." The writer means an *additional. Another* implies another sixteen tons.

2 more

Between/Among When referring to three or more people, ideas, or things, use *among: Among* the movie stars were reporters, agents, starlets, and my cousin Harvey. When referring to two people, ideas, things, or places, use *between:* There was an oak desk *between* the teacher and the student.

clear

Definite/Definitive A *definitive* argument is a final argument. A *definite* argument is *clearly* an argument.

distinct

Discreet/Discrete *Discreet* means "showing strong reserve in one's behavior or speech": The secret agent worked behind her boss's back. She was always *discreet. Discrete* means "distinct, individual": Each employee has *discrete* duties.

Disinterested/Uninterested *Uninterested* means "without interest": I am *uninterested* in football. *Disinterested* means "objectively interested, free of self-interest or bias": The referee must remain *disinterested* in the football game.

physically

Farther/Further Use *farther* when referring to physical distance: The village lies *farther* up the mountain. Use *further* when referring to extensions in time or degree: We will discuss this *further* at the end of the week.

Hopefully *Hopefully* means "full of hope" or "with hope." It does not mean "I hope." Thus, you may write "The defendant *hopefully* looked at the jury." You should not write *"Hopefully,* it will rain tomorrow." In ten more years, however, usage may permit it.

suggest   deduce

Imply/Infer I *imply* (suggest, hint at) when I speak or write. You *infer* (deduce, conclude) when you listen or read. I *imply* in the above sentences that you do not know the distinction between the two words. You *infer* that I think you do not know the distinction.

Irregardless *Irregardless* is not a word. *Regardless* is, and so is *irrespective,* a word that may have led to the "ir" tag of *irregardless.*

Its/It's *Its* is possessive: The dog licked *its* foot. *It's* is the contraction of "it is": *It's* a pretty day.

Lay/Lie *Lay* means "to place."

I *lay* the book on the table.
I *laid* the book on the table.
I *have laid* the book on the table.

Lie means "to recline."

I *lie* down every day.
I *lay* down yesterday.
I *will have lain* in that bed every night for five years.

[handwritten margin notes: lay / laid / have laid / lie / lay / have lain]

That/Which Use *that* to signal defining or necessary information: The shoe store *that* was built near the river will close on Saturday. Use *which* to signal nondefining, or parenthetical, information: The shoe store, *which* opened last Saturday, is the first in our town.

Here is a brief list of other words frequently confused because they look or sound similar:

adverse	averse
casual	causal
cite	site
deprecate	depreciate
desert	dessert
emigration	immigration
incredible	incredulous
interpellate	interpolate
judicial	judicious
moral	morale
past	passed
precede	proceed
purport	purpose
quiet	quite
sensual	sensuous

FOR PRACTICE

Identify and correct the misused words in the following:

1. Hopefully, we will make our quotas for the coming year.
2. I have written seven letters of application this week and plan to write another three letters over the weekend.

3. Ms. Austin received the largest amount of votes.

4. Their trip took them further west than anyone in the family had ever gone.

5. Mary inferred to me that she might be getting promoted next month.

Absolute Words

I heard a country-and-western singer bellowing through the static on my radio: "I won't stop loving you until an hour past eternity." As an exaggerated expression of love, I might accept it, but, as an utterance with any meaning, I cannot. Eternal is eternal, and by definition there can be nothing beyond—no hour, no nothing. We call such words absolutes, and they cannot be qualified. "Fatal" is another. Overexposure to radioactivity is fatal to human beings. It is not partially fatal or very fatal. Just fatal. By maintaining the subtleties in such words, we are sustaining the language's potential for acute clarity. If we permit someone to say, "This movie is *more* perfect than that movie," then we have eliminated the idea of "perfection." The most abused absolute word is "unique" which has fallen victim to advertisers who defy logic and clarity by insisting their deodorant, their automobile, their perfume, or their toothpaste is the *most* unique. Unique means "one of a kind." It does not mean rare, remarkable, or unusual. Of course, anything that is unique may well be rare and remarkable; but anything rare and remarkable is not necessarily unique. Here are some more absolute words: supreme, final, unanimous, total, equal, empty, dead, pregnant, summit, nadir, ultimate, utmost, infinite.

By the way, *absolute* is an absolute word.

FOR PRACTICE

Identify the misused words in the following:

1. The sexual policy of this company is total equality for all.

2. The most essential thing to remember when you are before the judge is to smile.

3. In a totally unanimous decision, the officers authorized the pay increase.

4. The drawer was completely empty.

5. The report reminds us that the toxic chemical is very fatal and should be handled with care.

Application:

ASSUMING THE EDITOR'S MIND

By applying these seven principles, you will quickly become familiar with the obstacles to clarity, those dangers lurking within our language and those bad habits that make writing more difficult than it need be. Like the artist who, with his trained eye, sees more than most of us in a painting, you, with your deeper understanding, will now see more in a piece of writing, even in one of your own. And this understanding, this outsight, will give you control when you write. Removing unnecessary words will make the movement of your prose quick and accurate, a courtesy your reader will appreciate. Removing all ambiguity and jargon and preferring concrete words and the active voice will ensure that your prose is precise and direct and, therefore, immediately communicable to the reader. In short, you will ensure that your writing is clear. The habit of applying these seven principles will make you more sensitive to prose—the first step in acquiring the editor's mind.

The final step in this section, however, is to assume the editor's mind by applying the principles of clarity to two writing samples: a student essay and a business letter. I've chosen two kinds of writing to underscore my point that the principles apply to all prose. The essay and letter are designed to help you quickly "get into" editing. The best approach to take with the assignment is to acquire a kind of tunnel vision. Ignore any mistake or trouble spot that does not directly involve one of the seven principles of clarity. You will get two more chances to edit each piece. What's most important at present is that you recognize the places where the principles of clarity should be applied.

Sample Essay

My roommate is named Robert. He is one of those kind of men who looks like a hero. He is all things to all men and the apple of the eye of all the girls; always in the limelight. Although not lanky, he is tall. It goes without saying that he is of slender build, but he's not really skinny. By the same token he has muscles like a statue and is not brawny. And he's confident, but not in a cocky way. And he doesn't need more suitable companions because everyone likes him because they think he is more perfect than most people they know. I thought he was too. I was green with envy. Breezing through life, he never seemed to have any problems. But then something happened.

It was a usual evening, I had been reading a French book while cooking my hamburger casserole that was putting me to sleep. I burned the casserole and scorched the skillet which was not supposed to scorch and while eating the charred debris, it occurred to me that something was wrong with Robert. He was not his usual self. He has a tendency to talk a lot and is a usually reliable source of small talk at supper time. But this time he appeared to be quiet as a mouse. He seemed introspective. He seemed further away, not all together.

After dinner was when he laid down on the dingy couch and stared at a poster on the wall. He hardly spoke two words. These surrounding circumstances are what caused me to, in a casual way, ask him whether or not if anything was wrong. He looked helplessly at me. There were tears in his eyes. His eyes were the color of a pearl-gray winter morning. He never talked to, even for a minute, me about his problems. Solutions were always his. I was the one with all the problems. All his problems were kept in his head. They had to come out sometime.

For the next couple of hours, we laughed and talked. We also cried about his problems. He looked like a sad dog. It occurred

to me that night that Robert was just like the rest of us. The end
result of this occurrence was that I ascertained that those of us who
envy handsome men are not fully cognizant of their kind of problems. There's always more than meets the eye.

This is a mess, isn't it? The student knows what he wants
to say, but not how to say it. The essay, as you can easily tell,
is neither clear, nor graceful, nor fresh. What can we do to
make it so? We will go through the essay three times—once
for clarity, once for grace, once for freshness—as we slowly
turn this student's prose into an essay that is all three. Our first
step is to make it clear. Don't worry about grace and freshness
for the moment. Given what you now know, apply the following principles of clarity to the essay.

Principles of Clarity

Remove Redundancy
Remove Wordiness
Remove Ambiguity
   Look for words with more than one meaning
   Properly place all modifying words, phrases, and clauses
   Check that each pronoun refers to only one noun
   Make sure each sentence is properly punctuated
Use Precise Words
Avoid Jargon
Use Active Voice
Use the Right Word

My roommate is named Robert. He is one of those ~~kind of~~ [wordiness]

men who looks like ~~a~~ *the* hero *on the cover of a harlequin romance*. He is all things to all men and [use precise words]

the apple of the eye of all the girls; always in the lime-

light. Although not lanky, he is tall. ~~It goes without~~ [wordiness]

~~saying that~~ he is of slender build, but he's not really

skinny. By the same token he has muscles like a statue and

is not brawny. And he's confident, but not in a cocky way.

[ambiguity/two meanings]

And he doesn't need more ~~suitable companions because~~ ev-   *friends since*

[misused words]

eryone likes him because ~~they think he is more perfect~~   *he seems more admirable*

[use precise words]

than most people they know. I ~~thought he was~~ too. I was   *admired him*

green with envy. Breezing through life, he never seemed

to have any problems. But then something happened.

[use precise words]   [ambiguity/punctuation]

It was a ~~usual~~ evening, I had been reading a French book   *typically quiet*

[ambiguity/misplaced clause]   [ambiguity/misplaced modifier]

(while cooking my hamburger casserole) that was putting me

to sleep. I burned the casserole and scorched the skil-

[ambiguity/pronoun reference]

let which was not supposed to scorch ~~and~~ while eating the   *I was*

[passive voice]

charred debris, ~~it occurred to me~~ that ~~something was~~   *I realized*   *Robert, who*

[use precise words]

~~wrong with Robert. He was not his usual self. He has a ten-~~   *tends to talk a lot, was not smiling and not as*

[wordiness]

~~dency to talk a lot and is a~~ usually reliable source of   *cheerful as usual.*   *he is*

[use precise words]

small talk at supper time. But this time he ~~appeared to~~   *was*

~~be~~ quiet as a mouse. He seemed introspective. He seemed

[misused word]

~~further~~ away ~~, not all together.~~   *far*

After dinner was when he laid down on the dingy couch

[use precise words]   [ambiguity/misplaced adverb]

and stared at ~~a~~ poster on the wall. He (hardly) spoke two   *the Pepto-Bismal*

[redundancy]   [wordiness]

words. ~~These surrounding circumstances are what caused~~

~~me to,~~ *I asked* in a casual way, ~~ask~~ him ~~whether or not~~ [wordiness] if anything

was wrong. He looked helplessly at me. There were tears

in his eyes. His eyes were the color of a pearl-gray win-

ter morning. He never talked to, even for a minute, me

about his problems. Solutions were always his. I was the

one with all the problems. ~~All his problems were~~ *He* kept *all his problems* in [passive voice]

his head. They had to come out sometime.

    For the next couple of hours, we laughed and talked, *and cried about his insecurity* [wordiness]
about his intelligence, his fear he would not be as good a lawyer as [use precise words]
~~also cried about his problems.~~ (He looked like a sad dog.)
his father. He worried, too, that he would never find the right woman. [wordiness] [use precise words]
~~It occurred to me~~ *I realized* that night that Robert was just like the [redundancy] [jargon]
rest of us. *Even though he looked like the hero of a harlequin* ~~The end result of this occurrence was that I~~
romance he still had problems. This experience taught me [jargon] [use precise words]
~~ascertained~~ that those of us who envy handsome men ~~are~~ *don't stop to consider that they are human too.* [jargon]
~~not fully cognizant of their kind of problems.~~ There's

always more than meets the eye.

Here is what the essay might look like after being edited for clarity.

    My roommate is named Robert. He is one of those men who looks like the hero on the cover of a harlequin romance. He is all things to all men and the apple of the eye of all the girls; always in the limelight. Although not lanky, he is tall. He is of slender build, but he's not really skinny. By the same token he has muscles like a statue and is not brawny. And he's confident, but not in a cocky way. And he doesn't need more friends since everyone likes him because he seems more admirable than most people they know. I admired him too. I was green with envy. Breezing through life, he never seemed to have any problems. But then something happened.

It was a typically quiet evening. While cooking my hamburger casserole I had been reading a French book that was putting me to sleep. I burned the casserole and scorched the skillet which was not supposed to scorch. While I was eating the charred debris, I realized that Robert, who tends to talk a lot, was not smiling and not as cheerful as usual. Usually he is a reliable source of small talk at supper time. But this time he was quiet as a mouse. He seemed introspective. He seemed far away.

After dinner was when he laid down on the dingy couch and stared at the Pepto-Bismol poster on the wall. He spoke hardly two words. In a casual way, I asked him if anything was wrong. He looked helplessly at me. There were tears in his eyes. His eyes were the color of a pearl-gray winter morning. He never talked to, even for a minute, me about his problems. Solutions were always his. I was the one with all the problems. He kept all his problems in his head. They had to come out sometime.

For the next couple of hours, we laughed and cried and talked about his insecurity about his intelligence, his fear he would not be as good a lawyer as his father. He worried, too, that he would never find the right woman. He looked like a sad dog. I realized that night that Robert was just like the rest of us. Even though he looked like the hero of a harlequin romance he still had problems. This experience taught me that those of us who envy handsome men don't stop to consider that they are human too. There's always more than meets the eye.

Well, what do you think? If you've noticed that the essay is less passive, less ambiguous, less wordy, more concrete, and thus clearer than the original, but that you're still bothered by something, then you're getting a sense of the editor's mind. The "what" that's bothering you is a lack of grace and freshness. In the next sections you'll learn the principles you need to edit out these shortcomings. However, before you turn to the next set of principles and your next editing assignment, read the following business letter, which, like the essay, needs to be edited for clarity. After reading the letter, apply the principles of clarity just as you have done with the essay. You will soon discover that the principles apply no matter the nature or purpose of the writing.

Sample Letter

September 14, 1983

Mr. Harry Snub
Vice-President
Snub Pencil Products, Inc.
P.O. Box 1009
Dearborn, Michigan 48121

Dear Mr. Snub:

You inferred in your letter re March 26 that every year you almost made 50,000 of the four different kinds of pencils that we were considering purchasing for our office use. The reason why we wanted this clarification was because at that point in time we were trying to reach a decision as to whether we should bring an end to our contract with Felt, Inc. and begin a new contract with Snub Pencil Products, Inc.

Prior to signing the purchase contract, we were informed by your business manager that your company could supply us 5,000 pencils by July 30. We ordered 5,000. This was May 19. This was our first contract with your company. We signed another contract three days later for 2,000 more.

Our draftsmen and designers here at Texton were very enthused about your new and very unique product concept. It is the consensus of opinion among our draftsmen and designers that they will enable our work to get done much quicker, hopefully you will have the ability to meet our needs, but if you cannot fulfill the obligation of the contract we'll have to cancel. Pursuant to our agreement, you are being informed by this letter of any disagreement. Apparently, we have only received 3,000 order items. In a July 28 phone call your distribution supervisor informed us that you make only 15,000 pencils per year.

So far, this is just between you and me. I hope you take it upon yourself to take positive steps in this matter. Thanking you in advance.

Sincerely,

Carol C. Crowley
District Manager

September 14, 1983

Mr. Harry Snub

Vice-President

Snub Pencil Products, Inc.

P.O. Box 1009

Dearborn, Michigan 48121

Dear Mr. Snub:

[misused word] *implied*
You ~~inferred~~ in your letter [jargon] ~~re~~ *of* March 26 that every year
[misplaced modifier]
you almost (made) 50,000 of the four ~~different~~ [redundancy] kinds of

pencils that we were considering purchasing, ~~for our of-~~ [wordiness]

~~fice use.~~ [redundancy/wordiness] ~~The reason why~~ we wanted this clarification

~~was~~ [wordiness] because ~~at that point in time~~ [wordiness] we were *deciding* ~~trying to reach~~ [wordiness]

~~a decision as to~~ [wordiness] whether we should ~~bring an~~ end ~~to~~ our con- [redundancy]

tract with Felt, Inc. and begin a ~~new~~ contract with Snub

Pencil Products, Inc.

[jargon] *Before we signed*
~~Prior to signing~~ the purchase contract, ~~we were informed~~ [passive voice]
informed us
~~by~~ your business manager that your company could supply

us 5,000 pencils by July 30. We ordered 5,000. This was

May 19. This was our first contract with your company. We

signed another contract three days later for 2,000 more.

[misused word] *enthusiastic*

Our draftsmen and designers here at Texton were ~~very en-~~
[absolute word]   [jargon] *pencil designs*
~~thused~~ about your new and ~~very~~ unique ~~product concept~~.
[wordiness] *They agreed*
~~It is the consensus of opinion among our draftsmen and~~
[ambiguity/pronoun reference] *your pencils would*   *them to work more*
~~designers~~ that ~~they will~~ enable ~~our work to get done much~~
[punctuation] [misused word]   [wordiness]
quickly. We hope you can meet
~~quicker, hopefully you will have the ability to meet~~ our
[punctuation]   [wordiness]
needs, but if you cannot, ~~fulfill the obligation of the~~
[jargon] *the contract   As agreed,*
~~contract~~ we'll have to cancel. ~~Pursuant to our agree-~~
[passive voice]   [use precise words]
I am notifying you of a breach of the contract.
~~ment, you are being informed by this letter of any dis-~~
[misused word]   [ambiguity/misplaced modifier]
~~agreement. Apparently,~~ we have (only) received 3,000
[jargon] *pencils*
~~order items~~. In a July 28 phone call your distribution

supervisor informed us that you make only 15,000 pencils

per year.

[wordiness]
So far, this is ~~just~~ between you and me. I hope you take
[wordiness]   [redundancy]   [use precise words]
to provide us the pencils
~~it upon yourself to take~~ positive steps ~~in this matter~~.

Thanking you in advance.

Sincerely,

Carol C. Crowley

District Manager

Here is what the letter might look like after editing for clarity.

September 14, 1983

Mr. Harry Snub
Vice-President
Snub Pencil Products, Inc.
P.O. Box 1009
Dearborn, Michigan 48121

Dear Mr. Snub:

You implied in your letter of March 26 that every year you made almost 50,000 of the four kinds of pencils that we were considering purchasing. We wanted this clarification because we were deciding whether we should end our contract with Felt, Inc. and begin a contract with Snub Pencil Products, Inc.

Before we signed the purchase contract, your business manager informed us that your company could supply us 5,000 pencils by July 30. We ordered 5,000. This was May 19. This was our first contract with your company. We signed another contract three days later for 2,000 more.

Our draftsmen and designers here at Texton were enthusiastic about your new and unique pencil designs. They agreed that your pencils would enable them to work more quickly. We hope you can meet our needs, but if you cannot, we'll have to cancel the contract. As agreed, I am notifying you of a breach of the contract. We have received only 3,000 pencils. In a July 28 phone call, your distribution supervisor informed us that you make only 15,000 pencils per year.

So far, this is between you and me. I hope you take steps to provide us the pencils. Thanking you in advance.

Sincerely,

Carol C. Crowley
District Manager

EDITING EXERCISES

A. Apply the principles of clarity to the following:

1. ~~Taking into consideration that~~ *Since* we have no ~~one~~ on our staff ~~who is an expert on regional planning,~~ *regional planning expert* we are announcing ~~that we will be creating~~ *the creation of* a new position ~~that will be~~ opening at the earliest possible date.

2. We will not accept COD packages from companies unless they are registered by our mail department.

3. There were ~~all together~~ *altogether* twenty problems addressed continuously this year.

4. The tour guide said that the ~~most~~ ultimate point of land was ~~very pretty.~~ *exquisite.*

5. *The* Weather ~~characteristics~~ in South America have caused reanalyzation of our price options and forced us to implement reciprocal increases in wholesale costs to our customers.

6. The reason that I did poorly on the test is ~~due to the fact~~ *because* that I had a ~~terrible ache in my head.~~ *headache.*

7. I ~~almost convinced every single~~ *had almost every* child ~~that I was Santa Claus.~~ *convinced*

8. The unsigned letter ~~was believed to have been sent by John Neal.~~ *It was thought that J. signed*

9. After ~~my parents~~ visited with my roommates, ~~they~~ *my parents* said they were ~~very nice.~~ *entertaining.*

10. We need to order fifty 100 foot pipes with 2 foot nipples.

11. Below, the people looked like little ants hurrying with their work.

12. ~~My final conclusion is that~~ *I finally concluded that* this experiment ~~not only~~ represents ~~a~~ major breakthrough in linguistic research, ~~but also~~ *and* promises to turn completely around today's ~~modern~~ textbook ~~as far as approach goes.~~ *general consensus*

13. It is the ~~consensus of opinion~~ of the legal department that ~~you hold~~ a meeting with Mr. Frazer pursuant to the agreement. We ~~deem it advisable to take~~ into consideration ~~that~~ Mr. Frazer ~~has~~ a history of tape-recording conversations.

[handwritten: it is illegal for the Fence to be so close to the street]

14. The close proximity of the fence to the street is an illegal violation of the city's zoning laws.

15. It is not unusual to hear swearing in many of Shakespeare's plays. *[handwritten: swearing is common in many]*

16. While resting, a shooting star could be seen in the distance. *[handwritten: I saw, past]*

17. Farmers depend upon information from the distant past in order to know how to provide for the family. *[handwritten: about, provision]*

18. The teacher only should evaluate the student's performance. *[handwritten: and only]*

19. Faulkner is the most unique of all American writers. *[handwritten: a, after studying]*

20. I matriculated at Yale University, having studied management contingency when interfacing with employees.

21. The alarm to our house was set off by our pet parrot.

22. I have taken into consideration the surrounding circumstances of Oscar Wilde's trial and am of the opinion that he was unfairly mistreated.

23. The inspector stopped the shipment of ovens because he discovered some bugs in the product.

24. Having written the story in first person, we see all the events through the eyes of one character.

25. We preceded to a quiet site where we past our time by eating desert.

B. Apply the principles of clarity to the following letter:

Ms. Frances McKnight
Personnel Director
M. R. I. Corporation
9384 Pecan Street
Austin, Texas 78722

Dear Ms. McKnight:

I am writing in regard to your ad in the *Austin American-Statesman* newspaper for a Computer Programmer. Currently I am a senior at the University of Nebraska and have two years' worth of experience in programming, having worked on three different kinds of computer projects. One was oil and gas exploration, one was on advertising marketing analysis, and one was for the library that stored information on their inventory.

I was born and have lived in Nebraska all my life. Upon my completion of high school, I received a letter of acceptance to the University of Nebraska where I have been studying Data Processing and Analysis. I will graduate this coming May.

The fact that your ad said experience was a necessary qualification is the reason why I made the decision to apply. And the fact that your company takes into consideration the grade-point average. Mine is 3.8. This is my overall average.

As you requested, I am enclosing a resume of my past employment, schools attended, and references. Taking into consideration that hundreds of other people will be applying for the new position, I know that you will have many applicants so I want to thank you in advance for any consideration you might give me.

I look forward to hearing from you.

Sincerely yours,

Pat Meadows

C. Apply the principles of clarity to the following two paragraphs:

1. In the old trunk I only found fragments of a diary that was an autobiography of my grandfather's life. The diary didn't hardly say anything about him, but dealt more with his poetry. All we learn about him is that after moving to France the English banished him from their country. He was not a threat because he was a poet. But he was the brother of a just convicted spy. My grandfather wrote poetry about his homeland, England, for two years after his exile. He wrote twenty poems the first year and another fifteen the next. His poems are full of implication. He wrote about interesting places in France and very unique people he met, and contrasted them with similar people and places in England.

2. The reason why short story writers take into consideration the point of view of their story is that it is the point of view that determines from what viewpoint the reader will see the story. If he writes it in first-person point of view the author is limited to only one point of view—that of the narrator—and thus he cannot take his readers on a journey into the minds of the other characters. If he writes in third-person point of view, he can go into the minds of all the characters, but we lose the immediacy and intimacy of being in the mind of only one character. In both cases the end result is the same, there is something to be gained and something to be lost irregardless of the point of view chosen.

2. Grace

Beauty of style and harmony and grace and good rhythm depend on simplicity.

—PLATO

Brevity is the charm of eloquence.

—CICERO

A work has form in so far as one part of it leads a reader to anticipate another part, to be gratified by the sequence.

—KENNETH BURKER

The fluid motion of a ballet dancer gliding across the stage or a professional basketball player darting and spinning and jumping toward the basket exhibits a seemingly effortless beauty of movement, form, and proportion. We call it grace. In good prose we find the same—a continuity of movement that is effortless to read, the words chosen being so accurate, the relationships between each sentence and its parts flowing into each other so smoothly that the reader never stops or pauses or steps out of his concentration to question *meaning*. Grace is that quality that makes prose clean, crisp, precise, and very smooth. To give you a quick understanding of this phenomenon, take a look at the following passage. Imagine, as you read through the passage, a young ballet dancer whose movements are choppy, sometimes unrelated, sometimes too ambiguous to convey meaning.

The artist appeals to that part of us that is not dependent on wisdom. He is also appealing to that in us which we're given and which we don't acquire. Because of this, it's more permanent. It's also more enduring. He speaks to our capacity for delight. He also is speaking to our capacity for wonder and our sense of mystery that surrounds our lives. Moreover, he speaks to our sense of pity as well as our sense of beauty. He also speaks to our pain.

Like our imaginary young dancer, this piece of prose is clumsy, awkward, and choppy. Prose that lacks grace fails to provide clear transitions and misses opportunities to balance ideas and to coordinate and subordinate meaning so that each word and phrase assumes its proper place. In graceful prose, on the other hand, everything works. Everything moves so smoothly that the reader—unaware of the effort required to produce such ease—is carried away by the continuous movement of your words. Now look at the same words rearranged.

> The artist appeals to that part of our being which is not dependent on wisdom; to that in us which is a gift and not an acquisition—and, therefore, more permanently enduring. He speaks to our capacity for delight and wonder, to the sense of mystery surrounding our lives, to our sense of pity, and beauty, and pain.
> —Joseph Conrad, *The Nigger of the Narcissus*

The ballet dancer, the athlete, the serious writer all know that beneath the appearance of natural grace lie years of hard work and practice.

But besides making our prose easier to read, grace does something else: it actually affects the meaning of what you read. To gain a better sense of what *I* mean you'll have to turn the following pages—gracefully, of course.

1. AVOID AWKWARDNESS

When I sit down to read an essay I have the same expectations as I do when I put on a favorite record album. From the very first word, or note, to the very last word, or note, I expect smooth, continuous movement—no distracting scratches, pops, or gaps. Writing is movement. The writer moves the mind of the reader with words the way a musician moves you with notes. In order for your prose to move smoothly and continuously, you must remove anything that disrupts the graceful *movement* of your information or thoughts—anything that makes the reader needlessly pause, even if it's just for a second, to contemplate the confusion or construction of a sentence. Such gaps, pops, and scratches in prose we call awkwardness. Here are the most common causes.

Failing to Put Parallel Ideas in Parallel Form

Think about the reader. You want to keep his reading quick and energetic—his mind always moving forward, each word, phrase, and sentence arranged so that there are no unnecessary jolts in rhythm. To help make his reading smooth and easy, put parallel elements in parallel form. Notice how lack of parallelism upsets the rhythm in the following statements.

> It doesn't matter if the owners paint the walls and a new bathroom is added and finance it themselves, I still don't like the house.

> Students from New York, California, and those from Texas made it to the finals.

> I swim, go to films, read, and many other things.

Awkward sentence rhythm makes the reader too conscious of your sentence structure when he is supposed to be preoccupied with your thought. The parallel rhythm of the following sentences, however, pushes the reader onward.

> It doesn't matter if the owners paint the walls and add a new bathroom and finance it themselves, I still don't like the house.

> Students from New York, California, and Texas made it to the finals.

> I swim, go to films, read, and do many other things.

FOR PRACTICE

Rewrite the following sentences, putting parallel ideas in parallel form.

1. To accept your advice is asking for trouble.
2. Ms. Wilson was the engineer, designer, and supervised the project.

3. Poems from the Renaissance, the Victorian period, and some from the sixteenth century will be included in the discussion.

4. We hope the merger will be friendly, smooth, and a benefit to all.

5. Practicing writing is to practice thinking.

Unnecessary Repetition of Words and Sounds

By reading aloud, you can catch this interrupter of continuous movement—the pop. By paying attention only to the meaning of words and not their sounds, a writer can inadvertently jerk the reader from his concentration. "There was a purple, plastic box, pea green and peeling, sitting precariously on the porch." Unintentionally, the writer calls our attention to those p sounds and away from the meaning of the sentence.

FOR PRACTICE _____

Identify the distracting sounds in the following:

1. He positioned himself in a dignified position.

2. It had just occurred to me that what was recurring in every dream was an allegory of my current problems.

3. There was a time when lime was unknown in this country.

4. He told me that I had better write a better letter if I wanted to impress the admission board.

5. Stan showed slides of his ski trip in Switzerland.

Splitting Constructions

Sometimes it is possible to split an infinitive without any loss of clarity. "It takes a good ear *to* fully *appreciate* Chopin." "*To* truly *understand* Arnold, you should read Delaura's book." Other times, split infinitives can create ambiguity and awkwardness.

This letter authorizes us *to,* next Friday, *sell* the stock.

Our teacher wants us *to,* with the exception of the afterword, *read* the whole book.

Generally, you provide smoother reading by keeping the parts of the infinitive together.

> This letter authorizes us to sell the stock next Friday.

> Our teacher wants us to read the whole book, except the afterword.

Occasionally in English we split the two parts of a verb. "I *have* never *been* a good dancer." "We *are* not *going* to the concert." But in general, keep your verb constructions together. Split constructions can create awkward rhythms that disrupt the movement of the sentence. "We *were,* when the shark first appeared, *looking* for starfish hidden in the coral." "I *was,* just when your letter arrived, *planning* to return your call."

In general, don't split infinitives or verb parts.

FOR PRACTICE

Rewrite the following sentences to remove the awkwardness.

1. Judith told us to as quietly as possible leave the room.
2. Shakespeare was, as we were told by the guide, considered to be the greatest poet of his time.
3. I will, even though you do not believe me, return before the fall.
4. My uncle is, from time to time, calling to check on me.
5. Ms. Macdonald made it clear that to, in just three months, acquire an appreciation of contemporary poetry would require a great deal of reading.

Faulty Punctuation and Grammar

Punctuation marks, like words, have meanings. A comma tells you to pause, a dash tells you to slow down further, a period commands you to stop. If you don't understand the meaning of each mark and just use them haphazardly, you will probably create an awkward rhythm for the reader who is following your directives to pause or stop. Placing a comma where it doesn't belong, for instance, creates awkwardness:

> I walked down to the polluted creek, that, if you recall, once teemed with small fish.

Misuse of grammar causes a different kind of distraction. When someone writes, "Me and John read the scene from *Hamlet,*" the reader's attention is immediately pulled away from the words and to the questionable literacy of the writer. Poor grammar makes an essay less graceful because it disrupts the continuous concentration of the reader.

The appendix in the back of the book offers a short review of grammar and punctuation. I also recommend that you get a handbook and review it carefully. The best on the market are:

Handbook of Current English, Sixth Edition (1981; Scott, Foresman)
The Little English Handbook, Fourth Edition (1984; Scott, Foresman)
Harbrace College Handbook, Ninth Edition (1982; Harcourt Brace Jovanovich)
Prentice-Hall Handbook for Writers, Eighth Edition (1982; Prentice-Hall)
The Little, Brown Handbook, Second Edition (1983; Little, Brown)

FOR PRACTICE

Here is a quick exercise to test you on the most common mistakes in punctuation and grammar:

Properly place commas in the following:

1. I did everything to find them but Jack stayed in camp.
2. Moreover she didn't speak to me for a week.
3. According to the *Wall Street Journal* more women are moving into higher management positions.
4. After reading *"The Rape of the Lock"* I turned to my mystery novel.
5. The new building will be on a beautiful tree-covered lot.

Underscore any improper punctuation in the following:

1. I will be out of town next week, I hope you will continue the hard work.
2. There are, however some poets who don't believe in rhyme.
3. I will—moreover—bring you up to date, when I arrive.

4. There are three kinds of boys my little sister doesn't like; tall, short, and medium.

5. I read the poem "Ulysses", but I can't remember much about it.

Underscore any grammatical mistakes in the following:

1. Between you and I, the meeting was a waste of time.

2. Censorship is when one group of people tells another what it can't read.

3. I saw on television where Robert Redford is retiring from acting.

4. Either John or I is going to win.

5. The reason why I didn't play football was that my parents wouldn't let me.

6. Some friends and myself strolled through the garden.

7. To who should we send the report?

8. I laid down under the tree and cried.

9. She sat her briefcase on the desk.

10. Please join William and I for lunch next Tuesday.

When I reread anything I write, I put my pencil tip, as if it were a record stylus, above the first word and start moving it above the sentences. I want the pencil to move continuously and smoothly forward. Anywhere the movement of my pencil stops I know I'm in trouble. Something is interrupting the flow of my words. I have usually misplaced a modifier, failed to put parallel ideas in parallel form, unintentionally produced distracting sounds, put a punctuation mark where it didn't belong, or didn't place one where it was needed. I immediately remove the awkwardness and start all over, my pencil point once more back at the first word. Just as you would not give a friend an album you know is full of scratches, gaps, and pops, don't give a reader an awkward piece of prose.

2. PROVIDE CLEAR TRANSITIONS

For one movement not to flow effortlessly into the next is the constant fear of the ballet dancer for whom there can be no hesitations, no jerks, no jolts. These breaks in graceful movement are often caused by lack of concentration; they are avoided by providing almost unseen transitional gestures and movements.

In prose, transitional gestures and movements are words and phrases that link one sentence to the next. Has someone ever been talking feverishly to you only to suddenly lose his "train of thought"? The metaphor is a good one because it makes the writing process more visual. Like the couplings between the cars of a train, transitional words and phrases are what keep the train of thought within a paragraph linked together. Take a look at this:

> You have not attended one of our meetings in three years. We are removing you from our roster of active members. You have not made your last two payments for *Business World.* We are cancelling your subscription. If you wish to remain on our active roster and keep receiving *Business World,* please fill out the enclosed form and send us $35 for the past-due subscription fees.

If you read this enough times, you get the meaning. But the reader should never have to work to discover the connection between any two sentences—to do so is to take his mind away from the flow of information. Always supply the transitions in thought for the reader. Notice how the transitional words in the revised version improve the movement in the paragraph:

> *Since* you have not attended one of our meetings in two years, we are removing you from our roster of active members. *Moreover,* since you have not made your last two payments for *Business World,* we are cancelling your subscription. *However,* if you wish to remain on our active roster and keep receiving *Business World,* please fill out the enclosed form and send us $35 for the past-due subscription fees.

You have to read this paragraph only once. The transitional words guide you through the meaning. Each sentence smoothly and logically flows into the next. Here is a brief list of words—the couplings between train cars—that will help you keep your thoughts moving:

and	these	first
but	those	second
also	still	third
finally	consequently	hence
moreover	for example	for
in addition	thus	or
likewise	then	that
however	since	this

Notice the careful wording in the following paragraph from the text of resolutions by the 118th (1981) Annual Meeting of the National Academy of Sciences, which states their position on the Senate's attempt to define life:

On Human Life

It is the view of the National Academy of Sciences that the *statement* in Chapter 101, Section 1, of U.S. Senate Bill S158, 1981, cannot stand up to the scrutiny of science. *This section* reads "The congress finds that present day scientific evidence indicates a significant likelihood that actual human life exists from conception." *This statement* purports to derive its conclusions from science, *but* it deals with a question to which science can provide no answer. *The proposal* in S158 that the term "person" shall include "all human life" has no basis within our scientific understanding. *Defining the time* at which the developing embryo becomes a "person" must remain a matter of moral or religious values.

This carefully worded reply to the United States Senate sustains its clarity and grace by precise selection of transitional words and an occasional repetition to ensure that the reader's mind doesn't drift away.

I want to underscore the use of repetition of a word or phrase as a transitional device because more often than not gracefully written paragraphs combine transitional words and phrases with the repetition of pronouns that refer to preceding nouns. Repetition of words also echoes the commitment of the paragraph, helping keep the reader's mind on the track. Notice the effectiveness of this combination in the following:

The *prejudices* of past generations do not die easily. Leading a life similar to *their* human creators, *they* come into existence, thrive, and ultimately die. *Racial prejudice* in the United States is like a sick, distant relative in his twilight years that the family would rather pretend had passed on long ago; yet *racism* still exists—both in the aged who sometimes fondly remember segregation, and in their offspring, who, despite self-induced visions of open-mindedness, carry with them a longing for the days of white dominance. Flannery O'Connor's "Everything That Rises Must Converge" dramatizes the fact that society is hardly free of *racial prejudice.*

—Robert Bush

I don't want to leave you with the notion that transitional words or devices must link every sentence. Indeed, to put transitional words where they are not needed can simply bog down the reading. Often there is such an intrinsic relationship in meaning from sentence to sentence that transitional words are not necessary to maintain the smooth flow of the sentences and paragraphs. Notice in the following that you cannot separate transition from meaning.

The wild creatures I had come to Africa to see are exhilarating in their multitudes and colors, and I imagined for a time that this glimpse of the earth's morning might account for the anticipation that I felt, the sense of origins, of innocence and mystery, like a marvelous childhood faculty restored. Perhaps it is the consciousness that here in Africa, south of the Sahara, our kind was born. But there was also something else that, years ago, under the sky of the Sudan, had made me restless, the stillness in this ancient continent, the echo of so much that has died away, the imminence of so much as yet unknown. Something has happened here, is happening, will happen—whole landscapes seem alert.

—Peter Matthiessen, *The Tree Where Man Was Born*

FOR PRACTICE

In the following paragraphs mark the transitional words or devices that keep the train of thought moving smoothly:

1. But this is not the way out. To accept passively an unjust system is to cooperate with that system; thereby the oppressed become as evil as the oppressor. Noncooperation with evil is

as much a moral obligation as is cooperation with good. The oppressed must never allow the conscience of the oppressor to slumber. Religion reminds every man that he is his brother's keeper. To accept injustice or segregation passively is to say to the oppressor that his actions are morally right. It is a way of allowing his conscience to fall asleep. At this moment the oppressed fails to be his brother's keeper. So acquiescence—while often the easier way—is not the moral way. It is the way of the coward. The Negro cannot win the respect of his oppressor by acquiescing; he merely increases the oppressor's arrogance and contempt. Acquiescence is interpreted as proof of the Negro's inferiority. The Negro cannot win the respect of the white people of the South or the peoples of the world if he is willing to sell the future of his children for his personal and immediate comfort and safety.

—Martin Luther King, Jr.,
"The Ways of Meeting Oppression"

2. As the long months passed, I began to live on the slower planes and to observe more readily what passed for life there. I sauntered, I passed more and more slowly up and down the canyons in the dry baking heat of midsummer. I slumbered for long hours in the shade of huge brown boulders that had gathered in tilted companies out on the flats. I had forgotten the world of man and the world had forgotten me. Now and then I found a skull in the canyons, and these justified my remaining there. I took a serene cold interest in these discoveries. I had come, like many a naturalist before me, to view life with a wary and subdued attention. I had grown to take pleasure in the divested bone.

I sat once on a high ridge that fell away before me into a waste of sand dunes. I sat through hours of a long afternoon. Finally, as I glanced beside my boot an indistinct configuration caught my eye. It was a coiled rattlesnake, a big one. How long he had sat with me I do not know. I had not frightened him. We were both locked in the sleepwalking tempo of the earlier world, baking in the same high air and sunshine. Perhaps he had been there when I came. He slept on as I left, his coils, so ill discerned by me, dissolving once more among the stones and gravel from which I had barely made him out.

—Loren Eiseley, "The Bird and the Machine"

3. Some say the cocoa bean, from which the taste and matter we call chocolate is made, originated in the Amazon basin of Brazil, others place it in the Orinoco valley of Venezuela, while others contend that it is native to Central America. Wherever it first grew, we know only for certain that it has been cultivated for three or four thousand years in hot, rainy climates, not more than twenty degrees north or south of the equator. However, no historical reference to chocolate existed until the year 1502 when Columbus, on his fourth voyage to the New World, came upon a cargo ship in the Mexican Pacific filled with silver, gold, rare jewels and food. Among the latter, cocoa beans were included. Sensing that they somehow must be special to have been included in such distinguished company, he took them back to Spain and presented them at the court of King Ferdinand and Queen Isabella. However, no one—not even Columbus—knew what these beans could be, and they were dismissed without a second thought. Yet Columbus officially and quite unknowingly introduced chocolate to Western civilization.*

—Richard David Story, "A History of Chocolate"

3. PROVIDE PROPER SUBORDINATION

The town of Lahita consists of a trading post, a saloon, and a hotel. It sits peacefully in the Chisos Mountains.

In these two sentences, the fact that Lahita "consists of a trading post, a saloon, and a hotel," and the fact that it "sits peacefully in the Chisos Mountains," are given equal importance. But this student actually meant the following:

The town of Lahita, just a trading post, saloon, and hotel, sits peacefully in the Chisos Mountains.

---

*From "A History of Chocolate" by Richard David Story in *American Way,* February 1977. Copyright © 1977 by American Airlines. Reprinted by permission of *American Way,* inflight magazine of American Airlines.

By looking at the entire paragraph, try to see why what Lahita consists of is subordinate to its sitting in the Chisos Mountains.

> The Big Bend has only three settlements. A trailer park hugs the edge of the Rio Grande. A mining camp, built by the Comanches, functions at the foot of the Chisos hills. The town of Lahita consists of a trading post, a saloon, and a hotel. It sits peacefully in the Chisos Mountains.

To give the details of Lahita a full sentence, and thus to give them value equal to that of the other "settlements" in Big Bend, is to stray from the opening commitment, is to upset the balance and rhythm already established by the second and third sentences, and is to not place words in their logical and most meaningful order.

We frequently see this in business letters:

> Federal regulation E484 requires that we audit all work we subcontracted, and it must be done every six months. It takes three or four days and will require your full cooperation. We have two accountants who work full time for us, and they will arrive in Boston on April 10. This will be a week before the deadline.

Now, think about the following questions: Do "Federal regulation E484 requires that we audit all work subcontracted" and "it must be done every six months" deserve equal emphasis? If the answer is no, then we must subordinate one element:

> Federal regulation E484 requires that we audit every six months all work we subcontracted.

Are "It takes three or four days" and "will require your full cooperation" of equal importance? If not, then we subordinate:

> We will require your full cooperation for three or four days.

or:

> Taking three or four days, the audit will require your full cooperation.

Which is more important: "We have two accountants who work full time" or "they will arrive in Boston on April 10"? Proper subordination answers the question.

Our two full-time accountants will arrive in Boston on April 10.

Does "This will be a week before the deadline" deserve equal emphasis with the other sentences? Probably not. Thus we write:

Our two full-time accountants will arrive in Boston on April 10, a week before the deadline.

Subordinating sentences into clauses and clauses into phrases and phrases into adjectives helps you say more precisely what you mean. By giving your main idea the most emphasis and subordinating accordingly the remaining elements of your sentence or paragraph, you are, in effect, organizing meaning through sentence structure. This means that you are thinking clearly, which is a prerequisite for writing gracefully. Just as our ballet dancer must know the dominant movement (a leap, say) and the subordinate movements (a pointed toe, a curved hand), so a conscientious writer must know his dominant thought, around which he will organize the modifying or subordinate elements so that every part of his thought receives its proper emphasis.

To underscore this point, consider the following paragraphs. Both say the same thing. Both are clear. But notice how gracefully the second paragraph flows. It does so because of careful subordination.

Emily Dickinson was fascinated with death and immortality. She often wrote about it in her poetry. There she struggles with her will to believe that there is an afterlife and her propensity to doubt it. This struggle became a daily battle. She handles this battle with death by personifying it. She makes death an occasional visitor. He becomes someone to whom she can speak frankly. This gives her a personal relationship with death. It also enables her to mock death. Often she treats him no more respectfully than a flattering suitor. This helps her overcome her fear of death as well as her awe of it. At the same time she can ignore any philosophical or theological consideration of it. Death for her is an emotional and personal experience. She has this experience with a frequent visitor named Uncertainty.

Emily Dickinson was fascinated with death and immortality. In her poetry she struggles with her will to believe in an afterlife and her propensity to doubt it. She handles this daily battle with death by personifying it, by making death an occasional visitor to whom she can speak frankly. Not only does this give her a personal relationship with death, but it also enables her to even mock death, whom she often treats no more respectfully than a flattering suitor. The result is that she can overcome her fear and awe of death and at the same time ignore any philosophical or theological consideration of it. Death for her is an emotional and personal experience with a frequent visitor named Uncertainty.

Two important notes: a) It is indeed true that subordination can improve the rhythm, gracefulness, and meaning of sentences. I can take a sequence of sentences like the following and, by subordinating, create a less choppy, more graceful, and more precise statement.

Shawn and I took a walk. It was midnight. We went along a brook that was murmuring. The brook moved like a snake through the forest.

Shawn and I took a midnight walk along a murmuring brook that moved like a snake through the forest.

But it is equally true that excessive subordination creates a monotonous cadence (made up of a sequence of modifiers, clauses, and phrases) that calls too much attention to itself.

The old, dilapidated, grey, two-story mansion rested at the edge of the river that was well known for its reptilian midnight visitors who crawled out of the water to feast on the debris left behind by the campers who had spent the weekend celebrating the Fourth of July.

He is the kind of counsellor who knows what to tell students who have problems with parents who won't talk to teachers who seek their cooperation.

You want, then, to arrange the parts of your sentence so that every part receives its proper emphasis—no more and no less than it deserves—but you do not want to do so at the expense of creating a droning rhythm that has as much variety as a ticking clock.

(b) You also want to make certain that you do not subordinate your main idea. Look at this sentence:

Just as the boy ran into the road, I turned the corner.

"I turned the corner" receives the full emphasis of the sentence when it should be subordinated to a clause.

The boy ran into the road just as I turned the corner.

If you do not place your subordinate ideas or information into clauses or phrases, you can easily mislead the reader. In the following, for example, we are led to believe that the boxer's exhaustion is more important than his signaling the referee to stop the fight:

Bill was exhausted from his opponent's powerful punches when he signaled to the referee to stop the fight.

If we subordinate properly, we arrange the same material into its more logical and graceful form.

Exhausted from his opponent's powerful punches, Bill signaled to the referee to stop the fight.

These subtle adjustments in prose, which the reader is never aware of, keep the reading smooth. By giving all your ideas their proper emphasis—by arranging them into sentences, clauses, phrases, and modifiers—you make the reading accurate and efficient—two important qualities in graceful movement.

FOR PRACTICE

Turn the following groups of words into a sentence, or sentences, with graceful and logical emphasis by subordination (turning sentences into clauses, phrases, adjectives or adverbs; turning clauses into phrases; turning phrases into adjectives or adverbs.)

1. Fayette Construction began pouring the foundation in May. This was two weeks after the date agreed upon. But they stopped. There was a disagreement between the architect and the engineer.

2. My favorite books are on the book shelf that is blue. It is against the north wall.

3. The assistant who helps the teacher will be holding meetings Monday in the afternoon. She will be helping the students prepare for the final exam. The exam will be three hours long.

4. The factory will be large. It will be surrounded by a wire fence. Trees will conceal the fence.

5. The song was first heard on the radio in two places. One was Boston, and one was San Francisco. It was Christmas Eve. The number of people who listened in each city was estimated to be just about the same. Twenty thousand in each city.

4. WRITE IN AN APPROPRIATE VOICE: AUDIENCE AND PURPOSE

When it comes to taking chances, some people like to play poker or shoot dice; others prefer to parachute jump, or go rhino hunting or climb a mountain. But I like to get drunk and drive like a fool .... There are three basic pieces of equipment that one needs to enjoy this art form. The first one is a car. It is very important to have the right car; you need a car that handles really well. This is a critical factor and there's a lot of debate on this subject—about what kind of car handles best. Some say a front-engine car; some say a rear-engine car. I say a *rented* car. Nothing handles better than a rented car. You can go faster, turn corners sharper, and put the transmission into reverse while going forward at a higher rate of speed in a rented car than in any other kind. It is also important that the car be big. This is because when something happens in a really big car, like speeding through a pack of pedestrians, it happens very far away—way out at the end of your fenders. It's like a civil war in Africa; you know about it, but it doesn't really concern you too much. On the other hand, when something happens in a little bitty car it happens all over. You get all involved in it and have to give everything a lot of thought.

You could probably tell from P. J. O'Rourke's tone in the above piece that the article did not appear in *Popular Mechanics.* The editors at *Popular Mechanics* know their audience intimately and would never risk offending it. The readers of *The National Lampoon,* however, expect to be offended. Keeping your audience in mind helps you find the "voice" in which you want to write.

In principle 5 under Clarity, I urge you to write in your own voice without using jargon, slang, or substandard English. Here, I want to qualify that principle a little. You actually have several voices as a writer, and the one you use is determined by your purpose and audience. Let me show you what I mean. Here is one of my students complaining (purpose) to her classmates (audience) in prose.

Technological Brat

Its perfunctory beeps speak, but do not hear, its cathode rays respond, but do not feel, and as I try to establish a rapport with this aloof creation of technology, it blinks and stares, but does not see. A nasty sibling in the family of electronic ingenuity, the computer is a senseless being which randomly deals its merciless blows. People who have not become well acquainted with these smug monsters may describe computers as a boon to progress, but I call them a nuisance.

—Carmen Hill

Now here is the same student informing (purpose) the public (audience) in the campus newspaper for which she is a reporter.

The most highly endowed university in the nation, The University of Texas, besides being in the business of higher learning, is also in the business of higher profits. Royalties from oil and gas profits, which finance the wealthy Permanent University Fund, investments in a variety of large companies, and a complex network of managerial functions make the University a place where "business as usual" means more than just holding classes.

And here she is reminiscing (purpose) to herself (audience) about a favorite haunt that had just been torn down.

But Hank's on the Hill lounge was more than a beer-only bar with slanted pool tables and a cracked, concrete floor; it was a hub of social diversity where hands calloused by hard work shook hands studded by diamonds. . . . And amid the numerous "no gambling" and "no hustling" signs that adorned the walls, I learned to do both.

And finally, here is the same student analyzing (purpose) a poem for her teacher (audience).

In "To a Waterfowl," William Cullen Bryant relates the character of a small bird to the life of mankind. Man's destiny, like the waterfowl's, is to pursue a solitary path. In search of a goal, which is determined by instinct, the bird strives for that which is unknown to him, "long wandering, but not lost." Man is also driven by this hidden force, faithfully abiding by his lot of solitude even as the dusk of his life grows near. As this guiding life energy leads the waterfowl to its "sheltered nest," it takes man to his eternal resting place as well.

As you can see, in each example this student writes in a voice appropriate to her audience and purpose. When she is giving information in the newspaper she avoids any distracting subjective, self-indulgent wit, any highly connotative words that would pull the reader's mind away from her purpose—to *inform*. But when she writes for her peers and about her own feelings, she chooses subjective, highly connotative words, she plays with sentence rhythm and imagery, all working in harmony with her purpose—to *express*. When she writes for her teacher, she maintains a serious, yet casual tone of voice fitting for her purpose—to *analyze*. What you never hear in the above paragraphs is that pompous, robot voice I cautioned against earlier. "It is incumbent upon me to articulate my observations and opinions about this poem. . . ." What you do hear is an honest voice—never the same voice, but always *her* voice. Write in a voice appropriate to your audience and purpose.

FOR PRACTICE

Consider the appropriateness of the voice in the following paragraphs. Which is appropriate? Why?

1. Sherwood Anderson's "I Want to Know Why" is a neat story with plenty of interesting characters. Unfortunately we don't get to know those other characters because Anderson limits our point of view to only one character. He puts blinders on us, so to speak. Had he told the story from the third-person point of view, we would gain some insight into his friends and the black horse trainer and especially Jerry Tilford. But no! Instead, Anderson gives us the world through one boy's eyes, and even if this point of view makes us empathize with the narrator, it frustrates the reader who, like a beggar at Thanksgiving, wants to see more on the table.

2. In Sherwood Anderson's "I Want to Know Why" a fifteen-year-old boy narrates an event that thrusts him from innocence to experience, from boyhood to manhood. We literally share the boy's reaction to the smell of coffee and manure and horses and the racetrack air: "It just gets you, that's what it does." And we endure the boy's profound disappointment as he watches his idol sneak into the "ugly" house. "Then, all of a sudden, I began to hate that man. I wanted to scream and rush into the room and kill him. I never had such a feeling before. I was mad clean through that I cried and my fists were doubled up so my fingernails cut my hands." But while this first-person point of view gives us an intimate relationship with the narrator, it also limits the possibilities for the story—we are left without knowing Jerry Tilford's motives, the black man's honest feelings toward the boys, and the reaction of the other boys who witness the narrator's coming of age.

3. One of the most important elements in the short story is the technical consideration of point of view. For it is the control of point of view that enables a writer to articulate his themes and determine the exact perspective from which the readers will engage the story. In a story like Sherwood Anderson's "I Want to Know Why," we witness a testimonial-like tone as the narrator, a fifteen-year-old boy, guides us through his landscape of emotion while we watch him move from the sensuous joy of innocence to the forboding, pondering state of experience and maturity—all punctiliously controlled by the author's manipulation of point of view.

5. KNOW YOUR DIRECTION:
Commitment and Follow-Through

It's all right to have a train of thoughts, if you have a terminal.
                                                        —BOWKER

"Follow through!" shouts the potbellied coach, whether teaching you how to swing a golf club, or throw a ball, or shoot a basket, or serve a tennis ball. "Follow through!" Committing himself to a certain stroke (say a backhand) and then following through, keeps the tennis player under control, and this control becomes grace when the player executes the stroke so automatically that the movement appears "natural." You can keep your writing under control by always following through on every commitment you make. This is precisely the reason your high-school teacher demanded you write topic sentences from which everything must follow. Your teacher wanted each paragraph to have a smooth direction, just as the tennis coach wants each stroke to have a smooth follow-through.

But some writers make commitments, creating anticipation for the reader, that they never fulfill.

The Chisos Mountains are terrifyingly beautiful. A muddy river runs through a deep gorge and a green cottage rests at the edge. Only a dirt road winds near the gorge.

I was expecting dark detail about those "terrifyingly beautiful" mountains, but my expectations were never satisfied. Do a muddy river, green cottage, and winding road create terror? Beauty? By not following through on his commitment, the writer leaves me hanging. The equivalent of a tennis player starting a stroke but never completing it.

Here, in prose, is the equivalent of a tennis player who starts a swing, then decides at the last second to change strokes.

> Wine is a far more healthful drink than beer. In the past five years Americans have consumed more wine than they did in the last fifteen. This sudden popularity can be attributed to a number of factors.

The writer made the commitment to tell us why wine is a "more healthful drink than beer," but immediately moves onto another commitment. Even though the writer may follow through on the second commitment, the reader has still had expectations created that are never fulfilled and *that* upsets the smooth movement of the thought.

And finally, here is the tennis player who, when the ball approaches him, does everything at once: he jumps and turns and starts to swing, then hesitates, then moves from backhand to forehand and commits himself to every possible tennis stroke, but follows through on none.

> The United States government should draft women. The present selective service laws discriminate against men. We are becoming a machine-computer-oriented society. Machines, not men, will fight our next wars. The threat of nuclear war is becoming more ominous every day.

Rather than giving us one commitment and fulfilling it, this writer makes a series of commitments, each of which could be a paragraph or even an essay in itself. By trying to say everything at once the writer ends up saying nothing.

Grace is smooth movement, and one element of such movement in writing is moving from the commitment to its follow-through. You create expectations for the reader and then fulfill them. Notice how commitment and follow-through make the following read smoothly.

> Although we are accustomed to thinking of the earth's crust as relatively stable, except in places where earthquakes or explosive volcanoes suddenly and visibly dislocate it, *the earth is continuously changing.* Streams erode the land and deposit large quantities of sand, silt, and clay onto lowlands or into the sea. Even the outer part of the solid earth, its crust, moves en masse. Careful observations on lake levels show that the land north of the Great Lakes has been rising at a rate of about 16 inches per century. Similarly, tidal-gauge records show that certain places beside the Baltic Sea have been rising at a rate of more than 3 feet per century. Fossil sea shells in rocks now thousands of feet above sea level indicate extensive movements of the same sort in the past.
> —William H. Emmons et al., *Geology: Principles and Processes*

You want to remember that you not only commit yourself to a certain topic, but also to a certain tone *and* certain types of paragraph development. If you begin informally don't drift into the formal. And if you tell your reader Brand X is better than Brand Y, then know that you have committed yourself to a comparison and contrast paragraph.

One effective way to establish clearly your commitment for the reader is to ask a question that is in turn answered by the essay. Here is an example.

> The abortion issue in our time has been likened to the slavery issue in the 1800s: emotions run high, and the citizenry is deeply divided over what is universally acknowledged to be more than a superficial issue. In fact, there is a more fundamental similarity: in both cases an important underlying issue is, *What is a human being?*
> —Roger Bissell, "A Calm Look at Abortion Arguments"

One final point. Always try to narrow your commitment. An essay entitled "The Way Advertisers Treat Men in Magazines" is the subject for a book. Narrowing it to "The Way Advertisers Treat Men in *Vogue* Magazine" doesn't help much since there will be a large variety of ads in the magazine. "The Way Men Are Depicted in Cigarette Ads in *Vogue*" is getting the topic down to size. Often, students commit themselves to do too much, and the result is a paper full of generalizations and very little detail—a lot of commitment and little fol-low-through.

FOR PRACTICE

Evaluate the commitment and follow-through within the fol-lowing paragraphs:

1. Students who come to college on an athletic scholarship assume a tremendous responsibility. They must demonstrate intelligence academically as well as physical ability. The coach-ing staff often denies athletes time for education as winning seems more important than studying. College athletes gear their minds towards learning plays rather than chemical formu-las. Workouts leave little time for other benefits of college such as maturing and experiencing. Whatever spare time remains should be consumed by studying, but too often, athletes must find their "release" and neglect the books. Athletes can break all records on the playing field and fail all their courses. And one day they might find themselves standing in the unemploy-ment line because they were never mature enough to accept the responsibility of getting an education.

2. Mary's room gives off a very warm feeling of home. Her bed rests just before her window, and on each side is a stereo speaker. The fifteen-hundred dollars of sound vibrates the floors. The floor is carpeted in white and the walls are light blue. Her television sits upon her dresser. On the walls are prints of her favorite paintings.

3. If students are going to get the most out of their college experience, they must prepare to do two things: 1) to disci-pline themselves for the long hours required for study, 2) to resist the numerous temptations luring them away from their studies. Discipline means staying at the library until closing and setting the alarm thirty minutes early so you can review that last chapter and learning to read while you eat. Resistance

means ignoring your best friend's plea to join you for a party and refusing to go to the movie the night before an exam and even, on occasion, saying "no" to someone who would like to be with you on a Saturday night.

6. KNOW YOUR DIRECTION:
Form and Organization

Writers organize their movements according to their material. It is their obligation to the reader to organize their ideas or information into the most efficient and effective form. If, for example, you are recounting the history of the Norman Conquest, the most efficient organizational form would be chronological. You would lose us if you jumped back and forth between years and events. If you are giving instructions for building a model airplane, you would organize your paragraph sequentially: first, second, third. If you are describing a scene, you might, as many movie directors do, begin with a panoramic view (the desert and the fort in the distance), move closer (the outside gate made of thick logs), and closer (the courtyard with watering trough and hitching posts), and closer (the captain's front door—"Captain" at the top), and closer still (John Wayne sitting in bubble bath). We call this *form* of organization spatial—the writer moving the reader's mind through space. Notice the movement of your mind's eye as you read the following:

> There was one star still burning in the sky. Beyond the flat roofs of the intervening houses the Sea of Galilee was lying cold and grey like an old mirror, unruffled by any wind of dawn. On the opposite bank the savage Gergesene hills halted at the water's edge like crouching beasts. Behind these hills a faint pink glow filled the sky, growing every second more powerful; it widened and spread, quenching the last star, and giving, even before the sun rose, the thinnest shadows to palm trees and houses.
> —H. V. Morton, *In Search of the Holy Land*

You can guide your reader's mind in an infinite number of ways. There is no such thing as one best way to organize a paragraph. But although the types of paragraphs, and thus means of organizing and presenting material, are infinite, certain kinds of paragraph strategies and organization appear again and again—just as traditional and frequently repeated movements reappear within ballet's endless variety of motion. The reason these movements appear so frequently is that they are very efficient ways to arrange the structure and movement of a paragraph. Moving from general statement to particular example is probably the clearest and most efficient way to say the following:

> Every landscape in the world is full of these exact and beautiful adaptations, by which an animal fits into its environment like one cog-wheel into another. The sleeping hedgehog waits for the spring to burst its metabolism into life. The humming-bird beats the air and dips its needle-fine beak into hanging blossoms. Butterflies mimic leaves and even noxious creatures to deceive their predators. The mole plods through the ground as if he had been designed as a mechanical shuttle.
> —Jacob Bronowski, *The Ascent of Man*

And comparison and contrast is probably the most effective and efficient way to say this:

> When a mother is afraid that her child will die when it has only a pimple or a slight cold we speak of anxiety; but if she is afraid when the child has a serious illness we call her reaction fear. If someone is afraid whenever he stands on a height or when he has to discuss a topic he knows well, we call his reaction anxiety; if someone is afraid when he loses his way high up in the mountains during a heavy thunderstorm we would speak of fear. Thus far we should have a simple and neat distinction: fear is a reaction that is proportionate to the danger one has to face, whereas anxiety is a disproportionate reaction to danger, or even a reaction to imaginary danger.
> —Karen Horney, *The Neurotic Personality of Our Time*

Comparison and contrast and moving from general to particular are just two of the ways we naturally and efficiently organize our thoughts or information for the reader. If you will look through a nonfiction book (anything from a gardening text to

a history of the Civil War) or any news and information magazine, I predict that, among the wide variety of kinds of paragraphs, you will discover a large percentage within each essay
or chapter or article that do one of the following:

Move from general statement to particular examples
Move from particular examples to general statement
Move spatially—description
Move through time—narration
Define a term
Use an analogy
Move from cause to effect or from effect to cause
Classify
Compare and contrast
Illustrate a point with an extended example
Explain a process
Any combination of the above

These strategies, coming from the natural way we all think,
improve the graceful flow of your prose because they are very
efficient ways to arrange the movement of material. When an
essay is composed of a series of *efficient* units of thought we call
paragraphs, the reader can move easily and pleasantly through
the prose. It is not enough, then, for each sentence to be gracefully written. The form or strategy within which the sentence
appears actually contributes to the graceful movement of the
entire essay.

Remembering these strategies for paragraphs also helps the
writer find his thoughts when he is uncertain in what direction
to move. Assume, for example, that you have been assigned
a paper in which you must explain American football to a foreign student from Africa. Instead of pondering for several minutes in search of a way to handle the topic, you ought to run
down the list of paragraph patterns and see if you can use any
of them to help you find your ideas. Can I compare football
to anything? Can I organize any information chronologically?
Can I use an analogy? And so on. Quickly, then, the answers
and ideas come back to you. Yes, I can compare football to

soccer—something the reader is familiar with; yes, I can devote a paragraph to the history of the game; yes, I can compare football to a war, complete with generals (quarterbacks and coaches), artillery (passing game), a front line and a goal line. Since you will naturally use the strategies I mention here, you might as well go to them to begin with, if for nothing else, to get you started thinking about your topic. I will explore paragraph development more completely in Part 2. For now, just remember that you can make your prose efficiently graceful by using the traditional paragraph forms. Write prose that has good form.

FOR PRACTICE

Even though there are an infinite number of ways to develop a paragraph, certain kinds of paragraph strategies appear again and again. See if you can identify the strategy in the following:

1. The middle- and upper-class Englishman, on the other hand, is brought up in a nursery shared with brothers and sisters. The oldest occupies a room by himself which he vacates when he leaves for boarding school, possibly even at the age of nine or ten. The difference between a room of one's own and early conditioning to shared space, while seeming inconsequential, has an important effect on the Englishman's attitude toward his own space. He may never have a permanent "room of his own" and seldom expects one or feels he is entitled to one. Even Members of Parliament have no offices and often conduct their business on the terrace overlooking the Thames. As a consequence, the English are puzzled by the American need for a secure place in which to work, an office. Americans working in England may become annoyed if they are not provided with what they consider appropriate enclosed work space. In regard to the need for walls as a screen for the ego, this places the Americans somewhere between the Germans and the English.

—Edward T. Hall, *The Hidden Dimension*

2. The sophomore had left college to "find herself," rather as if she were a set of misplaced keys. She had the notion that her mind was a collection of pockets and if she searched in each one of them long enough she would find the keys to unlock this self.

—Ellen Goodman, "Inward Bound"

3. He was born in Bad Ocheim, Germany, in 1829, and during the European political turmoil of 1848 decided to take his chances in New York, to which his two brothers already had emigrated. Upon arrival, Levi soon found that his two brothers had exaggerated their tales of an easy life in the land of the main chance. They were landowners, they had told him; instead, he found them pushing needles, thread, pots, pans, ribbons, yarn, scissors, and buttons to housewives. For two years he was a lowly peddler, hauling some 180 pounds of sundries door-to-door to eke out a marginal living. When a married sister in San Francisco offered to pay his way West in 1850, he jumped at the opportunity, taking with him bolts of canvas he hoped to sell for tenting.

It was the wrong kind of canvas for that purpose, but while talking with a miner down from the mother lode, he learned that pants—sturdy pants that would stand up to the rigors of the diggings—were almost impossible to find. Opportunity beckoned. On the spot, Strauss measured the man's girth and inseam with a piece of string and, for six dollars in gold dust, had them tailored into a pair of stiff but rugged pants. The miner was delighted with the result, word got around about "those pants of Levi's," and Strauss was in business. The company has been in business ever since.

—Carin C. Quinn
"The Jeaning of America—and the World"

4. Because of the way it came into existence, the solar system has only one-way traffic—like Piccadilly Circus. The traffic nearest the centre moves fastest; that further out more slowly, while that at the extreme edge merely crawls—at least by com-

parison with the fast traffic near the centre. It is true that even the furthest and slowest of the planets covers nearly three miles every second, which is about 200 times the speed of an express train, but this is a mere crawl in astronomy. The planets Mercury and Venus, which constitute the fast traffic near the centre, move, the former ten and the latter seven, times as fast. We shall find the reason for all this later; at present we are merely concerned with the facts.

—Sir James Jeans, "A View of the Solar System"

5. The quasi-official division of the population into three economic classes called high-, middle-, and low-income groups misses the point, because as a class indicator the source of money is almost as important as the amount. Key distinctions at both the top and the bottom of the class hierarchy arise less from degree of affluence than from the people or institutions to whom one is beholden for support. For example, the main thing distinguishing the three top classes from one another is the amount of money inherited in relation to the amount currently earned. The Top Out-of-Sight class (Rockefellers, du Ponts, Mellons, Fords, Whitneys) lives entirely on inherited capital. There, money is like the hats of the Boston ladies who, asked where they get them, answer, "Oh, we *have* our hats." No one whose ample money has come from his own work, like film stars, can be a member of the Top Out-of-Sights, even if the size of his current income and the extravagance of his expenditure permit him temporary social access to it.

—Paul Fussell, "A Dirge for Social Climbers"

7. KNOW YOUR PURPOSE

Compare the following:

Nothing is more detrimental to the health of the American mind than television. This medium, unlike all others, encourages conformity, mindlessness, and sloth.

—ANONYMOUS

Television is a vast, phosphorescent Mississippi of the senses, on the banks of which one can soon lose one's judgment and eventually lose one's mind. The medium itself is depressing. The shuddering fluorescent jelly of which it's made seems to corrode the eye of the spectator and soften his brain.

—JONATHAN MILLER, "MEDIUM"

Film art is the only art the development of which men now living have witnessed from the very beginnings; and this development is all the more interesting as it took place under conditions contrary to precedent. It was not an artistic urge that gave rise to the discovery and gradual perfection of a new technique; it was a technical invention that gave rise to the discovery and gradual perfection of a new art.

—ERWIN PANOFSKY, "STYLE AND MEDIUM IN THE MOVING PICTURES"

If you examine these closely, you will see that, while the three writers have chosen similar subjects, they have not chosen the same purpose. Anonymous is *arguing.* He wants the reader to understand his point of view which he will support with relevant facts. He does not want to distract from his central argument by making judgments he cannot support, or using words that call too much attention to themselves and thus lead the reader's mind away from the main point. In the second passage, however, Jonathan Miller seeks out those highly connotative words, that passionate sentence rhythm—for he is not arguing, but rather *expressing* himself. To introduce somber and serious tones would spoil the fun he and the reader are having, and would certainly make the reader ask "Is he serious?" In the last passage, Erwin Panofsky is not arguing or expressing, but rather *informing,* explaining and at times analyzing, the evolution of a twentieth century art form. To borrow the loaded and metaphorical words of Miller would distract from the genuine seriousness of his purpose. Knowing your purpose, then, helps you remain consistent.

Indeed a recurring problem in both business letters and college essays is a lack of clear purpose. Papers that begin as an argument, requiring a specific kind of development and demanding logic, somewhere near the middle wander into pure opinion or expression and never return to the initial purpose.

Or business people try to do two things in one letter when it would be better to send two.

A good way to keep your purpose in focus is to visualize this triangle:

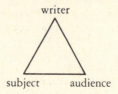

Every writing activity has three facets: writer, subject, audience. Always ask yourself "Which corner of the triangle am I *mainly* concerned with?" If you are mainly concerned with the subject matter before you, then you are probably *informing* (writing a newspaper story, a history essay, an annual report, a new law). If you are mainly concerned with your audience, then you are *persuading* or *arguing* or *entertaining* (writing a law brief, selling your firm's services, telling an anecdote). If you are mainly concerned with the writer—that is, your own feelings—then you are *expressing* (writing a diary, expressing your love, complaining in a letter to the editor). Often these purposes will overlap—information about lung cancer and cigarette smoking can be both informative and persuasive—but always isolate your *major* purpose. It keeps your thoughts on track. Let me give you a brief example of a writer confusing purposes:

> An art-history course should be required for every university graduate. Well-rounded graduates will serve as better ambassadors for our institution. Arts are the flowers amidst any academic jungle. It is by studying them that we come to understand ourselves for we recognize the artist's inner compulsion to create as our own. Art is not luxury, but necessity; not frivolous indulgence, but meaningful inquiry.

As you can see, the writer begins (in tone and substance) with an assertion that would demand logical support, but soon drifts toward mere emotion. Even an attentive reader cannot easily, if at all, discover the writer's main purpose and quickly becomes confused and irritated. Instead of being carried away by the forward movement of the words, he finds himself pausing to ask, "Where is this writer going?", and *that* pulls his mind away from the essay and makes him wonder if the essay is worth reading at all. By providing a clear purpose, you keep the prose moving forward and the reader subtly satisfied.

FOR PRACTICE

Isolate the main purpose in the following introductory paragraphs. Which paragraph lacks a clear purpose?

1. I had chosen to be alone that cold, snowy Christmas. I needed to "get away" from the world and think, and my grandfather's deserted farmhouse seemed just the right spot. I lit the old potbelly stove, boiled some water for coffee, and plopped down into the old, cane rocker that squeaked out memories with every shove. I was there just before the grey, wet window when I noticed it. The old tree. The gigantic oak where I hid from seekers and played my private games with the visiting birds and squirrels. The old tree was almost barren now, and I remember feeling almost embarrassed for its nakedness. Grandeur is indeed only transitory. As I sat and rocked, ignoring the whistle of the coffee pot, I recalled Edna St. Vincent Millay's sonnet, about the lonely tree in winter, and her words lulled me into a meditative state that would last until the coffee pot's whistle softened to a squeak.

2. The train and the river are for Thomas Wolfe two basic symbols in getting across to his readers his feelings about time—time at whose mystery Wolfe never failed to marvel. The river with its ceaseless flow, its continually new combination of particles, its irrevocableness, contained for Wolfe in its essence the sadness, the loneliness, and the loss that time passing brings. The river represented, although Wolfe would not have named it in this way, a sense of Heraclitean flux. Against the river, acting as its foil, stands the train. For the train, al-

though carrying with it a sense of sadness and loneliness as its whistle sounds in the Virginia night, is not irrevocable. There are always tracks leading in the opposite direction and trains traveling on them, and roundhouses where trains may be reversed.

—Margaret Church, *Time and Reality*

3. My point of view is that of a cancer researcher who has been working for the last 20 years with RNA viruses that cause cancer in chickens.

Since the early years of this century, it has been known that viruses cause cancer in chickens. In more recent years viruses have been shown to cause cancer not only in chickens, but also in mice, cats, and even in some primates. Therefore, it was a reasonable hypothesis that viruses might cause cancer in humans and that, if a human cancer virus existed, it could be prevented by a vaccine as so many other virus diseases have been prevented.

—Howard Temin, "A Warning to Smokers"

4. Robert Frost's "The Road Not Taken" is a poem about a traveler who decides to take the path less traveled rather than the one most people follow. The images remind me of a fork in the trail on my grandfather's farm. To take the less traveled path there would mean fighting your way through thorns and stickers. I think Frost wants us to believe that the less-traveled path is the best one, but I disagree. It's a nice romantic notion he has, but the fact is, if you want to get to your destination, you need to trust the path-makers that have preceded you.

5. During millions of years of evolution, plants have found many ways to survive; the bulb's way has been to go underground during adverse seasons and store food against the day when conditions are favorable for it to grow again. Today there are about 3,000 species of bulbs; and after many years of careful crossbreeding, thousands of varieties have been developed that bloom in almost every climate around the world. Although all these plants are loosely called bulbs, only about half of them are true bulbs; the others are either corms, tubers,

tuberous roots or rhizomes. Despite the differences in their structures, shapes and habits, they have one characteristic in common: all of them gather food from the leaves of the plants during the growth cycle and pack these nutrients into their own storage bins so that they can eventually provide food for future plants.

—James Underwood Crockett, *Bulbs*

Application:

ASSUMING THE EDITOR'S MIND

At the beginning of this chapter, I defined grace as seemingly effortless beauty of movement, form, and proportion. You determine your *movement* by a clear understanding of your *audience* and your *purpose,* and you control your *movement* by making clear *commitments* and *following through,* usually within a specific *form,* including a *voice* appropriate to your purpose and *transitions* which are smooth. You create *proportion* by *subordinating* the parts of your sentences until they all have their proper emphasis. Remember, however, that true grace results not from the application of one or two of these principles, but rather from the combination of all, and not from mere understanding, but from daily discipline.

In the first editing exercises, you made the following essay and letter clearer by applying the seven principles of clarity. Now enhance them with movement, form, and proportion by applying the seven principles of grace.

Principles of Grace

Avoid awkwardness
  Failing to put parallel ideas in parallel form
  Unnecessary repetition of words and sounds
  Splitting constructions
  Faulty punctuation and grammar

Provide clear transitions
Provide proper subordination
Write in an appropriate voice: audience and purpose
Know your direction: commitment and follow-through
Know your direction: form and organization
Know your purpose

Here is the essay after it has been edited for clarity.

Sample Essay

My roommate is named Robert. He is one of those men who looks like the hero on the cover of a harlequin romance. He is all things to all men and the apple of the eye of all the girls; always in the limelight. Although not lanky, he is tall. He is of slender build, but he's not really skinny. By the same token he has muscles like a statue and is not brawny. And he's confident, but not in a cocky way. And he doesn't need more friends since everyone likes him because he seems more admirable than most people they know. I admired him too. I was green with envy. Breezing through life, he never seemed to have any problems. But then something happened.

It was a typically quiet evening. While cooking my hamburger casserole I had been reading a French book that was putting me to sleep. I burned the casserole and scorched the skillet which was not supposed to scorch. While I was eating the charred debris, I realized that Robert, who tends to talk a lot, was not smiling and not as cheerful as usual. Usually he is a reliable source of small talk at supper time. But this time he was quiet as a mouse. He seemed introspective. He seemed far away.

After dinner was when he laid down on the dingy couch and stared at the Pepto-Bismol poster on the wall. He spoke hardly two words. In a casual way, I asked him if anything was wrong. He looked helplessly at me. There were tears in his eyes. His eyes were the color of a pearl-gray winter morning. He never talked to, even for a minute, me about his problems. Solutions were always his. I was the one with all the problems. He kept all his problems in his head. They had to come out sometime.

For the next couple of hours, we laughed and cried and talked about his insecurity about his intelligence, his fear he would not be as good a lawyer as his father. He worried, too, that he would never find the right woman. He looked like a sad dog. I realized that night that Robert was just like the rest of us. Even though he

looked like the hero of a harlequin romance he still had problems.
This experience taught me that those of us who envy handsome
men don't stop to consider that they are human too. There's always
more than meets the eye.

Now apply the principles of grace:

[subordination]

My roommate ~~is named~~ Robert. ~~He~~ is one of those men who

looks like the hero on the cover of a harlequin romance.

He is all things to all men and the apple of the eye of all

[punctuation]

the girls, always in the limelight. ~~Although not lanky,~~

[parallel ideas in parallel form]

but not lanky;

he is tall. ~~He is of~~ slender ~~build,~~ but ~~he's~~ not ~~really~~

[parallel ideas in parallel form]

skinny. ~~By the same token he has muscles like a statue and~~

muscular but,

~~is~~ not brawny. ~~And he's~~ confident, but not ~~in a~~ cocky ~~way.~~

[clear transition]

admired

~~And he doesn't need more friends since~~ everyone ~~likes~~

[proper subordination]

and, though green with envy, I must admit

him ~~because he seems~~ more admirable than most people

~~they know.~~ I admired him too. ~~I was green with envy.~~

Breezing through life, he never seemed to have any prob-

[clear transition]

-- or so I thought until last Friday night.

lems. ~~But then something happened.~~

[commitment and follow-through]

The evening was progressing quietly as usual

~~It was a typically quiet evening. While cooking my~~

[proper subordination]

I dozed through a French book while I scorched

~~hamburger casserole I had been reading a French book~~

my Hamburger Helper casserole in an unscorchable

~~that was putting me to sleep. I burned the casserole and~~

skillet.

~~scorched the skillet which was not supposed to scorch.~~

[repetition of words: while]

As I ate

~~While I was eating~~ the charred debris, I realized that

Robert, who tends to talk a lot, was not smiling and not
[repetition of sounds]

as cheerful as usual. ~~Usually he is~~ *always* a reliable source of
[proper subordination] [repetition of words: time]

small talk ~~at supper time~~ *on this occasion* ~~But this time~~ he was quiet as
[parallel ideas in parallel form]

a mouse. *and* He seemed introspective *and* ~~He seemed~~ far away.
[faulty grammar]

After dinner ~~was when~~ he ~~laid~~ *lay* down on the dingy couch

and stared at the Pepto-Bismol poster on the wall. He
[clear transition]

spoke hardly two words. ~~In a casual way, I~~ *when I finally* asked him ~~if~~ *what*
[commitment and follow-through]

~~anything~~ *my words became magic. up* was wrong. He looked helplessly at me. ~~There~~
[proper subordination]

with tear-filled eyes ~~were tears in his eyes. His eyes were~~ the color of a
[commitment and follow-through]   [form and organization]

In a weak, trembling voice, he said, "It's just everything." pearl-gray winter morning. ~~He~~ never talked to, ~~even for~~
[parallel ideas in parallel form]   *Robert*
[splitting constructions]   *The problems were always mine;*

~~a minute,~~ me about his problems. Solutions were always

his. ~~I was the one with all the problems.~~ He kept all his
[proper subordination]

problems *inside* ~~in~~ his head. *and it was time for them all* ~~They had~~ to come out ~~sometime.~~

For the next couple of hours, we laughed and cried and

talked about his insecurity about his intelligence, his

fear he would not be as good a lawyer as his father. ~~He~~
[parallel ideas in parallel form]

his worries ~~worried, too,~~ that he would never find the right woman.

He looked like a sad dog. I realized that night that Rob-

ert was just like the rest of us. Even though he looked

like the hero of a harlequin romance he still had prob-

[voice appropriate to audience and purpose]

His shining image of perfection had

lems. ~~This experience taught me that those of us who envy~~

changed to one of an ordinary person with ordinary

~~handsome men don't stop to consider that they are human~~

problems.

~~too.~~ There's always more than meets the eye.

Here's a recap of the essay after we've edited it for grace.

My roommate, Robert, is one of those men who looks like the hero on the cover of a harlequin romance. He is all things to all men and the apple of the eye of all the girls. Always in the limelight, he is tall but not lanky; slender but not skinny; muscular but not brawny; and confident but not cocky. Everyone admired him, and, though green with envy, I must admit I admired him too. Breezing through life, he never seemed to have any problems—or so I thought until last Friday night.

The evening was progressing quietly as usual. I dozed through a French book while I scorched my Hamburger Helper casserole in an unscorchable skillet. As I ate the charred debris, I realized that Robert, who tends to talk a lot, was not smiling and not as cheerful as usual. Always a reliable source of suppertime small talk, on this occasion he was quiet as a mouse and seemed introspective and far away.

After dinner he lay down on the dingy couch and stared at the Pepto-Bismol poster on the wall. He spoke hardly two words. When I finally asked him what was wrong, my words became magic. He turned and looked up helplessly at me with tear-filled eyes the color of a pearl-gray winter morning. In a weak, trembling voice, he said, "It's just everything."

Robert never talked to me about his problems. The problems were always mine; the solutions were always his. He kept all his problems inside his head, and it was time for them all to come out.

For the next couple of hours, we laughed and cried and talked about his insecurity about his intelligence, his fear he would not be as good a lawyer as his father, his worries that he would never find the right woman. I realized that night that Robert was just like the rest of us. Even though he looked like the hero of a harlequin romance he still had problems. His shining image of perfection had changed to one of an ordinary person with ordinary problems. There's always more than meets the eye.

When you compare the first edited version of the essay to the one above, I think you will notice quite readily that applying the principles of grace makes the current version read more smoothly. The reader's concentration is unbroken by awkward rhythms, lack of direction and follow-through, unsubordinated thoughts, or lack of transition between thoughts.

Of course, you can effectively apply these same seven principles to business prose as well. So proceed to edit Ms. Crowley's letter by applying the principles of grace. Here's the letter after we edited it for clarity:

Sample Letter

September 14, 1983

Mr. Harry Snub
Vice-President
Snub Pencil Products, Inc.
P.O. Box 1009
Dearborn, Michigan 48121
Dear Mr. Snub:

You implied in your letter of March 26 that every year you made almost 50,000 of the four kinds of pencils that we were considering purchasing. We wanted this clarification because we were deciding whether we should end our contract with Felt, Inc. and begin a contract with Snub Pencil Products, Inc.

Before we signed the purchase contract, your business manager informed us that your company could supply us 5,000 pencils by July 30. We ordered 5,000. This was May 19. This was our first contract with your company. We signed another contract three days later for 2,000 more.

Our draftsmen and designers here at Texton were enthusiastic about your new and unique pencil designs. They agreed that your pencils would enable them to work more quickly. We hope you can meet our needs, but if you cannot, we'll have to cancel the contract. As agreed, I am notifying you of a breach of the contract. We have received only 3,000 pencils. In a July 28 phone call, your distribution supervisor informed us that you make only 15,000 pencils per year.

So far, this is between you and me. I hope you take steps to provide us the pencils. Thanking you in advance.

Sincerely,

Carol C. Crowley
District Manager

Now try to apply the seven principles of grace to the letter. If we take a closer look at it, we see that the *purpose* of the letter is to formally notify Snub Pencil Company of a past due order for 5,000 pencils and to seek assurance that Snub Pencil Company can comply with the order. Having clarified the purpose, we can now control its direction through better organization, by deleting much of the irrelevant information, and by subordinating the remaining information. And with a purpose so straightforward as this one, a formal voice is not called for; yet neither should the voice be so informal that it detracts from the message, possibly even leading Mr. Snub to think Ms. Crowley insincere in her inquiry. With these points in mind, let's take another look at the letter.

September 14, 1983

Mr. Harry Snub

Vice-President

Snub Pencil Products, Inc.

P.O. Box 1009

Dearborn, Michigan 48121

Dear Mr. Snub:

[clear transition/proper subordination/appropriate voice]

When Texton placed its first order with Snub Pencil
~~You implied in your letter of March 26 that every year you~~
[commitment and follow-through/form and organization/purpose]
Products, Inc. for 5,000 pencils on May 19, we were confident
~~made almost 50,000 of the four kinds of pencils that we~~

that your company could deliver the pencils by
~~were considering purchasing. We wanted this clarifica~~

the date our draftsmen and designers needed them.
~~tion because we were deciding whether we should end our~~

And after reevaluating our needs, we placed a second
~~contract with Felt, Inc. and begin a contract with Snub~~

order three days later for 2,000. The delivery date on
~~Pencil Products, Inc.~~

both orders was July 30.
[clear transition/proper subordination]
We have received only 3,000 pencils. On a July 28
~~Before we signed the purchase contract, your business~~
[commitment and follow-through/form and organization]
phone call, your distribution supervisor stated that your
~~manager informed us that your company could supply us~~
[purpose]
company makes only 15,000 pencils per year. We
~~5,000 pencils by July 30. We ordered 5,000. This was May~~

wonder, therefore, if you will be able to deliver
~~19. This was our first contract with your company. We~~

the remaining 4,000 pencils.
~~signed another contract three days later for 2,000 more.~~

[proper subordination]
agree that
Our draftsmen and designers here at Texton ~~were enthusi~~

your
~~astic about your new and~~ unique pencil designs. ~~They~~

~~agreed that your pencils~~ would enable them to work more

quickly. We hope you can meet our needs, but if you can-

[commitment and follow-through]
not, we'll have to cancel the contract. ~~As agreed, I am~~

[form and organization]   [purpose]

~~notifying you of a breach of the contract. We have re-~~

~~ceived only 3,000 pencils. In a July 28 phone call, your~~

~~distribution supervisor informed us that you make only~~

~~15,000 pencils per year~~.

[purpose]
~~So far, this is between you and me~~. I hope you take steps

to provide us the pencils. Thanking you in advance.

Sincerely,

Carol C. Crowley

District Manager

Ms. Crowley's letter will now read as follows:

September 14, 1983

Mr. Harry Snub
Vice-President
Snub Pencil Products, Inc.
P.O. Box 1009
Dearborn, Michigan 48121

Dear Mr. Snub:

When Texton placed its first order with Snub Pencil Products, Inc. for 5,000 pencils on May 19, we were confident that your company could deliver the pencils by the date our draftsmen and designers needed them. And after reevaluating our needs, we placed a second order three days later for 2,000. The delivery date on both orders was July 30.

We have received only 3,000 pencils. In a July 28 phone call, your distribution supervisor stated that your company makes only 15,000 pencils per year. We wonder, therefore, if you will be able to deliver the remaining 4,000 pencils.

Our draftsmen and designers here at Texton agree that your unique pencil designs would enable them to work more quickly. We hope you can meet our needs, but if you cannot, we'll have to cancel the contract.

I hope you take steps to provide us the pencils. Thanking you in advance.

Sincerely,

Carol C. Crowley
District Manager

The essay and the letter now read clearly and gracefully. Even so, they still are just okay, aren't they? In good prose okay is not enough. So lastly, we'll enliven these two pieces of writing by making them fresh. And, as with Sunday dinner, the best part always comes (please forgive me) after grace.

EDITING EXERCISES

A. First, identify the obstacles to grace within the following sentences; then revise the sentences.

Failing to put parallel ideas in parallel form.
   1. Mr. Johnson was our father-away-from-home, our cook, our counselor, and he guided us through the dense forest.
   2. Our legal department advises us to study the contract, and they tell us to check Burke's legal history, and then to report to them no later than Tuesday.
   3. Losing in sports sometimes means to win in life.
   4. The course should be fascinating and will provoke a lot of thought.
   5. To hear her play is appreciating the subtlety of the violin.

Unnecessary and distracting repetition of words and sounds.
   1. I was alone in my room, noticing how softly the moon shone on my telephone, when the tap came at the window.

2. To tell a tale effectively takes time as well as a true tone of voice.

3. When it began to rain, the child began to cry. I just started toward her when she began to raise her hands high in the air in a gesture of frustration.

4. The visitor brought a book he believed would boost the mood of the prisoners.

5. As I entered the garden I couldn't quite adjust to the quiet, still air.

Splitting constructions.

1. The book was, even if you don't believe it, written over two thousand years ago.

2. There has never, at any time in history, been a library as important as the one that was in Alexandria.

3. It is better to, so my mother tells me, read poetry aloud than just look at the words on the page.

4. He was the one who painted, slowly and carefully, that landscape on the wall.

5. He was, just as we yelled, backing out of the garage.

Faulty punctuation and grammar.

1. I will be flying to the east coast next week and John will be sailing to Hawaii.

2. Between the F.B.I., and he is a curtain of informants.

3. It was him who stood outside the court.

4. If I were her, I would not take so many courses.

5. Ignition is when the spark meets the gas.

6. Neither the student nor teacher were present.

7. Everyone must pull their own weight.

8. There are however some problems we must discuss.

9. Today we will discuss Keats, tomorrow we will discuss Tennyson.

10. There is where he lives.

B. This paragraph reads gracefully even though it uses no transitional words or phrases. What holds it together so well?

So many different operations go into the production of greeting cards that even a glimpse of them boggles the mind, serene and simple as the cards look when they finally reach the store. Hallmark buys paper by the boxcar, paper of every imaginable texture and weight, parchment, deckle, bond, pebble-grained, leather-grained, cloth-grained, board, brown wrapping, hard-finished, soft-finished, smooth. Special committees earnestly debate the future popularity of roses or ragamuffins. An artist conceives a group of cards that feature cartoon mice, and the cards sell and the artist is rewarded with a trip to San Francisco. Down in the bowels of the building, behind a secret door, a master photographer labors as he has labored for most of a decade to perfect flat three-dimensional photography using a camera on which Hallmark owns the license, a camera that rolls around in a semicircle on model railroad tracks, its prisms awhirr. In California a contract artist makes dolls of old socks and ships them to Kansas City to be photographed for children's cards. Market-research girls carry cards mounted on black panels to meetings of women's clubs, where the ladies, at a charitable fifty cents a head, choose among different designs with the same verses, or different verses with the same design, helping Hallmark determine the very best that you might care to send. An engineer, a stack of handmade designs before him on his desk, struggles to arrange them on a lithography sheet to get the maximum number of designs per sheet so that they can be printed all at once with minimum waste of paper—"nesting," the process is called.

—Richard Rhodes "Packaged Sentiment"

C. As you read paragraph 1 carefully, look for ways to make the prose more graceful and more accurate by subordinating sentences to phrases and phrases to words. Then read paragraph 2 and look for the subordination that makes the sentences read more smoothly.

1. Ken Kesey in *One Flew Over the Cuckoo's Nest* sees society as a precise, mechanical environment. Its sole purpose is self-perpetuation. The machine of society is more important than the members of it. George Orwell, in *1984,* likewise sees a society drifting toward a mechanized system. This would be

a system whose leaders could "plug in your wire whenever they wanted to." In *One Flew Over the Cuckoo's Nest,* as in *1984,* the object of power is power. And power in society is like that in a factory. It is sustained by machine-like regularity as well as uniformity. There is no place for the individual who is eccentric. Both Orwell and Kesey want to underscore this point. They also want to satirize this cold, utilitarian, and dehumanizing factory called society. To do this the authors weave machine imagery throughout their novels.

2. Ken Kesey in *One Flew Over the Cuckoo's Nest* sees society as a precise, mechanical environment whose sole purpose is self-perpetuation. The machine of society is more important than the members of it. George Orwell, in *1984,* likewise sees a society drifting toward a mechanized system whose leaders could "plug in your wire whenever they wanted to." In both novels the object of power is more power. And power in society, like that in a factory, is sustained by machine-like regularity and uniformity. There is no place for the eccentric individual. To underscore this point and to satirize this cold, utilitarian, and dehumanizing factory called society, both Orwell and Kesey weave machine imagery throughout their novels.

D. Comment on the appropriateness of the voice in each of the following passages. Try to rewrite each piece by using the tone of the other. What problems do you encounter? Why?

1. The situation is this: When New York City found itself temporarily short of cash in the mid-nineteen-seventies, all municipal departments had to do some cutting back. The New York Public Library needed to cut a day out of the week; its officials decided that Saturday couldn't be spared, and axed Thursday. But last fall, thanks to the Chase Manhattan Bank, the historian Barbara Tuchman, and two anonymous donors, the Public Library was able to announce that, beginning this month, its general-research collections would once more be accessible on Thursdays. The main, Fifth Avenue library was to make its Thursday début at 10 A.M., and we were on hand. In the back of our mind was the picture of the first day of the hunting season—the thought that precisely at 10 A.M. burly men smelling of whiskey and wearing red hats with library cards pinned to the brim would pull up to the curb in station wagons, dash into the library, return shortly with large volumes, tie them to the roof racks of the station wagons, and drive off down Fifth Avenue, whooping and firing their guns in the air. Nothing like that happened.

—*The New Yorker* Staff, "The Talk of the Town"

2. Now, if I, as a black man, profoundly believe that I deserve my history and deserve to be treated as I am, then I must also, fatally, believe that white people deserve their history and deserve the power and glory which their testimony and the evidence of my own senses assure me that they have. And if black people fall into this trap, the trap of believing that they deserve their fate, white people fall into the yet more stunning and intricate trap of believing that they deserve *their* fate, and their comparative safety; and that black people, therefore, need only do as white people have done to rise to where white people now are. But this simply cannot be said, not only for reasons of politeness or charity, but also because white people carry in them a carefully muffled fear that black people long to do to others what has been done to them. Moreover, the history of white people has led them to a fearful, baffling place where they have begun to lose touch with reality—to lose touch, that is, with themselves—and where they certainly are not happy. They do not know how this came about; they do not dare examine how this came about. On the one hand, they can scarcely dare to open a dialogue which must, if it is honest, become a personal confession—a cry for help and healing, which is really, I think, the basis of all dialogues—and, on the other hand, the black man can scarcely dare to open a dialogue which must, if it is honest, become a personal confession which, fatally, contains an accusation. And yet, if we cannot do this, each of us will perish in those traps in which we have been struggling for so long.

—James Baldwin, "Unnameable Objects, Unspeakable Crimes"

E. In the following passage identify the strategy used in each paragraph and mark the transitional words and devices.

Ballet is a word that can cause some confusion when one is talking of dance. It is used in various contexts to mean different things. It originates from *ballo* in Italian and *bal* in French, meaning dance in the sense of "a dance" or "a ball"; that is to say, a social occasion at which people dance. The Italian word *balletto* was used in the sixteenth century for a series of social dances usually performed by, but not limited to, couples.

In the sixteenth and seventeenth centuries, some of these social occasions became so elaborate that they included entertainments of music, poetry, and dance, somewhat like a lavish cabaret at a private party performed by the host and his friends. In France, this entertainment came to be called a *ballet.* When these entertainments moved from the great halls of royal palaces into real theatres, the dance element was developed and eventually separated from the speech or poetry. It retained the name *ballet.* So, first of all, ballet means a stage performance of dance. It can be any kind of dance.

—Margot Fonteyn, *A Dancer's World*

F. In the following passages do three things: 1) identify the paragraph strategy or strategies used, 2) evaluate how well each paragraph follows through with its commitment, 3) mark the transitional words and devices that keep the reading smooth.

1. Why then, with all the problems and after all these years, are so many city people now moving to small towns? Some reasons are obvious: Industries and businesses are moving to small towns, so more jobs are available. Better communications and transportation make for easier access to the city's benefits. The crime rates in cities have soared to such heights that many people are simply afraid to stay; the incidence of aggressive assault is twice as high in cities as in small towns, and the rate of robberies is 13 times as high. Another factor is pollution. Too many cities have taken shortcuts in their race to profits, refus-

ing to spend the money necessary to make their products or produce their energy in a safe, clean way. The environmental mess is no longer just a rallying point for people who are enamored of causes; statistics show that many of the people who are fleeing cities have lung and heart diseases caused by pollution and are too sick to take any more chances.

—Susan Schiefelbein, "Return of the Native"

2. Animals seem to have an instinct for performing death alone, hidden. Even the largest, most conspicuous ones find ways to conceal themselves in time. If an elephant missteps and dies in an open place, the herd will not leave him there; the others will pick him up and carry the body from place to place, finally putting it down in some inexplicably suitable location. When elephants encounter the skeleton of an elephant out in the open, they methodically take up each of the bones and distribute them, in a ponderous ceremony, over neighboring acres.

—Lewis Thomas, "Death in the Open"

3. Both mathematics and writing are deliberate, self-conscious acts. They share a sense of discipline. The ordering of words on a sheet of ruled paper, or of numbers in an equation, belongs to a common process of "composition": the putting of parts in their proper places.

To write an essay or to solve an algebraic problem, a student must define key terms, must understand guidelines for ordering terms in a series, and must strive for uniformity of order and tone. Factoring a quadratic equation and developing a paragraph both require consistent procedures toward the end of working out the main idea. Indeed, math and writing require such similar skills, in many respects, that the two otherwise disparate fields could reinforce each other—particularly in teaching.

—Joan Baum, "The Reciprocity of Words and Numbers"

4. There are three essential qualities for vulture country: a rich supply of unburied corpses, high mountains, a strong sun. Spain has the first of these, for in this sparsely populated and

stony land it is not customary, or necessary, to bury dead animals. Where there are vultures in action such burial would be a self-evident waste of labor, with inferior sanitary results. Spain has mountains, too, in no part far to seek; and the summer sun is hot throughout the country. But it is hottest in Andalusia, and that is the decisive factor.

The sun, to the vulture, is not just something which makes life easier and pleasanter, a mere matter of preference. His mode of life is impossible without it. Here in Andalusia the summer sun dries up every pond and lake and almost every river. It drives the desperate frogs deep into the mud cracks and forces the storks to feed on locusts. It kills the food plants and wilts the fig trees over the heads of the panting flocks. Andalusia becomes like that part of ancient Greece, "a land where men fight for the shade of an ass."

All animals, both tame and wild, weaken in these circumstances, and the weakest go to the wall and die. The unpitying sun glares down on the corpses and speeds their putrefaction, rotting the hide and softening the sinews and the meat, to the vulture's advantage. But the sun plays a still greater part in his life. Its main and vital function, for him, is the creation of thermal currents in the atmosphere, for without these he would be helpless.

The vulture must fly high—high enough to command a wide territory, for, except at times of catastrophe, dead animals are never thick on the ground.

—John D. Stewart, "Vulture Country"

G. With the list of the possible paragraph strategies before you, consider which ones you might use if you were the composer of the following articles. What would be the best order in which to arrange your paragraphs? How would some of the paragraph strategies help you effectively present your material? What would the purpose of your writing be?

1. An article for a general-audience magazine explaining what happens when one has a heart attack.

2. An article for a travel magazine recounting a ski trip in Austria.

3. An article in a news magazine presenting a brief biography of a historically important figure (i.e., Albert Einstein, Teddy Roosevelt, Susan B. Anthony).

4. An editorial in a local newspaper arguing for or against free education for illegal aliens.

5. A college research paper on the history of the watch.

H. Edit the following letter by applying the principles of clarity and grace.

Dear Mr. Salinger:

I am writing in response to your February 12, letter to my office. In your letter you claim that it is not necessary for you to pay the finance charge for last month because you had made your payment by the due deadline. Our records show that your check arrived after the said deadline. The finance charge must have been added because your check was received during Christmas week when our offices are closed for business. The surrounding circumstances of this concern are being considered by the department manager who is the one who makes decisions in these matters.

Hopefully, the consequent results of all this will be favorable. Mr. Glass and myself will touch base with you by mail as soon as possible.

Sincerely,

Margaret Wilson
Assistant Manager

CHECKLIST FOR WRITERS

The most difficult thing about learning to write is that you need to know two things at once. You need to know what you want to say and how to say it. At first thought, it may seem only logical that a book on how to write begin with a discussion of the "what you want to say"—how to find ideas and develop them, how to isolate your purpose, how to make your commitment clear to your reader. But if you think about it a moment, it does you little good to know what you want to say if you cannot communicate it clearly. Thus, the dilemma: Some students know what they want to say, but not how to say it; others, especially those schooled in style, grammar, and punctuation, know how to make their prose clear, but don't know what to say. To make this obstacle less frustrating to my students, I have them move in both directions—by editing, they learn the "how to say it"; by writing, they learn the "what to say." By experiencing both, they learn to do both at the same time. Thus, as part of your first writing assignment, I ask that you take a trip backwards through the writing principles, this time using the principles of Grace and Clarity to help you discover your ideas, organize them, and, finally, communicate them gracefully and clearly. To begin, select one or more of the following suggested essay assignments and follow these steps:

1. Establish a clear purpose for your readers. They should know if you are mainly *expressing* your feelings, mainly *informing,* mainly *analyzing,* mainly *arguing,* mainly *evaluating,* and so on.

2. Provide a clear direction for your reader by organizing and arranging your material into the most efficient and effective form. Consider the most common paragraph strategies as means to develop your ideas.

3. Provide a clear direction for your readers by making a clear commitment and never deviating from it.

4. Write in a voice appropriate to your audience and your purpose.

5. Give every element of each paragraph its proper emphasis by providing proper subordination.

6. Provide clear transitions.

7. Avoid the most common causes of awkwardness: failing to put parallel ideas in parallel form; unnecessary repetition of words and sounds; splitting constructions; faulty punctuation and grammar.

8. Use the right word.

9. Use the active voice.

10. Avoid jargon.

11. Prefer precise words to words that are general, abstract, or vague.

12. Remove all ambiguity.

13. Remove wordiness.

14. Remove redundancy.

WRITING ASSIGNMENTS

1. Write an essay entitled "My Favorite Junk Food," in which you explain why you prefer your favorite above all others.

2. Write a thorough definition of one of the following words: charisma, spunk, charm, grace, snob, X-rated, obscene, gentleman, style, lady. cute, chivalry

3. Narrate the worst date in your life.

4. Write a review of a film or television program that you consider particularly bad or good.

5. Write a letter of application to a potential employer in which you explain your qualifications and background.

6. Explain how something works. Suggestions: clock, typewriter, camera, computer, iron, telephone, combustible engine, telescope. Or explain a process: for example, how to make wine, organize a protest, sail a boat, read a poem.

7. Write an essay entitled "My Favorite Cartoon Character," in which you compare your favorite character with other, less noteworthy cartoon stars.

8. Write a letter to your parents explaining why you wish to change your major. Or why you would like to drop out for a semester.

9. Write an essay in which you explain what kind of music you like best. Be sure to say why.

10. Write a letter to your local Better Business Bureau in which you complain about an unfair or unscrupulous business practice.

3. Freshness

*Words differently arranged have different meanings, and
meanings differently arranged have different effects.*

—BLAISE PASCAL

*Elegance in prose composition is mainly this: a just ad-
mission of topics and of words; neither too many nor too
few of either; enough of sweetness in the sound to induce
us to enter and sit still; enough of illustration and reflection to change the posture of our minds when they would
tire; and enough of sound matter in the complex to repay
us for our attendance.*

—WALTER SAVAGE LANDOR

*When we see a natural style, we are astonished and de-
lighted; for we expected to see an author, and we find a
man.*

—BLAISE PASCAL

While standing in line at my local grocery I noticed the following headline screaming from a national tabloid: I LED A
LIFE OF *HELL* AS A SEX SLAVE IN A WEIRD LOVE
CULT!!! If your essay is on a similar topic, then you won't need
much of the advice in this section. The subject matter itself is
so overwhelming that few will be bothered by any lack of clarity or grace. Most writing, however, is not so inherently titillat-
ing. In fact, much of it can be lifeless and dull, especially when
the author is not stirring with the poetic fervor of a Shakespeare scribbling out his sonnets. But even the most mundane
subject can be given life and vigor if you follow the principles
of Freshness.

Some quick advice. If you are given the opportunity to select what you will write about, *always* select something that genuinely interests you. That alone will go a long way in keeping your prose fresh, and it will prevent the kind of prose that appeared on a tombstone, probably penned by an unimaginative relative who needed to get back to work:

> *Hiram is buried here.*
> *He was born, he lived, he died.*

1. CONTROL THE RHYTHM OF YOUR PROSE

> *To think, then, in terms of words, rather than in terms of phrases, is an elementary mistake. It is as if one were to think, musically, in terms of a single note, rather than in terms of a phrase or a melody.*
> **—ISSAC GOLDBERG**

In prose this phrase or melody of which Isaac Goldberg speaks is not the meaning of words but their accents, the beat of the words as you read them aloud. Here, for example, is what poets call an iambic beat, a regular up and down, rise and fall of the voice: "I know I am but summer to your heart, / And not the full four seasons of the year" (Edna St. Vincent Millay). The following beat is called dactylic: "Just for a handful of silver he left us / Just for a riband to stick in his coat" (Robert Browning). In prose, of course, we don't use beats this regular, for the very regularity would unnecessarily restrict what could be said efficiently. But good prose, like poetry, has an element of musicality to it. Compare the "musicality" of the following passages.

> *Poetry is not a turning loose of emotion. Instead, poetry is an escape from emotion. Poetry is not the expression of personality either. Rather, it is an escape from personality.*

> *Poetry is not a turning loose of emotion, but an escape from emotion; it is not the expression of personality, but an escape from personality.*
> **—T.S. ELIOT**

In this second passage we do not hear the rhythmic regularity of poetry or music, but we *do* hear rhythm, and, as you might agree, the rhythm actually contributes to the effectiveness of what is being said.

You can develop a sense for rhythm in prose by reading aloud. Listen carefully to the beat and pace of your words. Rearrange them, several times even, and read them aloud again, always listening for the rhythm most appropriate to your meaning. Apart from cultivating an "ear" for rhythm in prose, you also need to learn how to control rhythm. For that I suggest four steps.

Maintain Sentence Variety

It might have something to do with the way we breathe, but we do not like to speak or hear an endless succession of sentences made up of only three words (See Jack run. Run Jack run. Jack runs fast.), and we do not like to hear or speak an endless succession of sentences composed of a hundred words. Short sentences are too monotonous, and long sentences make us breathless. People instinctively prefer sentence variety. Notice how choppy sounding this paragraph is:

> They were looking at a terrain. The terrain lived in a clarity of focus. It was unlike anything they had ever seen on earth. There was no air. There was no wind. There were no clouds. There was no dust. There was not the finest scattering of light. Not even light from the smallest dispersal of microscopic particles on a clear day. Nothing visible moved before them. Nothing invisible moved before them. All the light was pure. No haze was present. Objects did not go out of focus. They did not go out of focus in the distance.

Now compare it to this version:

> They were looking at a terrain which lived in a clarity of focus unlike anything they had ever seen on earth, and there was no air, of course, and so no wind, and no clouds and no dust, and not even the finest scattering of light from the smallest dispersal of microscopic particles on a clear day on earth, no, nothing visible or invisible moved in the vacuum before them and all light was pure and

no haze was present, not even the invisible haze of the finest day, therefore, objects did not go out of focus as they receded into the distance.

In the first you become bored; in the second you get lost. In the original version, notice the use of long and short sentences.

They were looking at a terrain which lived in a clarity of focus unlike anything they had ever seen on earth. There was no air, of course, and so no wind, nor clouds, nor dust, nor even the finest scattering of light from the smallest dispersal of microscopic particles on a clear day on earth, no, nothing visible or invisible moved in the vacuum before them. All light was pure. No haze was present, not even the invisible haze of the finest day—therefore objects did not go out of focus as they receded into the distance.
—Norman Mailer, *Of a Fire on the Moon*

By varying your sentences, you keep the reading active and the reader interested. And the rhythm of your prose created by this variety can, like the rhythmic beat of a popular song, pleasantly affect the reader.

FOR PRACTICE

Rewrite the following two paragraphs. Create more variety within the sentences.

1. The same sense of thievery which propelled the grackles, sent the roach away from my bare cupboard. He went across to the Bloomfield's kitchen for heartier meals. He was a pugnacious creature. He carried my last bit of food on his back. It was a half-eaten salami sandwich. He strolled casually by. He looked up at me. He smirked defiantly. He was full of belligerance. He seemed capable of accomplishing the toughest tests of courage and stamina. I felt angered by the roach's blatant audacity, yet, at the same time, I was in awe of it because as the brazen creature majestically sauntered away from me with his head held high as he tackled each porch step with unaffected ease and grace, and leisurely made his way down the aggregate sidewalk, I, ironically, was a bit saddened to see the

little guy leave since although I knew he had been eating all my food and crawling over my face at night, and hiding himself in my shoes and pants legs, and terrorizing my guests, I, admittedly, knew as well that it was his impudicity that added vitality to the boredom of everyday living.

2. After a short time, the roach reached the edge of the curb. He took his first step across the street. Suddenly, a young cyclist raced by. He sideswiped the roach. That propelled him high in the air. He looked like a ball out of a cannon. Helplessly, the injured roach somersaulted a few times. Then, he landed with a thump on the sidewalk. Without hesitation, I jumped from my chair. I ran to the stiff body. Minutes before, he had been so full of life. But there he was flat on his back. His four scrawny feet twitched above him. He was a pathetic victim of his own mortality. I stood over the roach. He was lifeless. I thought how pitiful it was that the strongest of all creatures known to me could die so suddenly and so tragically. He had escaped countless roach traps, cans of pesticides, fly swatters. Even my brother's shoe. Mournfully, I walked away. I turned back only once. This was just for a last glance. I wanted to preserve one final, memorable impression. But the site where the roach had once been was bare. In the distance I saw a familiar black spot. It was scurrying across the street. It went up the Bloomfield's sidewalk. It squeezed itself under their door. He seemed to say, "Oh yes, I am stronger than death is."

Use Punctuation to Create Rhythm

To punctuate is to puncture the monotony of words strung together. You, in effect, control the rhythm of your words with certain marks just as a composer uses symbols to control his melody. Notice how William Faulkner uses the semicolon, comma, and dash to modulate the rhythm of his prose.

He [the writer] must teach himself that the basest of all things is to be afraid; and, teaching himself that, forget it forever, leaving no room in his workshop for anything but the old verities and truths of the heart, the old universal truths lacking which any story is ephemeral and doomed—love and honor and pity and pride and compassion and sacrifice.

—"On Receiving the Nobel Prize"

With his punctuation symbols, Faulkner tells us where to pause and for how long. The dash is a longer pause than the comma, but briefer than the semicolon. Various combinations of punctuation marks create a variety of rhythmic effects. Here is Friedrich Wilhelm Nietzsche using the dash for an important pause and italics for an important emphasis.

It is my ambition to say in ten sentences what everyone else says in a whole book—what everyone does *not* say in a whole book.

And here is Rainer Maria Rilke using the hyphen to connect several words that, when combined this way, become another word entirely. Notice that the hyphens not only clarify meaning, but also add a rhythmic effect to the sentence.

Works of art are indeed always products of having-been-in-danger, or having-gone-to-the-very-end in an experience, to where man can go no further.

And, finally, here is Mark Twain using a period to stop the reader in order to give strong emphasis to the following phrase and thereby set up the reader for the humorous twist.

Man is the Only Animal that blushes. Or needs to.

Twain would not have been taking full advantage of punctuation's potential to create rhythm and effect had he written, "Man is the only animal that blushes or needs to."

Knowing how punctuation contributes to meaning and controls the sound and sense and rhythm of your words will put *you* in control of your own prose. For *you* are the composer of rhythm as well as the communicator of information or ideas. And you acquire this sense of rhythm, not by following rules of punctuation (which is an entirely different matter), but by using punctuation to its full effect.

FOR PRACTICE

Identify the punctuation marks that help create a subtle and pleasant rhythm in the following paragraphs.

1. Then it was off to "the war to end 'em all"—World War II. Alex barely had enough time to change out of his Yankees uniform before he was drilling and training for the ultimate act of survival—outlasting the deadly phenomenon of the trenches. How dashing, how noble Alex must have looked in his doughboy regalia—the clear-eyed, excitable, all-American kid, upright in his tight, pressed khakis, ready to live whatever was "over there." But, as is often the case, war was not fair to Alex. On a cold, unfriendly battlefield somewhere in France, surrounded by a hauntingly dark morning sky and an opaque drizzle, Alex died. What must have seemed like the most unlucky of coincidences to Alex, he was killed on his twentieth birthday—November 1, 1918.

—Eric Craven, "Alex"

2. Perhaps it was his childhood, growing up penniless and starving in the slums of São Paulo, Brazil—as a reward he and other Jewish people received during World War II for escaping Nazi Germany—that planted within him the unending drive and determination to better himself. Perhaps it was his life in America, the land of opportunity, where a person can succeed through persistence and effort, that encouraged him to continually strive and struggle for that better life. For whatever reason, Dad seemed always to be filled with an all-consuming need to capture that mythical Holy Grail, that vague will-o'-the-wisp, that elusive one-and-only "true answer," to finally rest and feel certain of himself.

—Joel Bogan, "Spirit"

3. The case of Giorgio de Chirico is one of the most curious in art history. An Italian, born in 1888 and raised partly in Greece—where his father, an engineer, planned and built railroads—he led a long, productive life, almost Picassian in length—he died in 1978. He had studied in Munich, and in

his early 20s, under the spell of a symbolist painter named Arnold Böcklin, he began to produce a series of strange, oneiric cityscapes. When they were seen in Paris after 1911, they were ecstatically hailed by painters and poets from Picasso to Paul Eluard; before long De Chirico became one of the heroes of surrealism.

—Robert Hughes, "The Enigmas of De Chirico"

Use Balance to Create Rhythm

You now know that readers innately do not like short choppy sentences or long coiling ones, and that they prefer, instead, variety in sentence rhythm. Moreover, you will discover they have a particular fondness for rhythmic balance—an aesthetic pleasure some say comes directly from the Latin influence on the language (the Roman love of symmetry), others from the iambic (up and down) beat of our syllables, others from the physical balance we experience when we walk or run or swim, and still others from the "one-two" of our heartbeat and breathing patterns. Regardless of the origin, this innate preference for balance appears, over the centuries, in our fondness of pairs: pots and pans, this and that, now and then, neither fish nor fowl, sink or swim, wind and weather, thick and thin, sticks and stones, neither hair nor hide, tit for tat. You see it in familiar maxims: "He knows not when to be silent who knows not when to speak"; "To do two things at once is to do neither." And you hear it in speeches: "Give me liberty or give me death"; "I must be cruel, only to be kind."

To give you a specific example of an instance in which you prefer this balance, consider the following:

We do not campaign stressing what our country is going to do for us as a people. We stress what we can do for the country, for all of us.

These are the exact words from a speech John Kennedy gave before his election as President. They lacked the memorable phrasing that *balance* can provide. Now, compare them to the

final version in the speech President Kennedy gave on inaugu-
ration day:

> *And so, my fellow Americans, ask not what your country can do for you;*
> *ask what you can do for your country.*

Balance makes the difference, doesn't it? The prose is now
more rhythmic, more vigorous, more memorable.

You balance words, phrases, or whole sentences by putting
them in similar construction. In this way, you balance one idea
with another. Such balance can sharpen a thought:

> *One aim of the physical sciences has been to give an exact picture of the*
> *material world. One achievement of physics in the twentieth century has*
> *been to prove that that aim is unattainable.*
> —JACOB BRONOWSKI, *THE ASCENT OF MAN*

Or it can produce wit:

> *Intelligence appears to be the thing that enables a man to get along without*
> *education. Education appears to be the thing that enables man to get along*
> *without the use of his intelligence.*
> —ALBERT WIGGAM, *THE NEW DECALOGUE OF SCIENCE*

Or it can convey emotion:

> They—Duty, Honor, Country—teach you to be proud and un-
> bending in honest failure, but humble and gentle in success; not
> to substitute words for action; not to seek the path of comfort, but
> to face the stress and spur of difficulty and challenge; to learn to
> stand up in the storm, but to have compassion on those who fail;
> to master yourself before you seek to master others; to have a heart
> that is clean, a goal that is high; to learn to laugh, yet never forget
> how to weep; to reach into the future, yet never neglect the past.
> —Douglas MacArthur, West Point Speech, May 12, 1962

Even in a sales pitch, balance can be important. Notice how
the lack of balance gives the following sentence two possible
meanings:

> Our firm offers not only the best technical equipment for tracking satellites, but also monitoring the latest NASA data.

Does this mean:

> Our firm not only offers the best technical equipment for tracking satellites, but also monitors the latest NASA data.

or:

> Our firm offers the best technical equipment not only for tracking satellites, but also for monitoring the latest NASA data.

Because they often appear together and because they often create a similar effect, balance and parallelism are frequently confused. Parallelism refers to the *grammatical* structure of sentences, clauses, or phrases, i.e., similar ideas expressed in exact grammatical structure: "Mary likes Tolstoy; John likes Twain." Balance refers to words, phrases, or clauses placed so that the ideas expressed appear in a *similar* (though not always precisely parallel) rhythm that has the effect of balancing one idea against another: "The memory of other authors is kept alive by their works; but the memory of Johnson keeps many of his works alive." In most instances, parallelism will contain balance, but all balance will not necessarily be parallel.

Perhaps you have noticed a close cousin of balance is repetition. After all, you are repeating a form, a sentence structure, or a kind of phrasing. The repetition of a word or words within a sentence or paragraph can make the statement more compact and forceful and can produce a rhythm that makes the communication more pleasant.

> *There is only one thing in the world worse than being talked about, and that is not being talked about.*
> —OSCAR WILDE

> *Wit consists in knowing the resemblance of things that differ, and the difference of things that are alike.*
> —MADAME DE STAËL

Our grand business is not to see what lies dimly at a distance, but to do what lies clearly at hand.
—THOMAS CARLYLE

You do not balance sentences and repeat words and phrases just for the sake of proving you can do it; nor do you do it to impress the reader with your mastery of technique. Rather, you watch for places where balance and repetition might enliven the prose and thus make the communication of your ideas or information more memorable—and often more emphatic.

FOR PRACTICE

While balancing your ideas by putting them into a similar construction can create a succinct and pleasurable rhythm, it can also distract the reader by calling too much attention to itself. Which of the following pairs of introductory paragraphs establish an appropriate rhythm and which do not?

1a. They inevitably will dredge out the creek bed to make it straight, lay down cement to make it smooth, increase efficiency to make it useful. And, they will still call it a creek bed. It is not a creek bed, but a drainage ditch; not an exciting, adventure-filled playground, but a boney, practical, plasticized imitation. Not beauty, but progress.

1b. Many call it progress, but few would call it beauty. To turn our creek into a drainage ditch was to turn the Niagra Falls into a faucet stream. They can take the wild beauty out of the creek, but they can't take the wild beauty from my memory. Some say this dredging of the earth is an example of what man can do to nature; I say it is an example of what man can do to himself.

2a. It's too bad we can't be honest with ourselves. It's too bad we can't be honest with others. It's too bad we can't be honest with something as innocent as the words we use.

2b. It's too bad we can't be honest with ourselves and it's too bad we can't be honest with others and it's too bad we can't be honest with something as innocent as the words we use.

Use an Occasional Periodic Sentence to Help Keep Prose Moving

Not only can well-structured sentences balance your thoughts and emotions and create a pleasing rhythm, but they can also hold your interest right to the end, as a murder mystery does, before you discover their meaning. We call these sentences periodic because to get their meaning we must read them right to the period.

> *When two people are under the influence of the most violent, most insane, most delusive, and most transient of passions, they are required to swear that they will remain in that excited, abnormal, and exhausting condition continuously until death do them part.*
> **—GEORGE BERNARD SHAW**

> *In 1706, Thomas Twining opened his coffee house in England on the Strand, near the site of the small church of St. Clement Danes and a stone's throw from Temple Bar. Twining, a weaver turned merchant, served not only the usual coffees and cocoas, but also a relatively unusual hot brew from China—tea.*
> **—JILL JONNES, "THE TALE OF TEA,**
> **A FRAGRANT BREW STEEPED IN HISTORY"**

Rhythm is movement, and you can lead the reader through your sound and sense by occasionally using a periodic sentence.

FOR PRACTICE

Rewrite the following sentences to make them periodic.

1. Jennifer discovered Shakespeare on a misty, grey morning, while reading through her mother's old textbook.

2. He was caught up and rushed through baseball and war, events paramount in the lives of most turn-of-the-century American males his age.

3. Five years after his death, Russell is a kaleidoscope of some distinct and some obscure memories.

4. According to my grandmother, "grace" and "kindness" were two words that always arose when she thought of her husband.

5. I do not know and do not wish to know the critics' judgment of Streep's performance last night.

Acquiring a good sense of rhythm in prose will make you more sensitive to the *how* of what you say and also more sensitive to an important way you can make your prose enjoyable to read. But to obtain a more complete sense of how rhythm alone can contribute to a prose piece, you need to read a longer and more complete passage. For practice I've chosen a feature article from a major magazine. As you read through it, pay attention to sentence variety, and punctuation, and balance and rhythm. My point is that effective prose rhythm is not the sole domain of the great writers of our time.

Jay, a carpenter who has worked for me on several occasions, is a barrel of a man, stout as an oak log. Though not yet 30 years old, his convictions are well seasoned; he is true to the grain of his own wood. On good days he shows up for work between 9 and 10 A.M. If it is raining, or his dog needs to go to the veterinarian, or he has promised to help a friend, or there is an exhibit of Zen art at the museum, he may not get here at all. As yet he hasn't called to say the day is too beautiful to spend working. But I wouldn't be surprised if he did. When he arrives, he unwraps his bundles of Japanese woodworking tools, removes the fine saws and chisels from their mahogany cases, puts some shakuhachi flute music on his tape deck, and begins methodically to sculpt the elaborate joints in the beams that will form the structure of the studio we are building. He works slowly, pausing to watch a hawk circle overhead, to tell a joke, to savor the smell of the wood. Occasionally I try to hurry him. "That looks close enough, Jay," I say. "May as well take the time to do it right the first time," he replies and goes on working at his own pace. After several days he announces that the beams are ready to be hoisted into place. We lift and tug and push. Notch joins notch. Tongue slips into groove. The puzzle fits together. We sigh with relief. A satisfying day.

Some would say Jay is an underachiever, a dropout, that he lacks ambition. A college graduate with honors in football, he works sporadically, for carpenters' wages. He has no pension, no health insurance, no fringe benefits. He drives an old truck and lives in a funky neighborhood near the industrial district of Oakland. When he doesn't need money, he tends his garden, writes poetry, paints, and studies Japanese and wood joinery. "I get by," he says. "It doesn't make any sense to sell your soul for security and have no time left to do the things you love."

—Sam Keen, "Lovers vs. Workers"

Sam Keen is not overwhelming us with a turn of phrase or aphoristic profundity; nor is he creating a rhythm as subtle and lyrical as some we find in Faulkner, Melville, or Mailer. But, by varying and balancing sentences, by repeating words and phrases, he does make the reading smooth and pleasing. His words ride in on the wave of his rhythm.

2. CREATE SUBTLE EUPHONY

Words have weight, sound and appearance; it is only by considering these that you can write a sentence that is good to look at and good to listen to.
—SOMERSET MAUGHAM

Under the first principle of freshness you read aloud for rhythm. Now read aloud for sound. Notice the repetition of sounds in the following:

The human tide pressed on, jostling and pushing. My bird had vanished under that crunching, multifooted current as remorselessly as a wounded duck under the indifferent combers of the sea. I watched this human ocean, of which I was an unwilling droplet, rolling past, its individual faces like whitecaps passing on a night of storm, fixed, merciless, indifferent; man in the mass marching like the machinery of which he is already a replaceable part, toward desks, computers, missiles, and machines, marching like the waves toward his own death with a conscious ruthlessness no watery shore could ever duplicate. I have never returned to search in that particular street for the face of humanity. I prefer the endlessly rolling pebbles of the tide, the moonstones polished by the pulling moon.

—Loren Eiseley, "One Night's Dying"

In English we create sounds two ways: by alliteration and assonance. Alliteration is the repetition of initial consonant sounds—the m sound in man, mass marching, machinery, in the passage above. Assonance is the repetition of vowel sounds—"past," "whitecaps," "passing." In the passage from "One Night's Dying," we actually hear the hard monotony of all those m's (man in the mass marching like the machinery) and the gentle abrasiveness of those soft p's, pushing and pulling us continually, like the tide ("I prefer the endlessly rolling pebbles of the tide, the moon-stones polished by the pulling moon."). You want to always be aware of how your prose sounds, but you do not want to abuse sound. Remember that application of the principles of freshness is determined by your purpose. A piece in a news magazine will probably have less euphony than an article describing a lion hunt in Kenya. To write, as one student did, "A crucial communication problem clearly creates a climate not conducive to constructive criticism," is calling more attention to sound than to meaning. It is distracting to the reader rather than pleasing to him. The following writer, on the other hand, is putting euphony to good use in a description of New York City.

> By this time Fifth Avenue is deserted by all but a few strolling insomniacs, some cruising cabdrivers, and a group of sophisticated females who stand in store windows all night and day wearing cold, perfect smiles. Like sentries they line Fifth Avenue—these window mannequins who gaze onto the quiet street with tilted heads and pointed toes and long rubber fingers reaching for cigarettes that aren't there.
> —Gay Talese, "New York Is a City of Things Unnoticed"

Look carefully for those opportunities when you can use euphony to good advantage. If not overdone, sound can make reading a more sensuous, and thus more enjoyable, experience. As Alexander Pope says:

> *True ease in writing comes from art, not chance*
> *As those move easiest who have learned to dance.*
> *'Tis not enough no harshness gives offense.*
> *The sound must seem an echo to the sense.*

FOR PRACTICE _____

Which of the following sentences demonstrate effective use of euphony and which are distracting and overdone? Why?

1. What once crackled with life now withers with decay. Bulldozers moved in and crunched over the majestic pines to clear space for a new subdivision.
2. Suspended high amid the cerulean distance, a V-shaped formation of white wings flew with overwhelming grace and synchrony.
3. Fear is the first feeling I remember wanting to forget.
4. It is sometimes hard to keep amused (in a taxicab) when business is slack. It is hard sometimes to find pleasure in doing nothing; it's hard to dabble in dullness.
5. Impatient motorists briskly weave dented volkswagons through the traffic with amazing dexterity and spunk.

3. SURPRISE THE READER

Getting through the night is becoming harder and harder. Last evening, I had the uneasy feeling that some men were trying to break into my room to shampoo me.
—WOODY ALLEN, *WITHOUT FEATHERS*

Always remember that your reader is taking time away from doing something else that may be more interesting than reading what you have to say; reward this kindness with a pleasant, occasional surprise. Since surprise relies entirely upon your imagination, there can be no easy guide, but here are a few suggestions.

Unexpected Syntax and Punctuation

Familiarity breeds contempt—and children.
—MARK TWAIN

Man lives *by* habits, indeed, but what he lives *for* is thrills and excitements.
—WILLIAM JAMES

Born into the weary, lethargic world of 19th century Dublin, James Joyce had nowhere to go but up—and away.

—ERIC CRAVEN

Wordplay and Wit

The only way to get rid of temptation is to yield to it. —OSCAR WILDE

New York is a town of thirty tattooists where interest in mankind is skin-deep, but whose impressions usually last a lifetime.
—GAY TALESE, "NEW YORK IS A CITY OF THINGS UNNOTICED"

They have already discovered that the Milky Way has some rather unruly neighbors—galaxies that cannibalize each other, punch holes in the galaxy next door and perhaps even hide enough matter in their darkest reaches to make the universe collapse. It's a few billion years too soon to worry about the latter, so researchers are peering at galaxies for clues to how the universe began and grew. Along the way, they are upsetting a certain amount of conventional wisdom. Galaxies, it seems, are not isolated islands in the sky, but often visit and mingle with each other. There is also a lot more to them than meets the telescope; most of their mass lies hidden in an invisible halo. **
—SHARON BEGLEY WITH JOHN CAREY,
"WORLDS PAST THE MILKY WAY"

Imagery

It was as if someone had taken a tiny bead of pure life and, decking it as lightly as possible with down and feathers, had set it dancing and zigzagging to show us the true nature of life.
—VIRGINIA WOOLF, "THE DEATH OF THE MOTH"

Millions of immigrants who once arrived by ships stopped off in New York for a generation or two while the city's digestive system tried to assimilate them before putting them into the great American bloodstream. New York is still trying to swallow large numbers of immigrants. They don't come by boat much anymore, and they may not even be from a foreign country. The influx of a million Puerto Ricans in the 1960s pro-

*From "Worlds Past the Milky Way" by Sharon Begley with John Carey in *Newsweek*, March 15, 1982. Copyright © 1982 by Newsweek, Inc. All rights reserved. Reprinted by permission

duced the same kind of digestive difficulties that the influx of the Irish did in the middle 1800s.
—ANDY ROONEY, "IN PRAISE OF NEW YORK CITY"

Flowers are seed machines—intricate, beautiful, efficient engines powered for one purpose: to make more flowers. Some years they work better than others, or more accurately, some years work better for them.

To the compound eye of a bee, a flower seen from afar (and that's about five or six feet) is a huge neon billboard flickering the message EAT HERE. As the insect canoodles amid the flower's private parts, it might nudge up against the stigma, drop a grain of pollen it has gathered elsewhere, and, if that pollen is compatible, thereby start the sexual process that will perpetuate the flower. *
—SUZANNE WINCKLER, "THE YEAR OF THE FLOWER"

The key to surprise in all of these examples is, of course, the unexpected. And a good place for the unexpected is your introductory paragraph. By surprising your reader right away, you spark his curiosity and foreshadow, in his mind, more surprises along the way. You create anticipation that will make him want to keep on reading. A few examples:

Sometime along in the nineteen-eighties, when the world has left us as far behind as we have left the years that followed the First World War, somebody is going to publish a piece called The Late Forties. *I hope to be dead at the time.*
—ARCHIBALD MACLEISH, "THE CONQUEST OF AMERICA"

"Would you let us have some cigars to take hunting with us tonight?"
—JEFFREY K. WILKERSON,
"MAN'S EIGHTY CENTURIES IN VERACRUZ"

In the sea green twilight the great jointed stalks of grass stand like jade columns supporting a submerged palace. The foot-thick culms glisten in the submarine light and rise for a hundred feet among dagger leaves that stir with a susurrus like surf on a distant shore. A passing breeze rubs the tapering stems together, and subdued groans, stuttering creaks, and a small scream fall from a moving canopy.

*From "The Year of the Flower" by Suzanne Winckler. Reprinted with permission from the June 1981 issue of *Texas Monthly.* Copyright © 1981 by Texas Monthly.

Are you Alice, sipping from the bottle labled "Drink me," and shrunk to elfin size? Or have you wandered into Gulliver's Brobdingnagian world, where even the grasses of the field reach for the sky?

No, you are of normal size, walking in a grove of bamboo, the giant tree grass that is the most versatile, and to me the most beautiful, plant on earth.
    —LUIS MARDEN, "BAMBOO, THE GIANT GRASS"

In general, you, as writer, are not an entertainer but an effective communicator who occasionally entertains the reader soley to assist the communication. Moments of surprise during one's reading keep him alert and establish a closer rapport with the writer—an important psychological device in effective communication.

4. CONTROL CONNOTATION AND DENOTATION

Once upon a time there was a woman named Hilda Hornbuckle. Hilda Hornbuckle was an unsuccessful concert pianist from the Southwest. One day she changed her name to Valentina Gudonov and quickly became a concert success, eventually marrying a distinguished conductor of a leading American orchestra. Ah, the power of connotation.

This anecdote, based on a true story, underscores the point that, apart from their sounds and meanings, words also have associations. It's difficult to accept Hilda Hornbuckle as a serious artist at the grand piano. Valentina Gudonov is Russianly distinguished. Hawthorne did not call his novel *The Red Letter*. Though red and scarlet *mean* the same thing, the latter possesses, like an aura, specific associations. Many movie stars learned about connotation at the beginning of their careers. Boris Karloff, John Wayne, Judy Garland, Doris Day, all suggest more than William Henry Pratt, Marion Morrison, Frances Gumm, or Doris Kapelhoff.

Denotation is the dictionary meaning of a word. The association surrounding a word is its connotation. Connotatively, a home is more than a house. Denotatively, Elavil, Asendin, and Placydill are all prescription drugs prescribed for depression; connotatively, they are mental states: elevating, ascending, and placid. Writers can say *more* by using connotation. Compare the two versions of the following:

> It was my mother who *governed* our house. She was always *giving orders* and *laying down* the rules. She *made certain* we never *broke* her *rule* not to accept rides from strangers.

> It was my mother who *ruled* our house. She was always *roaring commands* and *dictating* the laws of the house. She *ordained* that we never *violate* her *command* not to accept rides from strangers.

Though the words mean the same thing, isn't "violate" different from "broke," and "ruled" from "governed"? The role of the mother shifts from a governor/manager of the household in the first version to absolute ruler in the second. And it does so because of a shift in connotation.

Connotation is subtly at work in the business letter below as well.

> Dear Mr. Hudson:
> Your *lawyer* and I got into an *argument*. She *seems to think* that, since the company is *richer* than last year, we should *divert* some *money* to *charity*.

Now compare the version above to the following:

> Dear Mr. Hudson:
> Your *attorney* and I are in *disagreement*. She *believes* that, since the company is *more prosperous* than last year, we should *direct* some of our *assets* to *philanthropic causes*.

In the first version we hear an underlying tone of annoyance; the second version, by contrast, is ostensibly more objective in tone. For example, "lawyer," in this context, is a subtly weaker term than the official sounding "attorney"; "argument" more pugnacious than "disagreement"; "She seems to think" more equivocal than "she believes"; "richer" more ostentatious than "more prosperous"; "divert" more evasive than "direct"; and "charity" more diffuse and less purposeful than "philanthropic causes." Through attention to the connotation of words, the second writer is able to keep emotion out of the considerations of what to do with the company's earnings for last year.

In order to get the most possible from your words, pay close attention to their connotation and denotation. Notice how a writer like George Bernard Shaw manipulates both.

> Your friends are all the dullest dogs I know. They are not beautiful: they are only decorated. They are not clean: they are only shaved and starched. They are not dignified: they are only fashionably dressed. They are not educated: they are only college passmen. They are not religious: they are only pew renters. They are not moral: they are only conventional. . . . They are not even vicious: they are only "frail". . . . They are not prosperous: they are only rich. They are not loyal, they are only servile; not dutiful, only sheepish; not public spirited, only patriotic; not courageous, only quarrelsome; not determined, only obstinate; not masterful, only domineering; not self-controlled, only obtuse; not self-respecting, only vain; not kind, only sentimental; not social, only gregarious; not considerate, only polite; not intelligent, only opinionated; not progressive, only factious; not imaginative, only superstitious; not just, only vindictive; not generous, only propitiatory; not disciplined, only cowed; and not truthful at all: liars every one of them, to the very backbone of their souls.
>
> *—Man and Superman*

Two final points about connotation. First, misuse of grammar carries with it a specific connotation depending on where it appears. In a country and western song (I ain't got nobody; nothing's not going to bother me), for instance, it appeals to us average, common, unpretentious folk. But in a business letter or formal essay, misuse of grammar carries with it associations of ignorance, sloppiness, and unprofessionalism.

Second, there are writers who try to impress readers by using pretentious sounding or jargonistic words (the kind discussed in chapter 1). More often than not such words confuse rather than enhance meaning. One of the more recent illustrations of jargonistic gibberish is the word "guesstimate," probably invented with the intent of investing the simple word "guess" with the greater mathematical respectability inherent in the word "estimate." To guesstimate, however, is simply meaningless slang for "to guess." In controlling the connotation of your words, avoid jargon.

FOR PRACTICE

How does connotation control the differences in meaning in the following groups of sentences.

1. The woman gave a solemn speech.
   The woman gave a thoughtful speech.
   The woman gave an earnest speech.
2. She is an outspoken teenager.
   She is a candid teenager.
   She is a sincere teenager
3. The headline in the paper was astonishing.
   The headline in the paper was startling.
   The headline in the paper was surprising.

5. KEEP IMAGERY FRESH

The language you speak and write is inherently metaphorical. Just as you inherited that Latin preference for balance in your sentences, so, too, have you inherited the linguistic habit of making implicit and explicit comparisons between things of different worlds. Such comparisons conjure up mental pictures to help us *see* meaning. You *crawl* out from the *foot* of the bed, stare at the *hands* of the clock, *devour* the day-old muffin, pick up your comb by its *teeth,* and slowly prepare yourself to *face* the day—a day you will consciously and unconsciously spend creating images with your language:

I could just *kill* myself for believing that *fishy* story about the *choke* in the car.

He made me feel like a *million dollars,* like a *star.*

The *key* to success is pure luck.

I can't *stomach flowery* language.

I know I should give the *cold shoulder* to anyone who wears his *heart on his sleeve.*

He has to *shoulder* the burden.

I thought our romance was *skyrocketing.*

I swallowed their story, *hook, line, and sinker.*

I'll keep myself *busy as a bee.*

I'll make them *eat* their words.

I need to *iron out some problems.*

This habit of creating mental pictures by comparison is both bad and good. It is good because it enriches prose, keeps it fresh and alive. Notice the daring image by Norman Mailer as he describes man's first visit to the moon:

> It was almost three-thirty in the morning when the astronauts finally prepared for sleep. They pulled down the shades and Aldrin stretched out on the floor, his nose near the moon dust. Armstrong sat on the cover of the ascent engine, his back leaning against one of the walls, his legs supported in a strap he had tied around a vertical bar. In front of him was the eye piece of the telescope. The earth was in its field of view, and the earth "like a big blue eyeball" stared back at him. They could not sleep. Like the eye of a victim just murdered, the earth stared back at him.
>
> —*Of a Fire on the Moon*

This ancient habit, while it does make our perceptions and communications more vivid to the mind's eye, can possess, like the flash of a flash bulb, only temporary brilliance. If an image is overused, it quickly loses power to illuminate. You no longer *see,* for example, a god sleeping in a river when you hear the expression "the river bed," any more than you imagine a *shoulder* of the road, or a knife blade in "blade of grass," or a marble bust in "head of the company," or a bone in "bone of contention," or a shiny surface when the fullback runs a "brilliant" touchdown. And if you do not see, then what is the purpose of the image? Think about the following imageless images:

blanket of snow	like a sore thumb
a shot in the arm	sly as a fox
out in left field	checkered career
dark horse	mouth of a river
eye of the needle	pool our money
leaps and bounds	nipped in the bud
canvass a precinct	sow wild oats
chicken out	swan song
branch of the service	gave her my heart

All these mental pictures that were fresh when first used do little for your language except bog it down. Remove all deadwood from your prose and, as you write, keep your mind's eye alert for any image that will make communication more vivid and alive. In the following examples, notice how imagery not only adds freshness to the expository prose, but actually assists the reader in "seeing" what the writer is communicating. "Showing" how ring galaxies form:

Ring galaxies have a more violent genesis. When one galaxy flies through the middle of another, the gravity of the intruder pulls stars and dust to the center. Once it has passed, the stars bounce back in ripples, much like those made by a stone in a pond.*

—Sharon Begley with John Carey,
"Worlds Past the Milky Way"

Describing owl-courting behavior:

As the day grew lighter, the owl flew from tree to tree, aligning itself each time to face in the direction of the other owl's call. Now when it called, this male great horned bowed as deep as a Japanese ambassador and raised its whitish rump until its tail feathers stuck straight up in the air.

—Jonathan Evan Maslow,
"In the World of Owls, the Eyes Have It"

*From "Worlds Past the Milky Way" by Sharon Begley with John Carey in *Newsweek,* March 15, 1982. Copyright © 1982 by Newsweek, Inc. All rights reserved. Reprinted by permission

Explaining how bilirubin moves out of the liver:

> In the liver, bilirubin normally hooks up to a second chemical and is then shipped out in the bile—like hooking a garbage scow to a tug to be led out for dumping.
> —Michael Shodell, "The Curative Light"

If this doesn't come easy to you, remember that you create mental pictures two ways. You can make a direct comparison of two things by using the word *like* or *as:* He suddenly dropped, *like* a puppet with its strings cut. She looks *like* an unmade bed. We call such comparisons similes. Or, you can forego "like" or "as" and simply identify two things as one: She is the *flame* in his life. He *bottled* up his emotions. We call these metaphors. Let's look at two extended examples of each.

Simile

Using "as," James Baldwin created a vivid image that helps us understand a particular kind of hatred.

> That year in New Jersey lives in my mind as though it were the year during which, having an unsuspected predilection for it, I first contracted some dread, chronic disease, the unfailing symptom of which is a kind of blind fever, a pounding in the skull and fire in the bowels. . . . There is not a Negro alive who does not have this rage in his blood—one has the choice, merely of living with it consciously or surrendering to it. As for me, this fever has recurred in me, and does, and will until the day I die.
> —*Notes of a Native Son*

Kingsley Amis uses simile to help us *see* the results of a drunken night:

> His face was heavy, as if little bags of sand had been painlessly sewn into various parts of it, dragging the features away from the bones, if he still had bones in his face. . . . His mouth has been used as a latrine by some small creature of the night, and then as its mausoleum. During the night, too, he'd somehow been on a cross-country run and then been expertly beaten up by secret police. He felt bad.
> —*Lucky Jim*

Metaphor

Notice that Carl Gustav Jung does not say a dream is *like* a hidden door to the innermost recesses of the soul. It *is* a door.

> The dream is a little hidden door in the innermost and most secret recesses of the soul, opening into that cosmic night which was psyche long before there was any ego-consciousness, and which will remain psyche no matter how far our ego-consciousness may extend.

John Stuart Mill does not say social groupings are like molds. Instead:

> Persons of genius are . . . more individual than any other people—less capable, consequently, of fitting themselves, without hurtful compression, into any of the small number of molds which society provides in order to save its members the trouble of forming their own character. If from timidity they consent to be forced into one of these molds, and to let all that part of themselves which cannot expand under the pressure remain unexpanded, society will be little the better for their genius. If they are of strong character and break their fetters, they become a mark for the society which has not succeeded in reducing them to a commonplace, to point out with solemn warning as "wild," "erratic," and the like—much as if one should complain of the Niagara River for not flowing smoothly between its banks like a Dutch canal.
>
> —*On Liberty*

Simile and metaphor *do* enrich your prose. But use them sensitively. Remember that you are not creating an image just for the sake of creating an image—imagery is not mere ornamentation. It is, instead, another way of communicating meaning. And often, as C. S. Lewis says, a fresh image "starts forth, under the pressure of composition or argument. When this happens, the result is often as surprising and illuminating to us as to our audience." Your best imagery often will just mysteriously appear *as* you write.

One final point. Don't mix metaphors. To say "The ship of state crawls slowly in times like these" is to confuse the mind's eye and what it hears. See?

I leave you with a passage that will make you *see* and *think*—
George Orwell's lament about the sad condition of contemporary prose.

> Prose consists less and less of *words* chosen for the sake of their
> meaning, and more and more of phrases tacked together like the
> sections of a prefabricated henhouse. . . . there is a huge dump of
> worn-out metaphors which have lost all evocative power and are
> merely used because they save people the trouble of inventing
> phrases for themselves. . . . Modern writing at its worst . . . consists
> in gumming together long strips of words which have already been
> set in order by someone else.
> —George Orwell, "Politics and the English Language"

FOR PRACTICE

Evaluate the effectiveness of the images in the following sentences. Why are some effective and some not?

1. From the walls covered with posters many eyes follow my every movement—the pleading eyes of soft white seal pups, the steamy eyes of young men with open shirts and faces smooth as baby bottoms, the heavy-lidded, Ping-Pong ball eyes of Garfield the cartoon cat.

2. My date gave me the kind of hateful look I hadn't seen since the day I accidentally vacuumed up her hamster.

3. The dragon Despair is fueling the flames of inflation and there's no dragon-killer in sight. *Blech*

4. The batter was slow as molasses in stepping up to the plate.

5. The pinball and video games chime insistently like a squad of belligerent Tinkerbells.

6. REMOVE WORN-OUT EXPRESSIONS AND CLICHÉS

As a matter of fact, I'll cover this principle quick as a flash. Unoriginal metaphors and similes add no visual power to your prose; hackneyed expressions make your prose thinkless and bore the reader with sentence rhythms he's heard or read too many monotonous times before. Remove them all. A few examples:

each and every	pursuant to
food for thought	as acknowledged in
it goes without saying	ipso facto
words fail to express	labor of love
beneath contempt	moment of truth
heartfelt thanks	tower of strength
marked contrast	first and foremost
leave no stone uncovered	considered opinion
method in his madness	seat of learning
this day and age	by the same token
point with pride	last but not least
in no uncertain terms	few and far between

Oh, three more:

as a matter of fact
I'll cover
quick as a flash

FOR PRACTICE

Identify the worn-out expressions in the following sentences, then rewrite them.

1. The Jamestown company is trying to get its foot in the door at Easton, using each and every known sales tactic to win their account.

2. The soldiers left their quarters clean as a whistle and ready for the moment of truth from the inspector.

3. It goes without saying that next year's fashions will be in marked contrast to last year's.

4. The judges left no stone uncovered in their search for the essay that was the cream of the crop.

5. Words fail to express my gratitude.

7. WRITE FRESH INTRODUCTIONS AND CONCLUSIONS

Introductions

A good introduction establishes the tone and direction of your essay. From your first few words your reader should know where you're headed and the tone of voice you'll use to guide him there. But the introduction is also the first (and often the only) chance you have to peak his interest, to pull him into your mind. Most readers aren't quite awake when they start reading; they normally don't bring energy with them to your essay. Your opening words are the *starter* as well as the introducer of the essay and thus they, like spark plugs, have to ignite your readers' curiosity. Good introductions not only provide a clear purpose and tone for readers, but they also stimulate their interest.

The best review of the types of fresh introductory paragraphs belongs to Professor Reed Sanderlin of the University of Tennessee.

Open with a question and suggest the implications

Have you had the eerie feeling that you are *not* being left alone? That somebody unknown and unseen is spying on you? You were not imagining things. Our privacy is up for sale.
—Myron Brenton, *The Privacy Invaders*

Open with a hypothetical or representative incident or situation

A group of youngsters—the oldest was fourteen—formed a circle and solemnly inhaled on a Turkish water pipe until their eyes were glazed and distant. All of them were deep-tanned, sun-bleached, sports-playing California-affluent junior-high-schoolers, good students and normal children whose parents thought they were on a picnic.

—Albert Rosenfeld,
"Marijuana: Millions of Turned-on Users"

Open with an announcement of the topic and indicate important subtopics

This book is a collection of short stories by Southern writers. And that involves two questions which more than once had to be considered in the making of this book. What is a Southern writer? And what is a short story?
—Robert Penn Warren, *Southern Harvest*

Open with a bold, challenging assertion or provocative statement

The present chasm between the generations has been brought about almost entirely by a change in the concept of truth.
—Francis A. Schaeffer, *The God Who Is There*

Open with a story

A book as wide-ranging as this one needs a governing metaphor to give it at least the illusion that all is well:

It was said that in the old days that every year Thor made a circle around the Middle-earth, beating back the enemies of order. Thor got older every year, and the circle occupied by gods and men grew smaller. The wisdom god, Woden, went out to the king of the trolls, got him in an armlock, and demanded to know of him how order might triumph over chaos.

"Give me your left eye," said the king of the trolls, "and I'll tell you."

Without hesitation, Woden gave up his left eye. "Now tell me."

The troll said, "The secret is, Watch with both eyes!"
—JOHN GARDNER, *ON MORAL FICTION*

Open with quotations, either imaginary or by some historical person, or from some previous text.

" 'Your writing tells a reader whether you are bright or dull, prepared or lazy, precise or sloppy. It is even more important than the way you act or dress."
"It's harder to waffle on paper—what you write is like a window into your mind."

We're sure you've read or heard hundreds of statements like these, made by senior executives of national corporations. Our purpose is not to preach, once again, that writing is important; you already know that. We've written this book because writing is a process, like any other management process, and we want to show you some steps you can take to write more efficiently and effectively.

—Marya W. Holcombe and Judith K. Stein,
Writing for Decision Makers

Open with a personal experience

As a boy growing up in Monterey, Kentucky, during the 1930's and '40's, I thought almost every other place superior to where I lived. Monterey was rural, poor, and small, with a population of less than three hundred. We felt inferior to Owenton, our county seat, which was ten miles away and had over a thousand people and one movie theater; we definitely felt like hicks when we visited Frankfort, twenty miles away, with its twelve thousand people and three movie theaters. And as for Louisville and Cincinnati, somewhat further away and much larger, our occasional visits to either could be overwhelming."

—Charles Hudson,
Review of Wendell Berry's *Recollected Essays*

Open with a riddle or some problem or puzzle the reader can grapple with

A *riddle* is making the rounds that goes like this: A man and his young son were in an automobile accident. The father was killed and the son, who was critically injured, was rushed to a hospital. As the attendants wheeled the unconscious boy into the emergency room, the doctor on duty looked down at him and said, "My God, it's my son!" What was the relationship of the doctor to the injured boy?

If the answer doesn't jump to your mind, another riddle that has been around a lot longer might help: The blind beggar had a brother. The blind beggar's brother died. The brother who died had no brother. What relation was the blind beggar to the blind beggar's brother?

—Casey Miller and Kate Swift,
"Is Language Sexist? One Small Step for Genkind"

Open with an event, situation, or problem from the past

The 38 clerical employees in the trust department at First National Bank of Boston used to start work about nine A.M. and quit at five P.M. like their counterparts at most other offices. Beginning in 1973, they changed to a system of flexible working hours, or "flex-time," under which they put in their usual eight-hour day any time between 7:30 A.M. and 6:30 P.M. Except for a fixed period during the middle of the day when everyone must be on the job, they can come in, eat lunch, and leave whenever they like, provided they work the required number of hours per week and complete their assignments on time.

—Barry Stein, Allan Cohen, and Herman Gadon,
"Flextime: Work When You Want To"

Open with a direct statement of the main, or thesis, idea that is to be developed or argued

Of all areas of criticism today, the most bloodily contested is that of film criticism. There are several reasons for this. Film is now the most popular art form, outdistanced only by rock music and television, which, however, are not arts. So film has both the popularity that comes from easiness—just consider how much harder it is to absorb a concert, an art show, or a book than to let a movie wash over you—and the catchet of being a legitimate art form. It is now one of the most sought after college subjects, and English, theatre, art, and communications departments fight among themselves for the right to teach it. And since not all students of film can make films, the next best thing, presumably, is to write about them.

—John Simon, "The Bloody Sport of Film Criticism"

Open with important factual, statistical, or historical data

There was a time when the undertaker's tasks were clearcut and rather obvious, and when he billed his patrons accordingly. Typical late-nineteenth-century charges, in addition to the price of merchandise, are shown on bills of the period as: "Services at the house (placing corpse in the coffin) $1.25," "Preserving remains on ice, $10," "Getting Permit, $1.50." It was customary for the undertaker to add a few dollars to his bill for being "in attendance," which seems only fair and right. The cost of embalming was around $10 in 1880. An undertaker, writing in 1900, recommends these minimums for service charges: Washing and dressing, $5; embalming, $10; hearse, $8 to $10. As Habenstein and Lamers, the historians of the trade, have pointed out, "The undertaker had yet to conceive of the value of personal services offered professionally for a fee, legitimately claimed." Well, he has now so conceived with a vengeance.

—Jessica Mitford, *The American Way of Death*

Open with a descriptive scene or setting (past or present)

In the desert country the air is never still. You raise your eyes and see a windmill a hundred yards away, revolving in the sunlight, without any apparent beginning and for years to come without any end. It may seem to slow up and stop but that is only because it is getting ready to go round and round again, faster and faster, night and day, week in, week out. The end that is followed immediately by a beginning is neither end nor beginning. Whatever is alive must be continuous. There is no life that doesn't go on and on, even the life that is in water and in stones. Listen and you hear children's voices, a dog's soft padded steps, a man hammering, a man sharpening a scythe. Each of them is repeated, the same sound, starting and stopping like the windmill.

—William Maxwell, *The Folded Leaf*

Open with a definition (simple or extended)

Liberalism is not a dogma. It may only be, in fact, a temperament or an attitude towards other persons and society. This makes it difficult to provide a coherent statement of a philosophy. It becomes all the more necessary, therefore, tiresome as it may be, to begin with definitions.

—Daniel Bell, "Liberalism in the Postindustrial Society"

A region may be defined as any place that is bounded to some degree by barriers to perception. Regions vary, of course, in the degree to which they are bounded and according to the media of communication in which the barriers to perception occur. Thus thick glass panels, such as are found in broadcasting control rooms,

can isolate a region aurally but not visually, while an office bounded by beaverboard partitions is closed off in the opposite way."
—Erving Goffman, *The Presentation of Self in Everyday Life*

Conclusions

As in all journeys, even mental ones, the traveller anticipates not only the ending, but the "feeling" of the ending, something similar to the feeling musical compositions always provide at their conclusions. In many movies, music alone provides the sense of completion. Listen carefully the next time you're there. In prose you produce this "feeling" with sentence rhythm. You not only satisfy your reader by summarizing, but you summarize with a rhythm that feels like an ending. Two examples:

> In short, by recognizing what the past reveals to us about Indians and their culture, we are in a position to transcend our own history, and to recognize, in policy as well as in theory, that "the only good Indian" is a real Indian, not a white man with red skin.
> —Carl Degler, "Indians and Other Americans"

> You can't do that anymore, I thought. You can't do a lot of things anymore when you've definitely left your childhood behind. I felt a poignant stabbing in my heart as I watched the graceful black shadows wheel in the sky, but it was quickly followed by a comforting thought: they would win. Long after my mother and I would be gone, long after the plywood houses had turned to dust, long after mankind's tortured history had unfolded its last mystery—there would always be crows, I was sure. Clever, adaptable, endurable, *innocent* crows. They would survive. Somehow, that was a consolation.
> —Rudolph Chelminski,
> "Recollections of a Childhood Friend Named Crowcrow"

There will be other times, however, when you can do more in your conclusion than just balance and vary sentences. On some occasions you can actually make the conclusion provocative by posing a question or making a prediction.

> From his point of view and at the level where he had chosen to do his dreadful work, Hitler was perfectly correct in his estimate

of human nature. To those of us who look at men and women as individuals rather than as members of crowds, or of regimented collectives, he seems hideously wrong. In an age of accelerating over-population, of accelerating over-organization and ever more efficient means of mass communication, how can we preserve the integrity and reassert the value of the human individual? This is a question that can still be asked and perhaps effectively answered. A generation from now it may be too late to find an answer and perhaps impossible, in the stifling collective climate of that future time, even to ask the question.

—Aldous Huxley, *Brave New World Revisited*

Man has not yet grown up. He is not adult. Like a child he cries for the moon and lives in a world of fantasies. And the race as a whole has perhaps reached the great crisis of its life. Can it grow up as a race in the same sense as individual men grow up? Can man put away childish things and adolescent dreams? Can he grasp the real world as it actually is, stark and bleak, without its romantic or religious halo, and still retain his ideals, striving for great ends and noble achievements? If he can, all may yet be well. If he cannot, he will probably sink back into the savagery and brutality from which he came, taking a humble place once more among the lower animals.

—Walter Terence Stace, "Man Against Darkness"

A dancer *completes* the dance with a specific movement that brings everything together and signals the *ending* as well as THE END. Your conclusion is the last movement of your essay. As in dance, the movement is usually brief, clear, and compact and it satisfies the audience's sensibility to THE END.

Bookend Essays

The reader experiences a pleasant aesthetic satisfaction when an essay is framed with book ends—when the introduction and conclusion echo each other without repeating exactly; when they allude to one another either by image, sentence rhythm, repetition, or tone. Let me give you two examples.

INTRODUCTION

"Our case is going to be to you like a jigsaw puzzle," District Attorney Lewis R. Slaton, 59, told jurors during opening arguments in the long-awaited case of *Georgia vs. Wayne B. Williams.* The 23-year-old black freelance photographer has been accused of killing two of the 28 young blacks who were slain during Atlanta's notorious 22-month series of murders. "At the conclusion there will be enough pieces in the puzzle that you will see the truth." Meanwhile, he suggested folksily, "Sit back and enjoy yourselves as much as possible." Slaton even urged the jurors to show sympathy for the state's witnesses, warning about the sly tactics of the chief defense trial lawyer, Alvin Binder, 52, a white attorney from Mississippi.

CONCLUSION

Whether the eight black and four white jurors are convinced by Binder's trial skills will not be known until the end of the trial, which is expected to last at least six weeks. The jurors were selected in only five days, a short time considering the volume of pretrial publicity. A former Detroit policeman explained why he thought he could judge impartially. "I looked at Mr. Williams," he replied to questions during jury selection. "I looked at his mother and father. No one knows if that man is guilty. Nobody's heard the evidence." As the prosecution began assembling its "jigsaw puzzle" of evidence last week, the defense appeared to be pouncing effectively on some of the pieces.
—*Time* Staff, "A 'Shark' Goes After the Evidence"

Let me remind you that the beginning and the end are good places to apply the principles of freshness.

INTRODUCTION

Author Thomas Thompson measured his life by white, blank pages; filling them, he once said, is an agony and also a sort of ecstasy. His brow pensively crinkled up as his penetrating eyes gleamed. "Every morning a writer must start out fresh with an awful, yawning, white piece of paper." Then, eagerly, he went on: "In filling those blank pages, you follow a wacky, maddening search for truth; you approach it with wit, wisdom, courage, hard work."

CONCLUSION

Thompson had an obsession, a passion for bringing reality to life. He was intrigued by those aberrations of human nature that cause people to seek fame and fortune, to love—and to kill. He seemed to write, not with a pen, but with a paintbrush, as he took the stark qualities of the bizarre and transformed them into living color. Thomas Thompson has died, but he left behind those awful yawning pages that are no longer blank.

—Carmen Hill, "Yawning Pages"

FOR PRACTICE

How do the following introductory paragraphs spark the reader's interest?

1. There's a "country"—well, some regard it as a country—that has no citizens, inhabits about three acres of territory, issues coins, stamps and passports, maintains diplomatic relations with some 45 nations, and has been in uninterrupted existence since the 11th century.

—James Hansen, "Knights of Malta,
a Mini-Nation Based on Chivalry"

2. I am anxious to say a word about the potato. . . . We sing the flower, we sing the leaf: we seldom sing the seed, the root, the tuber. Indeed the potato enters literature with no very marked success. True, William Cobbett abused it, and Lord Byron made it interesting by rhyming it with Plato; but for the most part it enters politics more easily and has done more to divide England from Ireland than Cromwell himself.

—John Stewart Collis, "The Potato"

3. While I was still a boy, I came to the conclusion that there were three grades of thinking; and since I was to claim thinking as my hobby, I came to an even stranger conclusion—namely, that I myself could not think at all.

—William Golding, "Party of One—Thinking as a Hobby"

4. Palestine twitches on the small white mat, struggles to raise her head, and failing, falls back again; she cries, then stops. Some slice of light has caught her attention. The nurse in bright pink carries a bird cage to the mat, and for a moment Palestine is pleased by two jumpy canaries—one black, one yellow. Now she rolls back and forth. Her legs, still bowed,

kick out spasmodically. You cannot tell if she hears the music in the nursery or the murmurs of the other babies, stacked up in their double-decker box cribs. She acknowledges no one. But everyone knows Palestine—if not by her blue "Space Patrol" sleep suit, then by the dark brown bruise on her right heel, and, of course, by the circumstance of her birth.

—Roger Rosenblatt,
"Lebanon: A Legacy of Dreams and Guns"

5. Suppose there were no critics to tell us how to react to a picture, a play, or a new composition of music. Suppose we wandered innocent as the dawn into an art exhibition of unsigned paintings. By what standards, by what values would we decide whether they were good or bad, talented or untalented, successes or failures? How can we ever know that what we think is right?

—Marya Mannes, *But Will It Sell?*

How do the following concluding paragraphs create a sense of an ending?

1. At times, lying on my back on the plain with binoculars trained on the sky, I have seen vultures circling in two or three layers, each one high above the other. What can this mean? A hungry duplication, or triplication, hopelessly covering the same feeding ground and using the only available thermals? Or the opposite—idle and well-fed reserves standing by for surplus?

No one can tell me. But here in the vulture country there are no birds more spectacular, more fascinating to watch and to study. In time we may find out the last of their secrets. I lie on the plains and keep on watching them. And they, I know, keep on watching me.

—John D. Stewart, "Vulture Country"

2. The dump was our poetry and our history. We took it home with us by the wagonload, bringing back into town the things the town had used and thrown away. Some little part

of what we gathered, mainly bottles, we managed to bring back to usefulness, but most of our gleanings we left lying around barn or attic or cellar until in some renewed fury of spring cleanup our families carted them off to the dump again, to be rescued and briefly treasured by some other boy with schemes for making them useful. Occasionally something we really valued with a passion was snatched from us in horror and returned at once. This happened to the head of a white mountain goat, somebody's trophy from old times and the far Rocky Mountains, that I brought home one day in transports of delight. My mother took one look and discovered that his beard was full of moths.

I remember that goat; I regret him yet. Poetry is seldom useful, but always memorable. I think I learned more from the town dump than I learned from school; more about people, more about how life is lived, not elsewhere but here, not in other times but now. If I were a sociologist anxious to study the life of any community, I would go very early to its refuse piles. For a community may be as well judged by what it throws away—what it has to throw away and what it chooses to—as by any other evidence. For whole civilizations we have sometimes no more of the poetry and little more of the history than this.

—Wallace Stegner, "The Town Dump"

3. Is the funeral inflation bubble ripe for bursting? A few years ago, the United States public suddenly rebelled against the trend in the auto industry towards ever more showy cars, with their ostentatious and nonfunctional fins, and a demand was created for compact cars patterned after European models. The all-powerful auto industry, accustomed to *telling* the customer what sort of car he wanted, was suddenly forced to *listen* for a change. Overnight, the little cars became for millions a new kind of status symbol. Could it be that the same cycle is working itself out in the attitude towards the final return of dust to dust, that the American public is becoming sickened by ever more ornate and costly funerals, and that a status sym-

bol of the future may indeed be the simplest kind of "funeral without fins"?

—Jessica Mitford, *The American Way of Death*

4. Yet who reads to bring about an end however desirable? Are there not some pursuits that we practice because they are good in themselves, and some pleasures that are final? And is not this among them? I have sometimes dreamt, at least, that when the Day of Judgment dawns and the great conquerors and lawyers and statesmen come to receive their rewards—their crowns, their laurels, their names carved indelibly upon imperishable marble—the Almighty will turn to Peter and will say, not without a certain envy when He sees us coming with our books under our arms, "Look, these need no reward. We have nothing to give them here. They have loved reading."

—Virginia Woolf, "How Should One Read a Book?"

5. Superstitions are sometimes smiled at and sometimes frowned upon as observances characteristic of the old-fashioned, the unenlightened, children, peasants, servants, immigrants, foreigners or backwoods people. Nevertheless, they give all of us ways of moving back and forth among the different worlds in which we live—the sacred, the secular and the scientific. They allow us to keep a private world also, where, smiling a little, we can banish danger with a gesture and summon luck with a rhyme, make the sun shine in spite of storm clouds, force the stranger to do our bidding, keep an enemy at bay and straighten the paths of those we love.

—Margaret Mead, "New Superstitions for Old"

8. BALANCE THE PRINCIPLES OF FRESHNESS: A SUMMARY

In writing freshly, there is always the danger of overwriting—of piling on images and creating ostentatious sentence rhythms. But the principles of freshness should be used in subtle, almost unnoticeable ways. Consider these two paragraphs from Truman Capote's description of a train ride through Spain.

> The young soldier was one of many on the train. With their tasseled caps set at snappy angles, they hung about in the corridors smoking sweet black cigarettes and laughing confidentially. They seemed to be enjoying themselves, which apparently was wrong of them, for whenever an officer appeared the soldiers would stare fixedly out the windows, as though enraptured by the landslides of red rock, the olive fields and stern stone mountains. Their officers were dressed for a parade, many ribbons, much brass; and some wore gleaming, improbable swords strapped to their sides. They did not mix with the soldiers, but sat together in a first-class compartment, looking bored and rather like unemployed actors. It was a blessing, I suppose, that something finally happened to give them a chance at rattling their swords.
>
> The compartment directly ahead was taken over by one family: a delicate, attenuated, exceptionally elegant man with a mourning ribbon sewn around his sleeve, and traveling with him, six thin, summery girls, presumably his daughters. They were beautiful, the father and his children, all of them, and in the same way: hair that had a dark shine, lips the color of pimientos, eyes like sherry. The soldiers would glance into their compartment, then look away. It was as if they had seen straight into the sun.
>
> —"A Ride Through Spain"

Although you might note the clarity and grace of Capote's prose, concentrate now on his use of the principles of freshness.

SENTENCE VARIETY AND RHYTHM

The compartment directly ahead was taken over by one family: a delicate, attenuated, exceptionally elegant man with a mourning ribbon sewn around his sleeve, and traveling with him, six, thin, summery girls, presumably his daughters. They were beautiful, the father and his children, all of them, and in the same way.

IMAGERY

hung about the corridors/like unemployed actors/lips the color of pimientos/eyes like sherry/as if they had seen straight into the sun

BALANCE

Their officers were dressed for a parade, many ribbons, much brass.

As though enraptured by the landslides of red rock, the olive fields and stern stone mountains.

CONNOTATION

summery, shine, sherry

EUPHONY-ALLITERATION

stern stone mountains/smoking sweet black cigarettes/enraptured . . . red rock/swords strapped to their sides/as if they had seen straight into the sun

PUNCTUATION

The compartment directly ahead was taken over by one family: a delicate. . . .

They were beautiful . . . in the same way:

REPETITION

They were beautiful, the father and his children, all of them. . . .

PERIODIC SENTENCE

It was as if they had seen straight into the sun.

SURPRISE

snappy angle/It was a blessing, I suppose/It was as if they had seen straight into the sun.

DEAD IMAGES, CLICHÉS, WORN-OUT PHRASES

Since you haven't had much practice at consciously creating *freshness* with prose, you might try an exercise my students find very useful. I benignly force them to create at least one fresh spot in each paragraph—that is, each paragraph must possess a bright spot created by imagery or rhythm, surprise, suspense, or any of the other nine principles. Let me show you what I mean. Here are students *applying* a principle of freshness:

CREATING BALANCE AND RHYTHM THROUGH REPETITION AND PUNCTUATION

It was just another walk out to the woodshed, except for the knife in my hand—and it was just another brisk autumn day, except for my intentions.

—Peter Nassar

CREATING SURPRISE, RHYTHM, HUMOR

Ever since the vast age of fourteen, I've felt that youth without stupidity is like Bud Abbott without Lou Costello—a straightman without a comedian. So my senior year in high school I figured I had fought stupidity long enough. I was young and knew I'd have to make mature, sane judgments all too soon, so why not take advantage of youth while I could? So I was stupid.

—Shari Minton

CREATING EUPHONY AND SURPRISE

Label Language

It was late Saturday night, and I was having a few izods at this Mercedes on Sixth Street. I levied two channels calvin kleining by themselves in the corner—so I thought I'd try my luck. I got up and poloed to where they were.

"You shouldn't be izoding alone," I said. The fat channel gave me a cold levi. I tried again.

"What are two nice channels like you doing in a mercedes like this?" I was really hot.

"Go cartier yourself," the fat channel said.

—David Fuller

CREATING SURPRISE AND TONE

TV-aholics

Intravenously absorbing a Wednesday night smorgasborg of "Eight Is Enough," "Charlie's Angels," and "Vega$," the only exercise they receive is a five-yard down-and-out to the refrigerator, slam-dunking (drunking) a six-pack of beer, serving a bag of Frito

Lay's, stealing a ham sandwich, and putting in a piece of Duncan Hines chocolate cake.

—Brian Till

CREATING IMAGERY

We all seemed to take our pledge of allegiance a little more seriously during the hostage crisis in Iran. I wonder why? It seems somewhat facetious to remember our patriotic heritage only when it is questioned; rather like telling your grandmother you love her only after she finds the lid off the cookie jar.

—Scott Statham

PUNCTUATION TO CREATE RHYTHM, REPETITION, BALANCE

It was August '78—I was 17, had no cares, no problems, plenty of time, plenty of money, and plenty of friends. I also had a father who continuously reminded me that I have, or should have, lots of cares, lots of problems, not enough time, and certainly not enough money.

—Brian Till

IMAGERY, SENTENCE VARIETY, EUPHONY

Moo. Ever felt like mooing? You know—when you're just one of the masses standing in line, like cattle being angled into a corral to be fattened up before slaughtering. I've noticed I'm not the only one who gets this feeling while being herded into good ol' Jester Cafeteria for another soybean enriched feeding.

—Shari Minton

SENTENCE VARIETY, PUNCTUATION TO CREATE RHYTHM

The image still lingers in my mind's eye; those long, ground-gobbling strides of John Wayne as he pursued Maureen O'Hara down the street, she running, yet wanting to be caught, he fulfilling the expectations she had, that happiness would come to them both only after the completion of the game. Yes, the game.

—Gerry McKee

CREATING EUPHONY (ALLITERATION, ASSONANCE) AND RHYTHM

Shiny mirrors and glass shelves line endless miles of cabinets, each with its own dazzling array of potions and powders offering fleeting but exquisite beauty to any woman. Walking, stopping, finding, imagining, touching, trying, hoping—the women pass each counter mesmerized by its contents and fascinated by the fantasies that fill their minds.

—Steven Shoupp

The above examples come from students writing about themselves, their feelings, and their attitudes. I selected these deliberately to underscore just that point. You can always write more freshly if you write about yourself, about what you know, what you feel. And write in your own voice. Uniqueness, you see, is a subtle creator of freshness. But what if you aren't allowed to write about yourself? What if you have to write about something you don't want to write about—a book or poem, say? My reply is that you learn to write by writing about yourself so, if for no other reason, write on your own, just for practice. Keep practicing these principles. Then, when you are required to write about something like a book, you will still be able to keep the prose fresh. When thinking about the principles of freshness, remember this triangle:

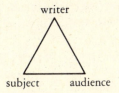

If you are concerned *mainly* with the "writer," that is, yourself, then you are probably *expressing,* and that means you would use many, if not all, of the principles of freshness. You would want to make your prose vivid with imagery, flowing with rhythm, and punctuated with surprise and wit. If you are mainly concerned with the audience (persuading them to vote for you, trying to convince them that American companies are causing the acid rain in Canada), then you are engaging in argumentation or persuasion which means you would sprinkle your main points with fresh spots in order to keep the communication lively and vivid. But if you are *mainly* concerned with the "subject," (a book review, a letter, for example) then you are probably *informing,* and that means you would use fewer of the principles of freshness. Imagery and too obvious a rhythm might detract from communication and your purpose. But fewer does not mean "none at all." You still should look for opportunities to make the prose fresh and pleasant to read. Notice what Don Graham does with punctuation, sentence variety, and balance:

> *Blanco,* Allen Wier's first novel, starts off well; the opening introduces us to the town in a manner reminiscent of Henry James' famous tally of what America did not contain: no established church, no peerage, no army, etc. Wier's Blanco contains even fewer marks of civilization: no newspaper, no hospital, no jail. The time is 1959. But the novel begins to get into trouble on the second page, when the characters are introduced. For Wier's characters, although they have impressed some reviewers as memorable, strike me as being unconvincing, derivative, drawn from literature rather than from life.

Some essays make me feel as if I'm trapped inside an unventilated, stuffy room and I'm being lulled into a drowsy state by a droning lullaby. Never write lullaby prose. Open the window and let in the fresh air—let in the principles of freshness.

SOME FINAL WORDS: FORTUNE-COOKIE WISDOM

1. You learn to write by writing. Practice, as with any skill, is the most important principle.
2. If given the chance, *always* select a topic that genuinely interests you. If not, keep practicing your Faulkner at home.
3. Write naturally. Don't affect a "high" style and don't write like anyone else. Write as you speak, then edit for the reader's sake.
4. Always write with the reader's mind. Try to keep the reader interested in every sentence of each paragraph.
5. Learn to trust your ear. Always read your prose aloud, listening for awkward phrasing and smooth rhythms. Your ear is often a good guide for punctuation.

6. Think of writing as movement like that of a phonograph needle, always moving forward. *Any* interruption (ambiguity, awkwardness, faulty grammar) of that smooth movement can disrupt the effect of the entire piece.

7. Think of editing as removing and adding. You remove wordiness, worn-out imagery, cliches, abstract words, jargon, ambiguity, awkwardness, and you add fresh images, new sentence rhythms, precise words, euphony, smooth transitions, meaningful coordination. As you edit, add and take away, always keeping the flow of the prose graceful.

8. Don't be afraid to cut. Cut out every word that doesn't make a direct contribution to the sentence or paragraph.

9. The writing process itself generates a special kind of energy: it puts you into another mental gear, and while there you will discover yourself refining your thoughts and seeking that ideal union of sound and sense, rhythm and meaning, image and idea. But you slip into this mental gear only after several minutes, at least, of writing. Make yourself write, even if you are not sure where you are going. The energy generated by writing will help you find your direction.

10. Relax. Memorize:

In language clarity is everything.
    —CONFUCIUS

A work has form in so far as one part of it leads a reader to anticipate another, to be gratified by the sequence.
    —KENNETH BURKER

Words differently arranged have different meanings, and meanings differently arranged have different effects.
    —BLAISE PASCAL

Or else:

Clarity

Grace

Freshness

Application:

ASSUMING THE EDITOR'S MIND

In this last application exercise, we'll take the essay and letter, which have been edited for clarity and grace, and try to invigorate them by applying the ten principles of Freshness.

Principles of Freshness

Control the rhythm of your prose
  Maintain sentence variety
  Use punctuation to create rhythm
  Use balance to create rhythm
  Use an occasional periodic sentence to help keep prose moving
Create subtle euphony
Surprise the reader
  Unexpected syntax and punctuation
  Wordplay and wit
  Imagery
Control connotation and denotation
Keep imagery fresh
Remove worn-out expressions and clichés
Write fresh introductions and conclusions
Balance the principles of freshness

You will recall from the discussion that expressive writing provides more opportunities than informative writing for applying the principles of freshness. We would, therefore, expect to use more of the principles of freshness in editing the essay than in the letter.

First, let's review the essay as it was after we edited it for grace.

Sample Essay

My roommate, Robert, is one of those men who looks like the hero on the cover of a harlequin romance. He is all things to all men and the apple of the eye of all the girls. Always in the lime-light, he is tall but not lanky; slender but not skinny; muscular but not brawny; and confident but not cocky. Everyone admired him, and, though green with envy, I must admit I admired him too. Breezing through life, he never seemed to have any problems—or so I thought until last Friday night.

The evening was progressing quietly as usual. I dozed through a French book while I scorched my Hamburger Helper casserole in an unscorchable skillet. As I ate the charred debris, I realized that Robert, who tends to talk a lot, was not smiling and not as cheerful as usual. Always a reliable source of supper-time small talk, on this occasion he was quiet as a mouse and seemed introspective and far away.

After dinner he lay down on the dingy couch and stared at the Pepto-Bismol poster on the wall. He spoke hardly two words. When I finally asked him what was wrong, my words became magic. He turned and looked up helplessly at me with tear-filled eyes the color of a pearl-gray winter morning. In a weak, trembling voice, he said, "It's just everything."

Robert never talked to me about his problems. The problems were always mine; the solutions were always his. He kept all his problems inside his head, and it was time for them all to come out.

For the next couple of hours, we laughed and cried and talked about his insecurity about his intelligence, his fear he would not be as good a lawyer as his father, his worries that he would never find the right woman. I realized that night that Robert was just like the rest of us. Even though he looked like the hero of a harlequin romance he still had problems. His shining image of perfection had changed to one of an ordinary person with ordinary problems. There's always more than meets the eye.

Now read through the final version by Brian Fest and notice how the principles of freshness enhance what was a mediocre paper.

[fresh introduction]

Do you believe in reincarnation? I've always envi-

sioned Robert, my roommate, as the reincarnation of one

[fresh imagery]   [remove worn-out expressions]

of those faultless heroes glossed onto the cover of a

[balance to create rhythm]

harlequin romance. You know the type: tall but not

lanky; slender but not skinny; muscular but not brawny;

confident but not cocky. Robert breezes through life
              [remove worn-out expressions]   [fresh imagery]
like most people breeze through the yellow pages—or so

I thought until last Friday night.

   The evening was progressing quietly as usual. I dozed
                        [euphony]
through an infinite, insipid chapter of my French book

while our economical but bland Hamburger-Helper casse-
                        [euphony]
role scorched my unscorchable Silver Stone skillet. As
              [euphony]
I crunched the charred debris of my casserole, I noticed
                              [punctuation to create rhythm]
something peculiar about Robert: his usually dimpled,
[fresh imagery]   [fresh imagery]
smiling face was shrouded by a sullen, somber mask. Al-

ways a reliable source of supper-time small talk, he was
[remove worn-out expressions]
very quiet and introspective—like a child being pun-
[fresh imagery]
ished for speaking out of turn.

   After dinner he lay down on the dingy couch and stared
                        [wordplay]
at the Pepto-Bismol-pink-flamingo poster on the living

room wall. When I finally asked him what was wrong, he
                              [control the rhythm of your prose]
shook his head, looked up helplessly at me with tearfil-

led eyes the color of a pearl-gray winter morning and

said in a weak, trembling voice, ""It's just every-

thing.''

Robert never really talked to me about his problems.

The problems were always mine; the solutions were always

his. He had always kept his problems stored inside his

[fresh imagery]
head like pennies in a piggy bank—finally there were too

many pennies, so the bank had to be emptied.

For the next couple of hours we laughed and cried and

discussed his insecurity about his intelligence, his

fear he would not be as good a lawyer as his father, his

worries that he would never find the right woman. Look-

[fresh imagery]
ing like a woeful little boy who didn't make the baseball

team, Robert transformed from my shining image of per-

fection to an ordinary person with ordinary problems.

[fresh conclusion]
But I must admit that I still think he belongs on the

cover of a harlequin romance.

The revised version balances the principles of freshness
throughout the essay creating a pleasant effect on the reader.
As you can see, expressive writing like this lends itself readily
to the application of the principles of freshness; informative
writing, like Ms. Crowley's letter, on the other hand, is less
amenable to them. Nonetheless I think that we can find a spot
or two that can be freshened. See what you think after you read
the letter over once again.

Sample Letter

September 14, 1983

Mr. Harry Snub
Vice-President
Snub Pencil Products, Inc.
P.O. Box 1009
Dearborn, Michigan 48121

Dear Mr. Snub:

When Texton placed its first order with Snub Pencil Products, Inc. for 5,000 pencils on May 19, we were confident that your company could deliver the pencils by the date our draftsmen and designers needed them. And after reevaluating our needs, we placed a second order three days later for 2,000. The delivery date on both orders was July 30.

We have received only 3,000 pencils. In a July 28 phone call, your distribution supervisor stated that your company makes only 15,000 pencils per year. We wonder, therefore, if you will be able to deliver the remaining 4,000 pencils.

Our draftsmen and designers here at Texton agree that your unique pencil designs would enable them to work more quickly. We hope you can meet our needs, but if you cannot, we'll have to cancel the contract.

I hope you take steps to provide us the pencils. Thanking you in advance.

Sincerely,

Carol C. Crowley
District Manager

And now the final version to which at least a few of the principles of freshness have been applied.

September 14, 1983

Mr. Harry Snub

Vice-President

Snub Pencil Products, Inc.

P.O. Box 1009

Dearborn, Michigan 48121

Dear Mr. Snub:

When Texton placed its first order with Snub Pencil
Products, Inc. for 5,000 pencils on May 19, we were confident that your company could deliver the pencils by
the date our draftsmen and designers needed them. And
after reevaluating our needs, we placed a second order
three days later for 2,000. The delivery date on both orders was July 30.

We have received only 3,000 pencils. In a July 28 phone
call, your distribution supervisor stated that your
company makes only 15,000 pencils per year. We wonder,

therefore, if you will be able to deliver the remaining

4,000 pencils.

Our draftsmen and designers here at Texton agree that

your unique pencil designs would enable them to work

[punctuation to create rhythm]

— *so, of course, we*

more quickly, ~~We~~ hope you can meet our needs, ~~but~~ if you

[maintain sentence variety]

however,

cannot, we'll have to cancel the contract.

I hope you take steps to provide us the pencils. ~~Thanking~~

[remove worn-out expressions]

~~you in advance.~~

Sincerely,

Carol C. Crowley

District Manager

EDITING EXERCISES

The following passages represent the diversity of effects that can be achieved when sensitively applying the principles of Freshness. Read each selection carefully, identifying each principle of Freshness as you go. Some selections will rely heavily on one principle (connotation or imagery, say), while others balance all the principles throughout. Which piece uses the principles most overtly? Which uses the principles most subtly?

THE NATION EMERGES FROM 25 DARK YEARS WITH TOO FEW FROGS

Many Now Mercifully Escape Dissection by Schoolboys; The Orbiting Frog Otolith

—JAMES STERBA

America's long national frog shortage is over.

Twenty-five years after the Russians caused it, the Reagan administration has quietly but firmly put an end to it. For the first time since Sputnik, U.S. demand for frogs no longer outstrips supplies.

Reaganomics, the recession, and cuts in federal funds for science education have combined to make it a littler easier being green.

"We have plenty now," says Roger Griedl, a Wisconsin frog merchant who has monitored the batrachian market's ups and downs for 30 years. "Demand is way down. There's not a lot of money out there these days to spend on frogs."

Although this may be good news down in the swamps, frog-supply companies are distressed and science educators worried. A nation that skimps on frogs today, they assert, will not lead the world in science tomorrow.

While it continued, the frog shortage touched the lives of millions of Americans. But for those who managed to pass the last quarter-century oblivious of the quandary, some background:

Sputnik started it.

Sputnik was the earth's first artificial satellite, and when the Soviets lofted it on October 4, 1957, the U.S. got scared. President Eisenhower launched a national campaign to beat the Russians in science. Declaring that science education was a matter of national security, he signed the National Defense Education Act in 1958, thereby circumventing opponents of federal aid to education. Federal dollars, including $50 million to $80 million annually for laboratory supplies, began to rain on high schools and universities. And what did these schools buy?

Frogs, by the millions. (They also bought textbooks, teacher training, student fellowships and lab equipment.) Pretty soon, virtually every student in every biology class in the nation got to take a frog apart.

"Those were the good old days," says Mr. Griedl, who is biology division operations manager of a frog-supply company called Nasco, a Ft. Atkinson, Wis., subsidiary of Geneve Corp. "Gosh, after sputnik every kid got his own frog."

Why frogs? Because taking them apart is a lot more exciting than looking at textbooks, says Roberta Hill, a biology teacher at Cyprus Lake High School in Ft. Myers, Fla. "It's an attention getter, a hands-on enrichment experience." She says lab work in comparative anatomy starts with taking apart a worm. Dissecting a frog is the culmination.

The idea was to lure students into science careers, using frogs as carrots.

A victory of sorts over Moscow came 12 years after Sputnik when Neil Armstrong set foot on the moon. In calling it a "giant leap for mankind," however, he obviously wasn't telling the whole story. Suppliers estimate that more than 100 million frogs gave their lives in the interim on behalf of U.S. science prowess, although no one is sure how many students they inspired to join the space program.

MEDIUM

—JONATHAN MILLER

Television is a vast, phosphorescent Mississippi of the senses, on the banks of which one can soon lose one's judgment and eventually lose one's mind. The medium itself is depressing. The shuddering fluorescent jelly of which it's made seems to corrode the eye of the spectator and soften his brain. It's quite different from the movies, which seem to be made of nothing except the images themselves. In television, the bodies and faces, the dances and games are suspended in a coldly glowing magma that must surely be repulsive to the touch: at once palpable and intangible—quite uncanny. It is like ectoplasm, in fact, which makes the term "medium" doubly appropriate. Television is a low-grade domestic séance in endless session, and the set goes to it with a vengeance, mouthing its gobbet of luminous cheesecloth until the tube burns out. Like a séance, too, it has a curiously limited repertoire, and it is certainly banal in the same way. There are no epiphanies to be had on television. There are none of the sometimes shattering apocalypses that one can get, even with the worst movies, in the dreamy caverns of the cinema. Possibly it's because Telly is so small and stingy. How could one ever hope to get an epiphany from it? Movies start with the advantage of an oceanic form, which can at least engulf the spectator and force him into a delicious surrender. Telly, on the other hand, is a mean, fidgeting irritant, far smaller than one's own field of vision, flickering away in the corner of the eye like a dull, damaged butterfly. It would be mad, perhaps, and certainly unfair, to expect consistent marvels from such a mingy little electronic

membrane as this. Not to mention all the other drawbacks of the instrument—the frame rolls, the flickers, the snowstorms, the ghosts,
the warps, the jumps, the judders, the chronic vibrato. Not to mention
the commercials, which inhabit the crevices of the programs like vile,
raucous parasites, jumping out all over the livingroom, nipping,
tweaking, and chattering unforgivably about joints, armpits, skin
wrinkles, bowels, and blocked-up nasal passages. And not, further-
more, to mention the way in which Telly slithers into the home and
stays in one corner of the room like a horrible electronic gossip. In
the suggestive gloaming of the darkened parlor, Telly is just one of
a number of bits of furniture vaguely discerned in the general moon-
glow. There is no sense of occasion, as there is with the theatre or
the movies—none of the mounting excitement that goes with buying
one's ticket, choosing the right candy, and shouldering one's way
blindly into the bosky auditorium. Telly is a sad, autistic experience
that rots the spine and sets one up as a willing customer for all
the sleazy remedies that are offered by the commercials. Just the
same, something comes across. After a period of intellectual
dark-adaptation, one begins to pick up glimmers of an unintended
message. This comes across *because* of television's banality rather than
in spite of it. Just as the dead make their revelations through the boring whine of some fat suburban medium rather than through an ex-
travaganza of supernatural effects, society mutters its anxious confi-
dences best through the bleak, unguarded monotony of modern TV.
In the endless sessions of transmission, the vigilance of the programs
must flag, so one can pick up all sorts of slips and betrayals.

THOUGH UNOFFICIAL, SPRING COMES EARLY IN SPOTS

—JAMES KILPATRICK

It is a well-known fact—at least it is well-known here in Rappahan-
nock County—that spring lives in a small swampy area just east of
the Shade Road; about a quarter mile south of the apple packing plant.
On the evening of Friday, March 11, spring made her first appearance.

The event is especially worth marking this year, for many discour-
aged Rappahannockers had begun to think the lady had moved away.

Under the heading of Mean and Dirty Winters, our winter certainly was small potatoes compared to the winter in Buffalo, Fargo
and Brainerd, but it was a mean and dirty one all the same.

The winter went on and on. It would not stop. Our whole country froze up like a tray of ice. Pipes burst and water pumps froze, and it was a backbreaking effort to get hay to the cattle. Nobody could remember anything like it.

But a few days into March, things began to thaw; and on this particular Friday evening, driving home from Washington, there was spring beside the Shade Road. How do I know? Because you could hear the peepers. They are the certain heralds of April on its way.

If you have never met a peeper, you should know that a peeper is a tree frog. He is not bigger than a minute—maybe three-quarters of an inch, greenish-brown, pop-eyed. His sole function is annually to announce the entrance of spring. This he does by puffing up his tiny throat, thrusting his head forward, and crying PEEP-er, PEEP-er, PEEP, PEEP, PEEP-er. The note is somewhere around B-natural above middle C; and after a winter like ours, it is the most welcome note ever sounded.

Spring turned up the next day, Saturday, in the great willow tree down at Woodville. Twenty-four hours earlier, the branches were bare. Now they had become a green cascade, a fountain of leaves as tiny as tears. People came to the Woodville Rural Independent Post Office to get their mail, and they looked at the willow across the road, and they all said the same thing: Spring!

After that, the lady turned up everywhere. The crocuses popped up, lavender and orange, and in the rock garden all kinds of tiny things began to lift their heads: Hepatica, aconite, dwarf daffodils.

The heather that had been given up for dead came back to life. The wild iris shouldered its sturdy frame above the ground. By Thursday, St. Patrick's Day, the fields were unmistakably green.

We hadn't seen a groundhog since October. Now, driving down the Rudasill's Mill Road, we saw four of them lumbering along: Four fat men out for a morning jog. They were sweating and complaining and saying, "Man, am I out of shape!" A dozen rabbits were on the lawn Wednesday evening, practicing sprints and hurdles. Chipmunks and squirrels appeared out of nowhere.

The past Tuesday, a pair of newly-wed bluebirds arrived, took one look at Apartment 4-D, our very best bluebird box, and promptly moved in. This is a truly elegant apartment, if you will forgive a little bragging, equipped with washer, drier, two ovens, air conditioning and wall-to-wall carpeting throughout. It rents promptly every spring.

A flock of 50 robins arrived. The killdeer is back, foolish bird, building a nest in a perilous spot right next to the driveway. Most of the juncos have gone, and the grosbeaks also, but we have a new visitor not registered before: A fox sparrow, and a handsome fellow he is.

With spring looking on, everyone has started plowing and planting and getting gardens ready. On the 12th, we planted onion sets and lettuce, and we raked up the backyard around the great chestnut oak that rules our hill. Once again we marveled at the sheer fecundity of nature. In an area perhaps 15 × 30 feet, we must have raked up—or pulled up—5,000 acorns. Half of them were trying to take root and turn into oak trees.

Down on your hands and knees, digging out these seedlings, you wonder what the chestnut oak knew what we didn't. A year ago, that tree saw the bitter winter coming; it produced more acorns than we ever have seen before, each fruitful with the germ of life. The winds of November scattered them, and the snow and ice watered them, and now spring warms them, and the wonder and the mystery all begin anew. Peepers and willows and bluebirds and groundhogs! The shut-in spirit opens like a crocus, lifting fragile petals to a welcome sun.

WRITING ASSIGNMENTS

1. Assume you are part of a group welcoming foreign students to the U.S. for the first time. Part of your duty is to write an essay explaining a social custom that might at first seem strange to someone who knows little about our culture. A few suggestions: gathering at the local drive-in, slumber parties, pep rallies, the car, the prom, blind dating, Halloween.

2. Select one of your favorite aphorisms and illustrate its truth by drawing upon your personal experience. A few suggestions: "The cruelest lies are often told in silence;" "Nothing so much prevents our being natural as the desire to seem so"; "Everybody wants to *be* somebody; nobody wants to grow." Don't forget about the lyrics of a favorite song.

3. Write a story about you and your pet. Use as many clichés and stale images as possible. Then rewrite the story replacing the dead clichés and images with fresh ones.

4. Write a vivid account of the most frightening time in your life.

5. Assume you have been given an opportunity to write a column for the local newspaper. You have been given total freedom to write whatever you wish. Decide on a title and

write your first essay as a columnist. Take a look at the work of several syndicated columnists to see what concerns they deal with.

6. Write an essay with the word "fad" somewhere in the title. Explain what fads are. Why do we have them? Why are they only temporary?

7. Compare the YOU today with the YOU as a pre-teen. Be as concrete as possible. Include physical as well as psychological differences.

8. Assume that with the wave of your hand you can make any twentieth-century invention or device disappear. What would it be? What would be the consequences?

9. What is your least favorite spectator sport? Boxing? Baseball? Football? Golf? Swimming? Explain why.

10. Assume you are to give a speech to the graduating class of your old high school. What would you tell them? Make your introduction and conclusion fresh and memorable.

PART • TWO

THE
• READER'S •
MIND

To be a good writer you must be a good reader—and by reader I do not mean someone who can understand every word. A careful reader sees beyond the words to technique, to structure, to the principles of clarity, grace, and freshness, just as the careful ear of the musician hears distinctly the chromatic harmony and transposition that those of us with untrained ears don't hear at all. Of course, to be a good reader you have to read. As Joseph Addison says, "Reading is to the mind what exercise is to the body." To develop the reader's mind, then, you must train yourself through appropriate exercises. The exercises I suggest are ones that have proved useful over the years in making my students more analytical readers and, concomitantly, better writers. When you *see* the principles of writing in the work of others, you can more easily see them (or see that they are not there, as the case may be) in your own writing. I do not propose that my way is *the* way to read an essay. I do know, however, that it is a very useful and efficient way to help you read and write with more confidence.

When you read you should look for two things: the places where the writer demonstrates the principles of clarity, grace, and freshness and the paragraph strategies the writer uses to organize his ideas. Looking at paragraph strategy is particularly important because it not only shows you how experienced writers efficiently organize their material into units of thought, but it also helps you see that these paragraph strategies come directly from the way we naturally organize our thoughts.

PARAGRAPH STRATEGY

Assume that you have just returned from a vacation to a remote Mexican cove where the gray whales are known to mate every December. While on your seven-day trip you witnessed the harpooning of several of the giant mammals, and the experience moved you to decide to join a protect-the-whales group. Back home again, you are visiting with a friend who is eager to learn of your trip. Your friend can stay only thirty minutes. To recount the entire seven-day trip hour by hour would take all night. How do you efficiently communicate your experience and your feelings in so short a time? Think a moment not about *what* you might say, but *how* you might organize what you say. Quite automatically you might do twelve things.

1. You might *narrate* your odyssey to the Mexican cove—the lost luggage, bouncing flight, cab ride through the countryside, and so on.

2. You might *describe* the inlet—the sparkling sand, the turquoise water, the smell of salt in the air, the shrieks of diving birds, and, of course, the barnacle-clad whales bobbing like buoys in the waters of the cove.

3. You might *classify* the particular whale you photographed—distinguishing it from the blue whale or the killer whale.

4. You might give the *cause* of the whales' congregation—to mate in warm waters before moving back out to sea and you might give the *effect* upon the species if the harpooning continues.

5. You might explain the *process* of killing and gutting the whales—men and machines carving up the mammal and sorting out its inventory.

6. You might give *examples* to *illustrate* the inhumanity of the killers—the cheers when a small man stabbed the open eye of the leviathan.

7. You might make an *analogy* between the whale-hunt and buzzards picking a carcass clean.

8. You might *compare and contrast* American policy toward the whales with Japanese and Soviet policy.

9. You might define a term like "endangered species."

10. You might argue with your friend—*moving from general statement to specific support*—that whaling should be stopped for the following ten reasons.

11. You might continue your argument—*moving from specific details to a generalization*—by citing five instances of Soviet and Japanese treaty violations and concluding that the United Nations should impose sanctions upon them.

12. Finally, you might use any combination of the above strategies—*comparing* the size of a whale's heart to that of a Volkswagen is *describing* as well.

In thirty minutes, then, you would have organized your experience and ideas in such a way that you could communicate efficiently with your friend. You would have arranged your information into parts and, thus, created a composition. In writing you do the same thing but with even more calculation. In other words, in order to communicate effectively with another person, writers constantly follow certain paragraph strategies because they are efficient means of communication. The following are the most common paragraph strategies for organizing and communicating information or ideas.

1. Narrating
2. Describing
3. Classifying
4. Giving the cause and effect
5. Explaining a process
6. Illustrating your point with examples
7. Creating analogies
8. Comparing and/or contrasting
9. Define a term
10. Moving from a general statement to specific examples
11. Moving from specific examples to a generalization
12. Combining any of the above.

These are not the only ways paragraphs can be organized. Some paragraphs do not follow these strategies, yet they are still efficient, clear, and coherent. The feelings or ideas themselves generate their own "organic" organization. Any paragraph that is unified (sticks to one topic) and coherent (moves smoothly from sentence to sentence) and does not follow one of the above strategies can be considered an organic paragraph—paragraphs often used as transitional paragraphs between those that follow a strategy.

EXAMINING AN ESSAY

The first thing I ask you to do in this reading exercise is to take a look at the articles in any of your favorite nonfiction magazines—*National Geographic, Smithsonian, Omni, Psychology Today,* for example. I predict that you will discover that either the essays follow almost entirely one of the strategies (usually narration) or that they are composed of a variety of these paragraph strategies with an occasional organic paragraph interspersed where necessary (usually as a transitional device). Select one of the essays and identify the strategy of each paragraph. The second thing I ask you to do is to keep the principles of Clarity, Grace, and Freshness in mind as you read and annotate the essay by indicating and identifying the principles the writer uses. To show you how this works, consider an article by Eric Drexler that appeared in the *Smithsonian.*

Drexler organized his material into thirty-three paragraphs, all but three following one of the most common paragraph strategies. These paragraphs, these units of thought, help him communicate a large amount of information efficiently. In addition, he looked for places in his prose where he could make it fresh and enjoyable to read. What follows is part of the article with the paragraph strategies identified and each paragraph annotated with references to the principles of clarity (C), grace (G), and freshness (F). Notice how the combination of paragraph organization and carefully applied principles makes the communication of information smooth and easy.

F: wordplay

SAILING ON SUNLIGHT MAY GIVE SPACE TRAVEL A SECOND WIND

—ERIC DREXLER

'Lightsails' made from super-thin aluminum could travel the solar system and beyond, and bring back precious payloads from space

DESCRIPTION

F: *euphony*

F: *sentence variety*

F: *introduce with description*

As the sun sinks from sight one summer evening in 1992, a spark appears in the fading light, rising and moving east. Faint at first, it climbs toward the zenith, shrinks to a line, then opens to a hexagon of light, slowly turning, sweeping across the sky to redden and vanish in the shadows of the east. The next night, it comes again.

As night follows night, the hexagon shrinks to a dot, then to a point drifting slowly across the sky circling higher and higher, now above both Earth and its cone of shadow. At last it vanishes, no longer circling, a fading glint among the stars.

ORGANIC—TRANSITION

F: *euphony*

F: *repetition*

Five centuries after Columbus, the hope of treasure calls once more and a ship sets sail for distant shores. And again, the ship has sails.

ORGANIC

G: *question to signal commitment*

But why, one may ask, should a spaceship use sails? On the seas of Earth, engines replaced sails generations ago, and engines of awesome power launch our spacecraft today.

NARRATION—CHRONOLOGICAL

G: *clear transition*

C: *precise, concrete detail*

Although rockets have been used for ages, light pressure has been known for scarcely a century. The source of the idea of using mirrors as sails to catch sunlight remains blurred. James Clerk Maxwell described electromagnetic fields in the 19th century; his equations indicated that light exerts a force when it reflects off a mirror. In 1924, Sir Arthur Eddington showed that light pressure helps keep stars from collapsing under their own weight (the light from our sun could support a weight of more than 100 trillion tons), and in that same year two Russians,

Tsander and Tsiolkovskiy, suggested using sunlight to drive large mirrors through space.

DESCRIPTION

F: imagery—metaphor
F: imagery
G: appropriate voice

C: concrete detail

F: euphony

F: imagery—simile

Another approach, which I have proposed, is to build a kind of solar sail, called a Lightsail, directly in space. If you imagine a network of carbon-fiber strings, a spinning spiderweb kilometers across with gaps the size of football fields between the strands, you will be well on your way to imagining the structure of a Lightsail. If you imagine the gaps bridged by reflecting panels built of aluminum foil thinner than a soap bubble, you will have a fair idea of how it looks: many reflective panels tied close together to make a vast, rippled mosaic of mirror. Now picture a load of cargo hanging from the web like a parachutist dangling from a parachute, while centrifugal force holds the web-slung mirror taut and flat in the void, and you should almost have it.

PROCESS

G: appropriate voice

Early in my work on Lightsails, I learned how to make thin films, to convince people (me, for example) that foil several hundred times thinner than kitchen foil could be made and handled. The process is simple, even on Earth, and had been developed by scientists doing basic research on other matters.

To make thin metal films, first take a glass microscope slide and smear it with detergent (some kinds work better than others). Let it dry, then wipe off all that is visible, leaving behind an invisible film. Then place the slide in a vacuum chamber and pump out the air. Next, run current through a tantalum strip in the chamber, until it glows white, to vaporize a bead of aluminum from its surface. This turns the slide and the vacuum-chamber window into instant mirrors. Finally, remove the slide and dip it slowly in water, which will creep under the metal film, following the detergent, with the result that the film floats off to turn a rectangular area of water into a smooth, rippling reflector.

COMPARISON/CONTRAST

G: clear direction and commitment

G: proper subordination

C: precise, concrete detail

Compare a Lightsail with an ordinary rocket. A one-ton rocket could push a cargo pod weighing more than a ton to a kilometer per second in a few minutes. A one-ton sail (more than a mile wide) would take all day to reach the same speed with the same cargo. But the next day the rocket would coast, drained of fuel, while the sail would add another kilometer per second to its speed. Accelerating just over one-thousandth as fast as a falling brick, it would pass 20 times the speed of sound (in air) in less than a week.

COMPARISON/CONTRAST

F: control connotation

C: concrete words

F: sentence rhythm—balance and repetition

F: punctuation to create rhythm

C: concrete detail

F: periodic sentence

The mighty engines of space gobble fuel in a way that steamships never did, and sails in space have other advantages over their relatives below. At sea, the winds shift, stop and storm unpredictably. In space, the "wind" is sunlight, and holds quite steady. At sea, winds give a ship a steady speed. In space, the "wind" blows at the speed of light and the "hull" has no drag; thus, speed can increase while light still strikes the sail. On seas of such vastness, high speeds are essential—circling the sun along Earth's orbit would take more than a century at the speed of a jet airliner.

GENERAL TO SPECIFIC/CAUSE AND EFFECT

F: imagery—simile

G: punctuation to create rhythm

Since Lightsails spin like a gyroscope, a Lightsail requires a steady twisting force to turn it to a new orientation. The sail can turn itself in two ways: it can shift the cargo off axis by

G: *sentence variety*

F: *balance sentences*

G: *parallel ideas in parallel form*

reeling and unreeling the connecting lines, or it can tilt its reflecting panels to shift the distribution of light pressure. The first turns the sail swiftly, for maneuvers near planets; the second turns it slowly, for maneuvers in orbit around the sun. In solar orbit, the sail can spin in one orientation for weeks at a time without moving a motor. Any panel can jam in any position with little effect, since there are so many of them; thus sails should run for decades without repair.

ANALOGY

F: *repetition for effect*

F: *euphony*

C: *precise, concrete detail*

Today, the solar system seems vast and inaccessible. But our sense of the size of the solar system reflects, in part, our sense of the cost of going places with rockets. From this viewpoint, developing Lightsails would be somewhat analogous to moving everything in the inner solar system to a thousand-kilometer orbit above the Earth, just outside the fringe of the atmosphere.

Among the most important changes would be access to asteroids. The planets themselves will remain deadly deserts, their gravity blocking access by Lightsails and handicapping industry. Planetary atmospheres block solar energy, spread dust, corrode metals, warm refrigerators, cool ovens and blow things down. Even the airless moon rotates, blocking sunlight half the time, and with gravity enough to ground a Lightsail beyond hope of escape.

EXAMPLE

C: *concrete detail*

Better yet, in some [asteroids] lie exposed metals of kinds made scarce here ages ago, elements that sank in the formation of Earth's metal core. Meteoritic steel, for example, is a strong, tough alloy containing nickel, cobalt, platinum group metals and gold. A kilometer-wide chunk of this material contains precious metals worth more than a trillion dollars, mixed with many years' supply of nickel and cobalt for

the entire world. Raw materials from the asteroids can provide most of the needs of an industrial civilization.

COMPARISON/GENERAL TO SPECIFIC

Still, the cost of space launches may make the
idea of mining raw materials in space seem absurd. But consider another perspective: what is
the cost of bringing down a meteorite? Nothing, of course: they fall by themselves, free samples from asteroids. Launches take rockets, but
plain rocks know how to fall. Material, once
gathered and guided to Earth, need cost little
to bring down. Since it makes scarcely more
sense to bring back a whole asteroid than to
bring back the moon, the chunks should be
small. Since things can be dropped with pin-
point accuracy (and since landing zones like salt
flats are often large), returning material can be
safe. Lightsails could bring robots and refining
equipment to an asteroid and return treasure
F: surprise   beyond the dreams of Cortés.

SPECIFIC TO GENERAL

C: concrete detail   In time, principles used in a sail for hauling a
                          satellite can serve in a sail large enough to haul
F: repetition for   an ocean liner to Mars in less than a year. In
effect   time, Lightsails can team with lasers to drive
                          starships. A sail pushed by sunlight can leave
G: proper   the solar system in less than two years, its speed
subordination   climbing past 100 kilometers per second before
                          the sun fades astern. A large laser orbiting the
F: periodic sentence   sun could better this, pushing the sail with its
                          beam of light far out into the interstellar dark-
F: sentence rhythm   ness, pushing the sail toward the speed of light.
                          . . . One way or another the stars themselves
                          lie within reach of sails.

ORGANIC

C: concrete words   Today, Earthbound governments growl at each
F: control   other, threatening nuclear war over the limited
connotation   resources of a single planet. Perhaps the great-

F: punctuation to create rhythm

F: imagery

F: punctuation to create rhythm

F: periodic sentence

F: fresh conclusion

est promise of space is the perspective it provides: that to fight over the resources of Earth is to fight over crumbs.

For a nation interested in prosperity and in peace, the challenge of space cannot be ignored. European, Soviet and Japanese efforts in space have grown even as the U.S. space budget continues its post-Apollo decline, and even the leaders of these countries still act as if the Earth were the whole "world." Perhaps, after 500 years, it is time the Copernican revolution came to global politics.

By examining an essay in this way, you will acquire the habit of "strategically" looking at your own prose. Before you write, you know you can run through the paragraph strategies to help you find your ideas. As you write, you constantly keep in mind that you must be clear and graceful and constantly look for places where you can make your prose fresh. Remember that an essay with at least one fresh spot in each paragraph creates an anticipation within the reader that the entire reading will be pleasant. Even though Eric Drexler's subject may limit his opportunities for freshness, he still does use description as an effective way to introduce expository material; he does use a question to signal his commitment; he does supply some occasional euphony and imagery; he does surprise us with an unexpected example; he does write in an appropriate tone of voice; he does create a sense of an ending in his closing paragraph; and, of course, by following the principles of grace and clarity, he does avoid awkward sentences, ambiguous phrases, and droning sentence rhythms. In short, he wants his material not only to be well organized, but also clear, graceful and fresh.

The purpose of this exercise is to make you a more analytical reader—a reader who sees beyond the words to technique, to structure, to the principles of clarity, grace, and freshness. By becoming a more careful reader, you are becoming a more careful writer. By discovering the hidden beauties within a piece of prose, you may discover within yourself the hidden desire and skill to delight *your* reader's mind.

EXAMINING A PARAGRAPH

Before you find your long essay or article, you may want to practice on the following paragraphs. Identify the paragraph strategy used in each excerpt, and annotate appropriately.

ZEN AND THE ART OF MOTORCYCLE MAINTENANCE

—ROBERT PIRSIG

A classical understanding sees the world primarily as underlying form itself. A romantic understanding sees it primarily in terms of immediate appearance. If you were to show an engine or a mechanical drawing or electronic schematic to a romantic it is unlikely he would see much of interest in it. It has no appeal because the reality he sees is its surface. Dull, complex lists of names, lines and numbers. Nothing interesting. But if you were to show the same blueprint or schematic or give the same description to a classical person he might look at it and then become fascinated by it because he sees that within the lines and shapes and symbols is a tremendous richness of underlying form.

A PRESENTATION OF WHALES

—BARRY LOPEZ

The sperm whale, for many, is the most awesome creature of the open seas. Imagine a forty-five-year-old male fifty feet long, a slim, shiny black animal with a white jaw and marbled belly cutting the surface of green ocean water at twenty knots. Its flat forehead protects a sealed chamber of exceedingly fine oil; sunlight sparkles in rivulets running off folds in its corrugated back. At fifty tons it is the largest carnivore on earth. Its massive head, a third of its body length, is scarred with the beak, sucker, and claw marks of giant squid, snatched out of subterranean canyons a mile below, in a region without light, and brought writhing to the surface. Imagine a 400-pound heart the size of a chest of drawers driving five gallons of blood at a stroke through its aorta: a meal of forty salmon moving slowly down 1,200 feet of intestine; the blinding, acrid fragrance of a 200-pound wad of gray ambergris lodged somewhere along the way; producing sounds more shrill than we can hear—like children shouting on a distant playground—and able to sort a cacophony of noise: electric crackling of shrimp, groaning of undersea quakes, roar of upwellings, whining of porpoise, hum of oceanic cables. With skin as sensitive as the inside of your wrist.

INSTRUMENTS OF DARKNESS

—LOREN EISELEY

Let me illustrate what I mean by a very heavy and peculiar stone which I keep upon my desk. It has been split across; carbon black, imprinted in the gray shale, is the outline of a fish. The chemicals that composed the fish—most of them at least—are still there in the stone. They are, in a sense, imperishable. They may come and go, pass in and out of living things, trickle away in the long erosion of time. They are inanimate, yet at one time they constituted a living creature.

Often at my desk, now, I sit contemplating the fish. It does not have to be a fish. It could be the long-horned Alaskan bison on my wall. For the point is, you see, that the fish is extinct and gone, just as those great heavy-headed beasts are gone, just as our massive-faced and shambling forebears of the Ice Age have vanished. The chemicals still about us here took a shape that will never be seen again so long as grass grows or the sun shines. Just once out of all time there was a pattern that we call *Bison regius,* a fish-like amphibian called *Ichthyostega,* and, at this present moment, a primate who knows, or thinks he knows, the entire score. In the past there has been armor; there have been bellowings out of throats like iron furnaces; there have been phantom lights in the dark forest, and toothed reptiles winging through the air. It has all been carbon and its compounds, the black stain running perpetually across the stone.

But though the elements are known, nothing in all those shapes is now returnable. No living chemist can shape a dinosaur, no living hand can start the dreaming tentacular extensions that characterize the life of the simplest ameboid cell. Finally, as the greatest mystery of all, I who write these words on paper, cannot establish my own reality. I am, by any reasonable and considered logic, dead. This may be a matter of concern to you reading these words; but if it is any consolation, I can assure you that you are as dead as I. For, on my office desk, to prove my words is the fossil out of the stone, and there is the carbon of life stained black on the ancient rock.

THE INFORMED HEART

—BRUNO BETTELHEIM

Another subtle, but most effective device the SS used to alienate the family from the prisoners, was to tell the wife or other relatives (usually only closest relatives were permitted to plead the prisoner's case), that not only was it the prisoner's own fault that he was in the camp, but that he would have been released long ago had he behaved there as he should. This led to recriminations in letters; relatives pleaded with the prisoner to behave better, which often outraged him, considering the conditions of his camp existence. He, of course, could not answer such accusations. At the same time he was resentful because what probably enraged him most was the family's own ability to act and move about freely when he was so helplessly unable to act for himself. In any case it was one more experience separating the prisoner from his few remaining ties to the non-camp world.

THE PHYSIOLOGY OF THE GIRAFFE

—JAMES V. WARREN

The subjects were wild giraffes captured by lasso from a fast-moving vehicle on the Kenya plains. After the giraffe was captured and tied down flat on the ground the pressure gauge was implanted in the animal's neck through a small slit made under local anesthesia in the carotid artery. In a giraffe the carotid is usually more than six feet long, is relatively straight and has few branches. The gauge was placed in the upper part of the neck near the head. At the same time a small ultrasonic flowmeter, measuring the velocity of blood flow by means of the backscattering of high-frequency sound waves from the red cells, was implanted. The apparatus, including a small transmitter and mercury batteries, was taped onto the giraffe's neck. At the end of the period of observation the animal was recaptured, the instruments were removed, the incisions were repaired and the giraffe was released unharmed to join its fellows in the bush.

THE SPIDER AND THE WASP

—ALEXANDER PETRUNKEVITCH

These solitary wasps are beautiful and formidable creatures. Most species are either a deep shiny blue all over, or deep blue with rusty wings. The largest have a wing span of about four inches. They live

on nectar. When excited, they give off a pungent odor—a warning
that they are ready to attack. The sting is much worse than that of
a bee or common wasp, and the pain and swelling last longer. In the
adult stage the wasp lives only a few months. The female produces
but a few eggs, one at a time at intervals of two or three days. For
each egg the mother must provide one adult tarantula, alive but paralyzed. The tarantula must be of the correct species to nourish the
larva. The mother wasp attaches the egg to the paralyzed spider's ab-
domen. Upon hatching from the egg, the larva is many hundreds of
times smaller than its living but helpless victim. It eats no other food
and drinks no water. By the time it has finished its single gargantuan
meal and become ready for wasphood, nothing remains of the tarantula but its indigestible chitinous skeleton.

THE ASCENT OF MAN

—JACOB BRONOWSKI

The fossil lemur has some essential marks of the primates, that is, the
family of monkey, ape and man. From remains of the whole skeleton
we know that it has finger nails, not claws. It has a thumb that can
be opposed at least in part to the hand. And it has in the skull two
features that really mark the way to the beginning of man. The snout
is short; the eyes are large and widely spaced. That means that there
has been selection against the sense of smell and in favour of the sense
of vision. The eye-sockets are still rather sideways in the skull, on either side of the snout; but compared with the eyes of earlier insect
eaters, the lemur's have begun to move to the front and to give some
stereoscopic vision. These are small signs of an evolutionary development towards the sophisticated structure of the human face; and yet,
from that, man begins.

MATCH

—FROM *THE WAY THINGS WORK*

In the manufacture of safety matches, softwood logs (e.g., poplar) are
peeled into a thin continuous shaving, or veneer, about $\frac{1}{10}$ inch thick
(veneer process). The ribbon of wood is then cut up into splints at
a rate of about two million per hour. These splints are soaked in a
bath of sodium silicate, amonium phosphate or sodium phosphate and
then dried. This impregnation prevents afterglow. Next, the splints
are fed into a continuous match machine in which the splints, standing
on end in wide belts, are passed through a paraffin bath, which treat-

ment aids ignition. Next the machine dips the ends of the matches in a liquid composition which becomes the striking head when dry. This composition consists of the oxygen carrier (potassium chlorate, lead oxide, potassium chromate, manganese dioxide, etc.), the inflammable ingredient (sulphur, etc.), frictional additives (powdered glass), colouring matter, and binding agents (dextrin, gums). The striking surface on the matchbox consists of powdered glass, red phosphorus, colouring matter, and binding agents.

Safety matches are so called because they can be ignited only by friction against the striking surface of the box. On the other hand, there are universal matches which have heads of such composition that they can be lit by striking them on any friction surface. The heads of such matches have a somewhat different chemical composition from ordinary safety matches. The round wooden matches manufactured in America have two-colour heads and are produced by a double dipping process. The large bulb of the match consists of mainly inert substances, while the "eye" contains the readily ignitible ingredients. The bulb having the larger diameter prevents the sensitive "eyes" from rubbing together after packing. Another American invention, now in worldwide use, is the paper book match. These matches are packed in printed cardboard folders with a striking surface on the outside.

When the head of a safety match is rubbed against the striking surface, frictional heat is generated at a small area of the head. The heat liberates oxygen from the oxygen carrier ingredient, and this oxygen combines with the sulphur (sulphur dioxide is formed in this reaction), whereby additional heat is evolved, causing more oxygen to be liberated and react with sulphur. The chemical process thus initiated by friction proceeds very rapidly, so that the entire match is soon alight. The paraffin-impregnated splint also catches fire. The impregnation of the splint prevents it from continuing to glow after the flame is extinguished.

THE MOUNTAINS OF CALIFORNIA

—JOHN MUIR

The color-beauty about Shadow Lake during the Indian summer is much richer than one could hope to find in so young and so glacial a wilderness. Almost every leaf is tinted then, and the goldenrods are in bloom; but most of the color is given by the ripe grasses, willows, and aspens. At the foot of the lake you stand in a trembling aspen grove, every leaf painted like a butterfly, and away to right and left round the shores sweeps a curving ribbon of meadow, red and brown dotted with pale yellow, shading off here and there into hazy purple. The walls, too, are dashed with bits of bright color that gleam out on the neutral granite gray. But neither the walls, nor the margin meadow, nor yet the gay, fluttering grove in which you stand, nor the lake itself, flashing with spangles can long hold your attention; for at the head of the lake there is a gorgeous mass of orange-yellow, belonging to the main aspen belt of the basin, which seems the very fountain whence all the color below it had flowed, and here your eye is filled and fixed. This glorious mass is about thirty feet high, and extends across the basin nearly from wall to wall. Rich bosses of willow flame in front of it, and from the base of these the brown meadow comes forward to the water's edge, the whole being relieved against the unyielding green of the coniferae, while thick sun-gold poured over all.

IN PRAISE OF GADGETEERS

—JOHN J. ROWLANDS

In case you have never looked it up, a gadget is defined as "a contrivance, object or method—often used of something novel or not known by its proper name."

A gadget is nearly always novel in design or concept and it often has no proper name. For example, the semaphore which signals the arrival of the mail in our rural mailbox certainly has no proper name. It is a contrivance consisting of a bamboo pole, two copper right-angles, some wire and a piece of shingle. Call it what you like, it saves us frequent frustrating trips to the mailbox in winter when you have to dress up and wade through snow to get there. That's a gadget!

SELECTED SNOBBERIES

—ALDOUS HUXLEY

Most of us are also art-snobs. There are two varieties of art-snobbery—the platonic and the unplatonic. Platonic art-snobs merely "take an interest" in art. Unplatonic art-snobs go further and actually buy art. Platonic art-snobbery is a branch of culture-snobbery. Unplatonic art-snobbery is a hybrid or mule; for it is simultaneously a sub-species of culture-snobbery and of possession-snobbery. A collection of works of art is a collection of culture-symbols, and culture-symbols still carry social prestige. It is also a collection of wealth-symbols. For an art collection can represent money more effectively than a whole fleet of motor cars.

BULBS

—JAMES UNDERWOOD CROCKETT

For all the lovely innocence that bulbs display in bloom, they have been involved in some strange goings-on during the course of history. Undoubtedly the most bizarre of these was the "tulip mania," a tidal wave of speculation in which tulips were traded for profit in the manner of corporate stocks, commodity futures or real estate. Tulip mania engulfed Western Europe early in the 17th Century, peaked in Holland between 1634 and 1637 and had such a sorry outcome that thereafter a professor of botany at Leiden, one Evrard Forstius, used to beat tulips to death with his walking stick whenever he encountered any. Before the wave crested, an otherwise sensible brewer had swapped an entire brewery for one bulb, a miller his mill for another. At its height the frantic trading in tulips made the Florida land boom and Wall Street speculations of the 1920s look almost colorless by comparison.

PART THREE

THE
·WRITER'S·
MIND

Even though looking for the principles of Clarity, Grace, and Freshness as you read will sharpen your writing skills, practicing writing is still your best instructor. It is one thing to recognize the writing principles and quite another to apply them as you write. So to complete this book's approach to writing, I offer three suggestions that over the years have proved efficient and effective ways to provide the practice needed to hone a burgeoning writer's prose. Practice three kinds of writing: *writing feeling, writing seeing, writing reasoning.* Writing feeling (expressing your emotions) will quickly make you sensitive to tone of voice and to sentence rhythm—two qualities often overlooked by writers who have been writing monotone what-I-did-last-summer prose. Writing seeing (describing and narrating) will make your prose more visual and fresh—and often more precise. Writing reasoning will make you acutely aware of organization, of clear, logical movement and, incidentally, will give you practice in the most common paragraph strategies. Having practiced communicating your feelings, your perceptions, and your thoughts, you will have become familiar with the skills required to effectively communicate information. I'll explain just how at the end of each of the following sections.

4. Writing Feeling

*The object of Truth, or the satisfaction of the intellect,
and the object of Passion, or the excitement of the heart,
are although attainable, to a certain extent, in poetry, far
more readily attainable in prose.*

—EDGAR ALLAN POE

It's right there embedded within the word, but few people see it. Motion. Emotion. Emotion in writing is movement, and without movement your prose becomes, as you would, lifeless. Here is a writer who probably feels emotion, but does not translate it into words:

> Baseball is an American game that I cannot bring myself to like. There is not enough activity to peak my interest, and the managers who are always walking onto the field take up too much time arguing with the umpires even though they know they will not win the argument.

The writer with real conviction says this:

> I hate baseball. I have always hated baseball. As a matter of fact, I have a hard time liking anyone who *does* like baseball.
> . . . I don't like managers in sports either, and there is no other game where the manager is as important as in baseball. . . . But what's managing got to do with a game? They sit in the dugout like little kings, waving, gesturing, spitting. They rush out on the field to challenge a decision by an umpire even though no decision has ever been changed in the hundred years the game has been played. When a manager storms out on the field, does he think this is going to be the first time? Why do they let the managers out on the field at all?
>
> —Andy Rooney, "Baseball"

173

As you can see, hear, and feel, Andy Rooney's version "moves" with the energy of honest emotion.

Perhaps it all started in high school or even junior high, but somewhere in your career as student, you suppressed your emotions when you wrote. Your honest feelings became something you reserved for after-school hours. Yet, nothing will teach you more about writing more quickly than writing with sincere conviction about something that stirs your emotions. As T. S. Eliot recognized, emotion plays a vital role in writing:

> For a mind of such agility, and for a sensibility so reticent, the minor subject, such as a pleasant little sand-coloured skipping animal, may be the best release for the major emotions. Only the pedantic literalist could consider the subject-matter to be trivial; the triviality is in himself. We all have to choose whatever subject-matter allows us the most powerful and most secret release; and that is a personal affair.

When you write for yourself, when you "release" your emotion, you will begin to feel the rhythm of your sentences and hear the tone of your voice. The more you express your feelings, the more you will understand that, as a writer, you have many rhythms and voices and all are transferable to prose. Thus, I encourage my students to get in touch with rhythm and tone in prose by writing from their hearts, by releasing some emotion into their sentences.

EXAMPLES OF WRITING FEELING

I don't know why, but when college students write from their hearts, they usually do one of three things. They moan and complain; they reflect upon their world; they (and these are my favorite) reminisce about people and times whose memory poignantly stirs their emotion. So, I ask you to do the same: complain, reflect, reminisce. Permit the mood of your mind to govern the rhythm of your sentences and the tone of your voice. The models given below, which are taken from

my students' work, may give you a better idea of what I mean.
Listen for rhythm and tone of voice as you read.

A quick note: Giving students the freedom to express themselves means that there can be no restrictions on what they
write—for to do so is to supress that honest emotion that is
so necessary in creating rhythm and tone. Several of the following selections reflect honest emotion about the one thing many
college students have on their mind—each other. I do not, of
course, expect you to agree with or even like the points of view
expressed, but I do want you to notice carefully how these writers let their emotions and mood influence their prose. Read
these pieces carefully. I'll be waiting on the other side with
more to say.

Complaining

I have enjoyed the new rise in country and western music's popularity. Being a direct descendent and lifelong fan of good ole
"twang-twang honky" songs, I was thrilled to have a large number
of people "finding" country music. Honky-tonks are where my
roots stem from.

Then the foe of this paper entered the stage—the obnoxious,
overbearing smartass that fits in a honky-tonk like a vulture in a
pet store. These people still holding on to their disco tendencies,
entered the country and western set to shake up its newly built
dynasty. The country-thèques (discos that play country music) were
filled with these obnoxious critters that do nothing but show how
fake they can be, while trying desperately not to be aware of
it—every one a Terry Toughguy that steps out of his $350 Reyn-
olds Penland suit at 5:30 and makes the scene by 7:30, decked out
in his quasi-Dior, country-cut, western shirt and tight-fitting Calvin
Kleins with the $150 Silver Belle ten-gallon felt hat, and obnoxious
ostridge-hide boots. The pseudo-cowboys in the country-thèques
also wear exquisite jewelry, like $1000 Rolex quartz wristwatches
covered with diamonds, and of course, the great standbys—
18-karat gold chains that get tangled in the hair transplanted into
his chest, class look-alikes for Bobby Ewing from "Dallas," but boy
are they country *and* cowboy.

The women that hang out at these country-thèques do just that
. . . hang out. The "polyester princesses" and "maybelline queens"

that wear their best satin shirt, unbuttoned to the navel and tied at the bottom so they can be sure to flaunt their stuff (usually just a lot of cleavage) to some poor ole "cowboy" that has been couped up in the office all day.

—Tony Moos

After groaning about the food, the herd usually resigns itself to passively eating the pulverized pulp plopped on their plate without looking at it. Most have trained themselves to consider any little "crunchy surprises" as just extra protein. However, few can reconcile a loud crunch of roach caliber in their "Beef Paprika" (soggy meat-flavored soybean) without stampeding for the nearest exit.

—Shari Minton

Few things in this world turn my stomach quicker than Cathy Rigby on television discussing how "natural" it is for a celebrity to talk about—feminine protection. Let's face it, the average tampon or sanitary napkin advertisement on television is about as tasteless as joke-telling at funerals. Most of these commercials are tacky, idiotic, insulting to intelligent life, and embarrassing as hell. It is extremely annoying when I am enjoying a quiet evening watching the tube, and I find myself being reminded every twenty minutes about something I'd rather forget. Contrary to popular belief, not every woman discusses why she likes "Pursette" tampons, while holding the box over her head in the middle of the New York Stock Exchange.

—Shari Minton

Reflecting on the World Around Them

Each major sport has its own technique for immediate post-win player celebration. After a touchdown is scored, all hands pile on the scorer—after he performs his little end-zone dance—everyone trying to be the highest on the stack. For a sport apparently dedicated to such piling-on activity, you might think the players would get enough during the game. Perhaps this permits the bench warmers to see some action.

—Bill Groce

Headlines in lemon yellow and glossy white reveal titles "How to Have a Beautiful Body"—"Skiing, Saunas, Sex"—"Seduction Update"—"Eighty-Five Sexy-Hot Looks"—"You in Action." Paging through *Harper's Bazaar,* the readers see photographs which show green-eyed blonds in virgin-white lace gowns, peach complexions, moist lips, long naked legs and deep cleavage. Advertisements read "Sensual—but not too far from innocence—Jontue." "About as far as you can go—The HCC Collection." "He still knows how to send chills up and down my spine—De Beers." These articles and advertisements reflect beautiful, sensuous women who serve as models for every woman. They tell women how to pour the foundation, build the exterior, and polish the finished product. Through this process women become competitors—one hating the other for the ability to capture any resemblance to the ultimate "model." Someone said that it is because of women that women hate each other, but he was mistaken. It is because of other women that we hate ourselves.

—Lynda Curik

The thanks-drive can be seen in action during any encounter with a salesperson or cashier. Thank you's fly back and forth across the counter like a heated volley over a net. A typical example: with goods in hand, you approach the cashier at your local supermarket. He casually serves:

"Thank you, will there be anything else?"

"No, that's all, thanks," you smartly lob back. He recovers by thanking you for your credit card. As he returns the card, you spike a quick, unexpected "Thanks," then pause for a short time-out while he rings things up. When he hands you the receipt, you thank him smugly, knowing the end is near. It's game point now and he pathetically tosses you his last gasp of thanks while handing you your change. You lift the package from the counter as one might raise a trophy, deliver the final phrase with a tone that says "Thank you!," period.

A while back the word "Trash" or "Refuse" was sufficient. Soon, however, that was considered a bit crude and so was replaced with a directive, "Push" or "Pull." But the idea has definitely gone too far when a trash can is labeled "Thank You." Obviously, this is not a label for the garbage, nor is it a message *from* the garbage. Instead, it means "Thank you for cleaning up after yourself." The thank-you is "in advance" of your going along with the hidden request. If you're the suspicious type, you might feel you're being manipulated.

—Kathy Blackbird

Reminiscing

Yet I knew that tonight I would be able to stall my future and escape my past—I would find love, lust, and paradise by the dashboard light.

It is strange that all I can remember now are bits and pieces of our hours spent together. I remember the scent of her hair—the fresh, clean fragrance of Gee Your Hair Smells Terrific. The sonata under the stars that the crickets played, dutifully serenading us every evening. Her light-red lipstick glistening against her creamy complexion by the light of the moon. I remember Andy Gibb playing continuously, track after track, every song stirring our emotions. I remember my arm sticking to the vinyl seat, and my feet hanging out the window. And I remember most of all her holding me close and whispering, "What are you thinking of?" when we both knew what I was thinking of.

Does growing up mean not having the time to enjoy the virtues of parking: sharing a starlight night, warm smiles, wet kisses, and very importantly, releasing the perception of time? Inside the car, in each other's arms, time stood still, measured only by the occasional click of the 8-track player; outside, time moved quickly—people died, babies were born, parents argued, robberies occurred, in short, reality.

Too many college students are afraid to let time rush past them. They are afraid they will be left out, that they will miss something important—perhaps a football game, a burger burn, a sorority meeting, or something equally earthshaking. For many, the transition from high school to college means fast-food sex squeezed in while the roommate is gone, or a drunken orgy—couples beating a path to the bedroom like an ant trail leading to some cache of goodies.

I *am* growing up, but, unlike many other students, I still search for another romantic, someone who appreciates the beauty of hot summer nights. Until then, I can always go into a drug store, open a bottle of Gee Your Hair Smells Terrific, and slip back two years, butterflies in my stomach and all.

—Brian Till

"Arizona Jack" is what people around Gila Bend, Arizona called him. Jack Waters was a Pima Indian—born, raised, attached, and confined to the reservation. He raised five kids and buried two wives there. Jack picked cotton when he could and drank whiskey all the time. Jack was dying . . . from breathing dust. But it wasn't just dust that killed him. Fate found him face down in a shallow irrigation ditch . . . the ditch that fed the fields in which he worked. It was too much whiskey and too little luck that killed "Arizona Jack."

—Bob Asmussen

Some say Ben was born there . . . No one, not even old Mrs. Catchet down the street, can remember when he did not live in the old two-story house on the corner. Not that he seems old—he still meets the paperboy at five every morning and mows his yard every Saturday wearing his floppy straw hat and his baggy green shorts and his black dress socks in folds around his ankles. He just seems permanent—like the cottonwood tree in his backyard.

—Jeff Kobs

They put me in the ambulance box and took me to Honey Grove. To stop the bleeding in my stomach they flew me back to Dallas in an army helicopter. Before I went into chemical sleep I asked where you were. The eyes behind the green mask looked away and said nothing.

My mother drove me back along that same highway. I was still laced together with synthetic thread. The water tower in Bonham didn't look so strange in the daylight. Passing a big oil spot in the middle of the road, my mom told me that's where it happened. Broken glass twinkled on the ground.

—Russell Scott

Jolly Polly was the Fat Lady for a carnival I saw when I was eight years old. She was only part of the freak show, a small menagerie of the malformed, but she amused me more than any of the other freaks. I could stand for hours, laughing with the rest of the crowd as Polly waddled over to her throne, which hung from a huge scale, and plopped herself down, serene and secure in her mightiness. A short, blue-and-white sailor dress fought to restrain Polly's army of flesh, but rippling rolls of fat draped over each other and hung over the sides of Polly's throne like a huge down quilt. Her marshmallow head seemed to sit directly on top of her shoulders, with no trace of a neck; I think her neck was hidden by her chins which hung loose like the skin of a Brahman bull. Jolly Polly's full red lips were always smiling, even when we all laughed at her as if she were something less than human. The only pain or irritation I could sense in Polly was in her rough voice when she spoke the words I would have nightmares about thirteen years later.

I guess sometimes it takes years to realize what we've been

through; when I remember Polly's less than jolly voice, I finally realize she had been laughed at, pointed at, and gawked at so many times that it didn't bother her anymore—she knew she was watching the *real* freak show, and I was part of it.

—Brian Fest

VOICE

As you can see, and perhaps feel, there is no one perfect way to express emotion. On the contrary, one sure way to judge the writer's sincerity is to consider the idiosyncracies of his style. Still, if you look carefully at these students' passages, you will notice that they all vary their sentence length, and they all use punctuation to create rhythm. I need to particularly stress their use of punctuation. As students become sensitive to the rhythm and tone of their voices, they discover—to their surprise—that they habitually use certain kinds of punctuation marks more than others. Some discover the semicolon; others become fond of the dash; and some even develop an affection for parentheses. As they hear the sound, rhythm, and pauses in their own voices, they *feel* the need for a symbolic way of properly communicating these to the reader. At last, then, punctuation becomes a useful part of language and not a set of cumbersome, dusty rules they have to memorize to please the teacher.

TONE

This sensitivity to the rhythm of their own voices leads students directly to the *tone* of their own voice, and tone of voice establishes and controls a writer's style. For style is the writer's personality governed by his purpose and audience. Although many things contribute to it, style is carried by form and rhythm and is made emphatic by tone of voice—the writer's attitude toward his subject, purpose, and audience. In the passages you've just read you can not only point out numerous examples of writers using punctuation or varying sentence length to control prose rhythm, but you can also identify each writer's attitude toward audience, purpose, subject. Think back to Jolly Polly with her marshmallow head and smiling red lips or to the vinyl seat and 8-track tape that glowed by the dashboard light. In each case we know how the writer feels about his memory, we know his reminiscing is sincere, we know he assumes his audience will be sensitive enough to appreciate the honesty. In short, each passage has a unique and appropriate tone.

Practicing controlling your tone of voice can help you gain control of your prose. Of course, most of the time you will not be writing about yourself; you will not be complaining or reminiscing. Instead you will be informing or evaluating or arguing or expounding upon something—kinds of writing that require different kinds of tone. But what tone? How do you learn to create it? The answer is the same for all writers: always keep in mind your attitude toward your subject, your purpose, and your audience. I will illustrate this with a few examples.

Franklin D. Roosevelt owned a quick wit and an engaging sense of humor—something he called upon frequently during interviews with reporters and friends. However, in a speech at Harvard University during Hitler's conquest of Europe, Roosevelt assumed a formal tone, one befitting the audience (American people/scholars) and his *purpose.*

> We, too, born to freedom, and believing in freedom, are willing to fight to maintain freedom. We, and all others who believe as deeply as we do, would rather die on our feet than live on our knees.

Compare Roosevelt's tone to this:

> I ran into my brother today at a funeral. We had not seen one another for fifteen years, but as usual he produced a pig bladder from his pocket and began hitting me on the head with it. Time has helped me understand him better. I finally realized his remark that I am "some loathsome vermin fit only for extermination" was said more out of compassion than anger. Let's face it; he was always much brighter than me—wittier, more cultured, better educated. Why he is still working at McDonald's is a mystery.
>
> —Woody Allen, *Without Feathers*

Woody Allen's attitude toward his *audience* (his fans) and his *purpose* (to entertain with his usual, absurd humor) and *himself* (he knows he is not a president, a Joyce, or a Faulkner) is just as clear and distinct as Roosevelt's. Both men select an appropriate tone even though both have other tones they would use on different occasions. Your style, made most manifest through your tone of voice, can vary greatly. Writing well is not just organizing and punctuating correctly, but finding the most appropriate tone of voice.

Most expository prose, especially the kind you will be writing most often, is not as formal as Roosevelt's nor as informal as Allen's, but somewhere in that vast area in between. In fact, imagine a continuum of possible tones. At one end we have the formal (Roosevelt), at the other end the informal (Allen), and in between an infinite range of other tones. Somewhere near the center is a kind of middle tone—something with form but not formal, something casual but not slang.

Roosevelt	Middle tone	Allen

Let's move toward that middle tone by looking at two more passages. In the first expository piece, Loren Eiseley—a poet, scientist, naturalist—informs the reader about research on the purpose and speculates about what such research can tell us about ourselves. Not as formal as Roosevelt, he is just as serious toward his audience and about his purpose.

There is nothing more alone in the universe than man. He is alone because he has the intellectual capacity to know that he is separated by a vast gulf of social memory and experiment from the lives of his animal associates. He has entered into the strange world of history, of social and intellectual change, while his brothers of the field and forest remain subject to the invisible laws of biological evolution. Animals are molded by natural forces they do not comprehend. To their minds there is no past and no future. There is only the everlasting present of a single generation—its trails in the forest, its hidden pathways of the air and in the sea.

Man, by contrast, is alone with the knowledge of his history until the day of his death. When we were children we wanted to talk to animals and struggled to understand why this was impossible. Slowly we gave up the attempt as we grew into the solitary world of human adulthood; the rabbit was left on the lawn, the dog was relegated to his kennel. Only in acts of inarticulate compassion, in rare and hidden moments of communion with nature, does man briefly escape his solitary destiny. Frequently in science fiction he dreams of worlds with creatures whose communicative power is the equivalent of his own.

It is with a feeling of startlement, therefore, and eager interest touching the lost child in every one of us, that the public has received the recent accounts of naval research upon the intelligence of one of our brother mammals—the sea-dwelling, bottlenosed porpoise or dolphin.

—*The Star Thrower*

Compare Eiseley's tone of voice to H. L. Mencken's who, in the following excerpt from his regular column in the *Baltimore Sun,* reviewed President Warren G. Harding's inaugural address.

On the question of the logical content of Dr. Harding's harangue of last Friday I do not presume to have views. The matter has been debated at great length by the editorial writers of the Republic, all of them experts in logic; . . . But when it comes to the style of a great man's discourse, I can speak with a great deal less prejudice, and maybe with somewhat more competence, for I have earned most of my livelihood for twenty years past by translating the bad English of a multitude of authors into measurably better English. Thus qualified professionally, I rise to pay my small tribute to Dr. Harding. Setting aside a college professor or two and half a dozen dipsomaniacal newspaper reporters, he takes the first place in my Valhalla of literati. That is to say, he writes the worst English that I have ever encountered. It reminds me of a string of wet sponges; it reminds me of tattered washing on the line; it reminds me of a stale bean-soup, of college yells, of dogs barking idiotically through endless nights. It is so bad that a sort of grandeur creeps into it. It drags itself out of the dark abysm (I was about to write abscess!) of pish, and crawls insanely up the topmost pinnacle of posh. It is rumble and bumble. It is flap and doodle. It is balder and dash.

—"Gamalielese"

Mencken is not as serious as Eiseley or as informal as Woody Allen, but he is not afraid of informality, nor of passion or humor. Both Mencken and Eiseley are reporting; both are writing expository prose, but each uses a different tone of voice, a tone that is governed by attitude toward subject, audience, purpose and, of course, himself. Eiseley leans toward Roosevelt; Mencken toward Allen. Our continuum of tones, therefore, might appear something like this.

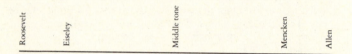

With this in mind, let's turn to that middle tone—a safer kind of tone, one not as expressive as Mencken or Allen's, not as formal and serious as Eiseley or Roosevelt's. Safe expository prose.

Let's, in fact, return to Eric Drexler's article on lightsails in Part 2. Drexler is writing to the readership of *Smithsonian* magazine, educated people interested in the past as well as the future, who enjoy reading about science and art. They expect to be informed, to be given knowledge about the world around them. Drexler is interested in his subject because he has worked on the project he is explaining. Thus, he must adopt a tone of voice that does not distract from the communication of his information—something Woody Allen's tone would do—and yet he must not assume a high and formal tone of voice that is not appropriate for his subject—sailing into space is not as solemn a proposition as Roosevelt's war with Hitler. So Drexler must find a voice away from those extremes. Mencken's voice is, however, too informal and Eiseley's voice is still too serious. So he writes in a voice that is casual, but not informal, persuasive, but not emotional. For the most part he keeps his own voice out of the prose, but on occasion we hear him politely intrude ("Now picture a load of cargo hanging from the web like a parachutist dangling from a parachute, while centrifugal force holds the web-slung mirror taut and flat in the void, and you should almost have it."/"Early in my work on Lightsails, I learned how to make thin films, to convince people (me, for example) that foil several hundred times thinner than kitchen foil could be made and handled.") Drexler's tone, then, is friendly, cordial, yet serious—an idealist informing readers about his dream for the future. It fits his purpose, his audience, his subject, and himself.

If you recall, I said that I am applying the words "middle tone" not to anything specific, but to a general range of prosaic voices. I do not want to leave you with the notion that Drexler's tone is somehow the perfect expository tone—there is no such thing. There is no perfect tone any more than there is a perfect man or woman. To underscore this point, consider the tone of another writer writing on a similar subject and for a similar audience: Tom Wolfe's "Columbia's Landing Closes a Circle," a descriptive report on the flight of the Columbia space shuttle for *National Geographic* magazine. He, like Drexler, avoids the extremes of either Roosevelt, Mencken, Eiseley, or Allen, and he, too, gives us paragraphs of technical and historical information.

> The problem with the X-20 program—the political problem—was the Titan rocket. The Titan III was to consist of a Titan II ballistic missile, ten stories high and 150 tons in weight, capable of 430,000 pounds of thrust at lift-off and boostered by two large solid-propellant rockets, each ten feet in diameter, attached to either side of the Titan II. Atop the Titan II would be the X-20. But this great brute of a rocket assembly was at least two and perhaps three years away from development.

But Wolfe does something more with his tone. His voice is a little more informal and witty and his prose a little more visual.

> The test subject would be placed inside a small shell—a capsule barely six feet across—and the shell would be placed on top of the Redstone. It was the human cannonball approach. All that was required was a test subject who could sit and stand the strain.

Because the poor devil couldn't control his own flight, entire fleets of ships and aircraft, plus a worldwide network of radio tracking stations, had to be mobilized in order to be sure of finding him when he hit the water. Afterwards, neither the capsule nor its rocket could be used again. It was like buying a new Buick Electra 225 every time you drove over to the Seven-Eleven.

If you compare these passages from Wolfe with those of Drexler's piece, you'll see that, while they both fit into that broad middle tone, they are both distinctly different. Our continuum of infinite tones might look something like this.

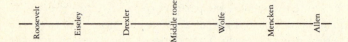

Most of the writing you will be doing will fall into that large middle tone range from Drexler to Wolfe. Yet your tone will be distinctly yours, one that reflects the mood of your mind, your attitude toward your subject and audience. You will find that distinctive tone by writing sincerely to your audience.

The purpose of writing about your feelings, therefore, is not to make you a great reminiscer or complainer, but to make you sensitive to tone, to help you gain control of it—no matter your subject, purpose, or audience. Once you can write in different voices and with different rhythms, you can keep your tone consistent and appropriate, and at times even modulate it to add freshness to your prose. Two paragraphs from Noel D. Vietmeyer's "Our 90-year War With the Boll Weevil Isn't Over," taken from *Smithsonian* magazine, provide a good example of modulating voice. In the first paragraph, as Vietmeyer introduces his essay, he refrains from intruding too much with his personal feelings.

A century ago the boll weevil was an obscure insect living a tenuous existence on scattered wild plants in Mexico. It was barely known to science when, in the 1880s, it began gobbling up cotton fields so quickly that the growing of cotton soon had to be abandoned in central Mexico. American entomologists had to write to

France to find the boll weevil's scientific name, *Anthonomus grandis.*
Only three specimens were available in all the world's insect collections.

But only four paragraphs later, while still giving us information, Vietmeyer varies his tone a little as he has found an occasion in expository prose where a little feeling is not only permissible, but refreshing.

> Boll weevils are inoffensive-looking critters: grayish-brown, humpbacked blobs of living hunger, related to the weevils that infest stored grain. Two or three of them could stand comfortably on your little fingernail, but when these resourceful saboteurs are disturbed or threatened, they characteristically pull in their legs, drop to the ground and play dead.

This varying of rhythm and tone is precisely what I mean when I speak of *controlling* your own prose—you modulate it, so to speak, and that makes the reading more pleasant.

Of course, sometimes the subject matter and audience require that your tone remain fairly consistent. You do not want to detract from an article on open-heart surgery by calling too much attention to the author, for example. But even in mainly middle-tone essays, you may find an opportunity for a little of the author's feeling. This is particularly likely in concluding paragraphs where the writer can not only pull everything together for the reader, but also satisfy the reader's sense of ending—a sense that rhythm and tone convey. Here are two examples. The first concluding paragraph comes from an article entitled "The Ears of the Earth," a report in *Esquire* magazine, by David Noonan on the world's largest radio telescope. After almost entirely middle-tone paragraphs that give us technical information, he concludes with this:

> A gathering in the hills. The slide rule johnnies are cruising through space, dynaflow all the way. It's mind over universe, and one single set of eyes is all it takes to explore the heavens, one set of ears to hear. Lean back in your chair and stick your head into the night, stick your head into space. Lean back out of the light

and listen well. You'll hear more than frogs and the rain, you'll
hear the hum of the universe, the cool sound of everything there
is, everything there was, everything there will be.

The second concluding paragraph comes from "The New Age
of Reason," an essay by John Culkin appearing in *Science Digest.*
Here Culkin argues for a new alphabet, one that is more efficient and practical. Although his concluding tone is not as
overt as that of Noonan's, he still satisfies the reader's need
for that sense of ending. After paragraphs of technical information about the UNIFON alphabet and consonants and diph-
thongs, he writes this:

> To many, the idea of reforming things as familiar as the alphabet,
> the typewriter and the calendar is comparable to tampering with
> the law of gravity or taking a referendum on the tides. We have
> a cultural and psychological investment in these institutions that
> discourages change. But as a planetary culture evolves and the in-
> terdependence of people becomes more crucial, the reasons for
> simplifying English, typing and the calendar will become even
> more compelling. We can't inflict on the next generation an ineffi-
> cient alphabet, an illogical keyboard and an untidy calendar. We
> wouldn't fly an airplane with the 20 percent efficiency rate of our
> alphabet. Is human communication any less important?

An effective writer, then, learns when its appropriate to shift
rhythm and tone and how to do so. The how-to-do-so is what
practicing writing feeling provides. Once you have written
about your emotions at their extremes, then you can easily get
in touch with those feelings that are not as passionate, but just
as real. You move from an overt tone and rhythm to that more
subtle middle tone. And still, the sound does echo the sense.

For your first writing assignment, then, I encourage you to
use the student paragraphs to guide you in expressing your
own emotion. Complain or moan or whine about something
that bothers you; communicate some observation that, for
whatever reason, affects you emotionally; remember poignantly a friend or relative or moment. But in all cases, let the
mood control your *rhythm* and tone. In other words, write
from your heart.

An important footnote. Writing feeling not only helps you learn to control your prose rhythm and tone, but it also can help you learn something about the writing process itself.

THE WRITING PROCESS

Writing is not nearly as conscious an act as some may lead you to believe. If I may borrow several words from Brewster Ghiselin (whose book *The Creative Process* I recommend), writing is full of "tension and tendency," full of "ill-defined impulses." You're never sure *exactly* what you are going to say or how you are going to say it. You have a feeling, an impulse, a notion—but never absolute certainty. Like confluent rivers, these seem to converge at some unanticipated time during the writing process to become the *direction* and *purpose* of your thoughts.

According to Ghiselin, most writers testify that their work is rarely the "production by process of purely conscious calculation." Rather, it is "spontaneous and involuntary" cooperation with the conscious calculation. This means that two of you actually write your essay—the alert and aware editor who searches for redundant words and slips in grammar, and the impulsive, often mysterious, writer who simply takes dictation from those inexplicable impulses within. So don't assume you have to know everything you're going to say before you say it. If you're really writing, you won't. Too many students look at a blank piece of paper as if it were a Chinese puzzle—they can't get started because they don't know where to begin and don't know where they're going. But begin and go. Don't dam up your thoughts and feelings before you write—let them flow like a river *as* you write. The act of writing can help you find your direction. Waste some paper—you won't be wasting your time.

Of course, this conscious and unconscious act of writing does pose problems for the student. First of all, it does little good to have an awareness of this spontaneous and calculating process if there is no sincere will on the part of the writer. The *will* to write provides the discipline that in turn permits the conscious and unconscious to "do their thing"—to even surprise the creator with their work. Few students have this will, and understandably so. You didn't go to college to become a Shakespeare or Sappho. So you, and your teacher, are stuck with a discipline in which, to truly master it, you must possess what you don't possess, namely, will. Writing has this in common with playing the piano: unless you sincerely want to learn to play the piano, you probably won't ever play it very well. One way to overcome this obstacle is to introduce yourself to writing by writing about yourself, about what you feel and think. What you learn as you write about your feelings can be used when you begin writing about other, more impersonal matters. Most important, you will acquire an understanding of the constant and exciting interplay between the calculated and the spontaneous that all professional writers know so well. One important facet of the Writer's Mind.

Exercises

Identify the tone in each of the three following essays. What contributes to it? What is each writer's attitude toward his subject, his purpose and his audience?

WOOLEY

—MARK STRAND

I speak of George Wooley, my friend. Wooley the watchful. Wooley the wily. Wooley the warm. I speak of him because he is dead. The world never knew him, never gave him a chance, and he passed unacknowledged into his grave.

Wooley was a dashing figure—a sportsman, an inventor of games, a poet, a tireless lover. He moved with the ease of the famous—as if a red carpet were unrolling perpetually before him. He wore tailored tweed jackets, faded cotton shirts. Italian corduroy pants, Justin

boots. His wavy hair, which he combed straight back,
colored and matched his eyes. Women adored him, but n
He always moved on. He was Wooley the wild to some. Wooley the
weird to others. To me he was Wooley the wonder.

It is the shadow of Wooley's voice that you hear in mine. I was
nothing until I met Wooley; I remember his words when he described
his Rocky Mountain retreat to some dinner guests one night. He
looked up to the ceiling. His hands were before him as if he were
holding an invisible basketball. And he began: "There you would see
cloud towers, floating bushes of shade, great scoops of vapor, milky
mountains of air, blouses blown up and away, buttocks adrift,
bleached wigs, powdery potatoes, albino clods, blurred faces of everybody you ever knew, all the paraphernalia of sleep—eiderdowns, pil-
lows, and nimble sheep—strung along high winds, hissing their long,
unfinished histories, passing from east to west day after day, with monotonous comic appeal and mysterious pomp, over hot, haze-filled cities. . . ." I tell you he was out of sight! When he finished, there was
silence except for me, his old friend, who began to weep. It was not
only the beauty of his speech but the odor of Gorgonzola sauce rising
from the gnocchi on my plate that undid me. Unparalleled, heavenly
incongruity!

Compared with Wooley's, the lives of all my other friends seemed
aimless. They complained of boredom. An excess of afternoons, Wooley would have said. Tom and Harriet, Pete and Greeny, Phil, Floss,
Willis, Milly—the whole gang, they never understood him. They
were shocked when he challenged Monty Bianco, the tennis star, to
a match at the field club. They were concerned when an ambulance
pulled up at courtside and a heavily bandaged, wobbling Wooley was
helped to the court, with racquet in hand. When Monty saw him, his
eyes bulged in disbelief. He didn't know what to do until Wooley,
his voice cracking with anguish, told him to serve. Monty served three
double faults. On the fourth point Wooley returned Monty's first service but released a scream of such hideous magnitude that if an elephant with a human voice had watched its children slaughtered it
would not have sounded as pained. Monty was stunned and missed
his shot. At this moment the hired ambulance driver and attendant
rushed out to help the brave Wooley back into the ambulance. What
a breath of fresh air his humor was!

Wooley was a fabulous inventor of games, but they were often mis-
understood. Death, his greatest, was probably ahead of its time. It
was played on a Monopoly-like board, and each player picked at random a card telling him what disease he would have for the duration
of the game. The object was to avert death as long as possible, and
the winner was the one who outlived the others. Wooley, why did
you have to die!

He loved children especially. The dolls he invented for them—beautiful dolls—could never be marketed. They came in little sickbeds or in wheelchairs, and, reversing the usual fate of dolls, were programmed to get well or to walk again if given love and encouragement. Some would reward the child with heartfelt utterances like "I can walk! I can walk!" or "I can see! I can see!" Oh, shortsighted parents! If only you had known him!

I remember asking him about the days when he was in love with Isabel Bell and his saying, "That was another season of the year—a vague indefinable season, whose trees were neither with leaves nor without, whose air was neither warm nor cold. I have no memory of the days or of the time." Not a mean word about Isabel, who left him for the flashy Monty Bianco. How considerate, how selfless.

When I asked him how he felt after his father cut him off without a penny, he said, "I would go out under the stars and enter the smallness of being that was mine, and I would disappear into the emptiness within, and it seemed enormous." Again there was no anger.

Once, while we were swimming, I asked him if things came easily to him. He said, "I see the world through a small eye, an eye so small the world does not notice." I was so moved by his answer I almost drowned.

But it was Wooley who drowned, a few years later, while skating with Milly and Pete and Greeny and Floss and me. We were out on the lake at night, standing around a fire, smoking cigarettes, listening to Wooley tell us about the dark towns of Central Europe, each with its own muddy main street over which chickens strutted aimlessly. Suddenly he skated away over the endless black pane of ice. None of us followed him. Under the stillness of the night sky, we stood together, a shivering, frightened little group, and through the cold dark flew the sound of our voices calling, "Wooley, Wooley, Wooley!"

PRINTED NOISE

—GEORGE WILL

The flavor list at the local Baskin-Robbins ice cream shop is an anarchy of names like "Peanut Butter 'N Chocolate" and "Strawberry Rhubarb Sherbert." These are not the names of things that reasonable people consider consuming, but the names are admirably businesslike, briskly descriptive.

Unfortunately, my favorite delight (chocolate-coated vanilla flecked with nuts) bears the unutterable name "Hot Fudge Nutty Buddy," an example of the plague of cuteness in commerce. There are some things a gentleman simply will not do, and one is announce in public a desire for a "Nutty Buddy." So I usually settle for a plain vanilla cone.

I am not the only person suffering for immutable standards of propriety. The May issue of *Atlantic* contains an absorbing tale of lonely heroism at a Burger King. A gentleman requested a ham and cheese sandwich that the Burger King calls a Yumbo. The girl taking orders was bewildered.

"Oh," she eventually exclaimed, "you mean a Yumbo."

Gentleman: "The ham and cheese. Yes."

Girl, nettled: "It's called a Yumbo. Now, do you want a Yumbo or not?"

Gentleman, teeth clenched: "Yes, thank you, the ham and cheese."

Girl: "Look, I've got to have an order here. You're holding up the line. You want a Yumbo, don't you? You want a Yumbo!"

Whereupon the gentleman chose the straight and narrow path of virtue. He walked out rather than call a ham and cheese a Yumbo. His principles are anachronisms but his prejudices are impeccable, and he is on my short list of civilization's friends.

That list includes the Cambridge don who would not appear outdoors without a top hat, not even when routed by fire at 3 A.M., and who refused to read another line of Tennyson after he saw the poet put water in fine port. The list includes another don who, although devoutly Tory, voted Liberal during Gladstone's day because the duties of prime minister kept Gladstone too busy to declaim on Holy Scripture. And high on the list is the grammarian whose last words were: "I am about to—or I am going to—die: either expression is correct."

Gentle reader, can you imagine any of these magnificent persons asking a teenage girl for a "Yumbo"? Or uttering "Fishamagig" or "Egg McMuffin" or "Fribble" (that's a milk shake, sort of)?

At one point in the evolution of American taste, restaurants that were relentlessly fun, fun, fun were built to look like lemons or bananas. I am told that in Los Angeles there was the Toed Inn, a strange spelling for a strange place shaped like a giant toad. Customers entered through the mouth, like flies being swallowed.

But the mature nation has put away such childish things in favor of menus that are fun, fun, fun. Seafood is "From Neptune's Pantry" or "Denizens of the Briny Deep." And "Surf 'N Turf," which you might think is fish and horsemeat, actually is lobster and beef.

To be fair, there are practical considerations behind the asphyxiatingly cute names given hamburgers. Many hamburgers are made from portions of the cow that the cow had no reason to boast about. So sellers invent distracting names to give hamburgers cachet. Hence "Whoppers" and "Heroburgers."

But there is no excuse for Howard Johnson's menu. In a just society it would be a flogging offense to speak of "steerburgers," clams "fried to order" (which probably means they don't fry clams for you unless you order fried clams), a "natural cut" (what is an "unnatural" cut?) of sirloin, "oven-baked" meat loaf, chicken pot pie with "flaky crust," "golden croquettes," "grilled-in-butter Frankforts [sic]," "liver with smothered onions" (smothered by onions?), and a "hearty" Reuben sandwich.

America is marred by scores of Dew Drop Inns serving "crispy green" salads, "garden fresh" vegetables, "succulent" lamb, "savory" pork, "sizzling" steaks, and "creamy" or "tangy" coleslaw. I've nothing against Homeric adjectives ("wine-dark sea," "wing-footed Achilles") but isn't coleslaw just coleslaw? Americans hear the incessant roar of commerce without listening to it, and read the written roar without really noticing it. Who would notice if a menu proclaimed "creamy" steaks and "sizzling" coleslaw? Such verbal litter is to language as Muzak is to music. As advertising blather becomes the nation's normal idiom, language becomes printed noise.

SCIENCE, A WELLSPRING OF OUR DISCONTENT

—WALTER ORR ROBERTS

But above all else, the thing for us to realize about the scientific revolution is simply that *it is here.* We are now deep into the age of science. It cannot be ignored. Jet airplanes circle the globe in hours. Images of wealth or poverty, or of particular political ideology flash into millions of homes everywhere, instantly. Weapons systems can eradicate hundreds of millions of lives in minutes, and we have not been the only nation diligently applying technological skills to the problem of how to design and manage such weapons systems.

My voice can be embossed for my great-grandchildren, yet unborn, on thin mylar and ferrous oxide tape. I can listen, as I did a few nights ago, to Sviatoslav Richter's magnificent playing of Moussorgsky's *Pictures at an Exhibition* recorded on February 25, 1958, at Sofia, Bulgaria. In the background of this music I can hear the coughs of men I shall never know, whose language I cannot speak, but who are my brothers listening with me in my living room.

I can strip a tiny fleck of skin from my body, and have it preserved, intact, alive and growing indefinitely in a laboratory test tube, so that a curious inquisitor can examine microscopically the genetic code that makes me most of what I am, even long after I am through being it.

I can place my eye to the viewing screen of a giant telescope and peer into the silent depths of the Virgo Cluster of island universes, noting the soft glow of the 1000 billion suns that there generate the strange life processes of a hundred million planets, where thinking creatures think out their days, forever beyond communication with us.

It is here, this age of science, and with it some of the most compelling ideas of mankind: The magnificent structure of the relativity theory of Einstein, a notion that has stirred the very foundations of our thought, a creation of beauty that ranks with the greatest of Beethoven. Or the incredible principle of indeterminacy of Heisenberg, with its idea of the unavoidable uncertainty of definite knowledge about particular events in nature. This is a challenging notion that sets limits on the knowable.

Or the thrilling concept of the continuous creation of the universe, with its picture of stars and men coming and going through an infinite span of time—yet living always in a place in space that appears to its inhabitants but a few billion years old.

It is here, this age of science, and with it comes its promise of what the life of man can be, with food for all, with education, with human freedom, with a stable population. With this age of technology comes the realistic expectation that even the added billions can live in harmonious equilibrium with a natural environment of quality, and one that man can appreciate the more because he knows what a rare thing it is in the universe. For man, life need not be nasty, brutish, short—but a life rich with peace of mind and rewarding leisure tasks, with comfort and health, and with a language that transcends political ideology.

But to bring to substance this great dream for humanity we must know that this is what we really want and be willing to work to achieve it. To a tragic degree we in the West have drifted, not so much for lack of willingness to pay the price, but for lack of knowing what it is that we have really wanted—aside from factories, and a rise in the standard of living.

In our explosively changing world it is no longer sufficient to live with philosophies or religions simply handed down from an older generation. We must take up a vital, flexible, and ever-evolving concern about the nature and purpose of man, and about what constitutes a good life and a good society in the light of today's communications, population growth, races, political systems, weapons. We must exhibit a concern with philosophy that is geared to the chain-reacting growth of science, and that is consonant with the impact of science on man's changing conception of himself and his world.

Rather than simply fight for the preservation of the old things that are good, we must plan creatively also to shape the new. We must commit ourselves to dare to build the world we want, knowing that it is possible if we but demand it—and if we use intelligently all the potent forces of science, the arts and the humanities that are at our disposal.

There will always be dangers. But I hold with Thornton Wilder, who said, "Every good and excellent thing stands moment by moment at the razor edge of danger, and must be fought for." To be what we can be, we must be unafraid to place ourselves, our ways of life, our economic systems, in the microscope of science; and, we must have the courage to put into practice the findings that come out, no matter how hard they hit at the patterns of our folkways. To be what we can be, we must first and foremost know what we want to be.

WRITING ASSIGNMENTS

1. Either make an observation about or complain about something that bothers you—junk mail, dormitory food, parking on campus, child-resistant bottles, the blind date, phone calls from solicitors, gum chewers, etc.

2. Reminisce about a relative or friend who affected or influenced you in some way.

3. Reminisce about a time in your life you would like to forget. Perhaps something outrageous you did as an adolescent.

4. Make an observation about contemporary billboards. What do they say about American culture?

5. Reminisce about a place that has been special to you.

6. Make an observation about the teenagers of America. Assume the role of sociologist and characterize the modern teenager.

7. Complain about what you think is the worst movie you've ever seen. The worst TV commercial.

8. Explain how you feel about funerals.

9. Considering contemporary society, speculate about what you think our society will be like in the year 2000.

10. Reminisce about the worst or best pet you ever had.

5. Writing Seeing

My task . . . is, by the power of the written word, to make you hear, to make you feel—it is before all, to make you see.

—JOSEPH CONRAD

Helen Keller said that if she were president of a university, she would require a course called "How To Use Your Eyes," the purpose of which would be to force students to "really see" the world before them, to "awake their dormant and sluggish faculties." And Thomas Huxley, writing in *On Science and Art in Relation to Education,* held a similar view, arguing that all students should be taught to draw so that their minds would be trained in "attention and accuracy, in which all mankind are more deficient than in any other mental quality whatever." As you might have guessed, I would support Keller's and Huxley's proposal—for as a writer and a teacher I know the value of seeing. Seeing, really seeing, does more than sharpen your perception of the physical world—it makes you far more sensitive to words. And *that* is the fundamental aim of all writing courses. Thus, the second writing assignment I suggest is to communicate to a reader what you see—a word I am going to use in its broadest and most profound sense. While it is true we perceive and react to reality with our minds and hearts, we fundamentally perceive and react to reality through our senses: sight, sound, touch, taste, and smell. To see, then, means to comprehend and discern the world through all the senses—the most dominant, of course, being sight.

DESCRIBING AND NARRATING

For years textbooks have made distinctions between two kinds of seeing: describing and narrating. Narration, as tradition has it, is movement through time—the writer advances the action. Description is movement through space—the writer stops the action to set the scene or describe a character. Here is an example of narration:

> It was not long till I began to lose my sense of time, for the colors of evening never gave way to darkness. Instead they traveled, amber, rose, gold, around the mountaintops and became the colors of dawn as I trekked down the valley. I passed gorges that opened into awesome unnamed side valleys whose ends I could not see. I crossed and recrossed the river on bridges of turquoise ice, their edges crumbling away in the late May breakup. I hiked on, sometimes on snow, sometimes on bare, wind-scraped ground, and always past new peaks and canyons. When not moving, I lived as if I were a lichen, curled small and out of the fierce, freezing wind behind some boulder or low rise, facing the sun to absorb whatever I could.
>
> Alone, with no familiar sign of man in all these miles, I found my sense of place becoming blurred too. I paused to eat from a tin of sardines and rubbed the oil on my wind- and cold-chapped lips. Then I checked my map and the route I had taken.
> —Douglas H. Chadwick, "Our Wildest Wilderness"

And here is pure description:

> Two mountain chains traversed the republic roughly from north to south, forming between them a number of valleys and plateaus. Overlooking one of these valleys, which is dominated by two volcanoes, lies, six thousand feet above sea-level, the town of Quauhnahuac. It is situated well south of the Tropic of Cancer, to be exact, on the nineteenth parallel, in about the same Latitude as the Revillagigedo Islands to the west in the Pacific, or very much farther west, the southernmost tip of Hawaii—and as the port of Tzucox to the east on the Atlantic seaboard of Yucatan near the border of British Honduras, or very much farther east, the town of Juggernaut, in India, on the Bay of Bengal.

The walls of the town, which is built on a hill, are high, the streets and lanes tortuous and broken, the roads winding. A fine American-style highway leads in from the north but is lost in its narrow streets and comes out a goat track. Quauhnahuac possesses eighteen churches and fifty-seven *cantinas*. It also boasts a golf course and no fewer than four hundred swimming-pools, public and private, filled with water that ceaselessly pours down from the mountains, and many splendid hotels.

—Malcolm Lowry, *Under the Volcano*

Although understanding the distinction between these two kinds of seeing is useful and informative (indeed, I do it myself to distinguish paragraph strategies), it is nonetheless a distinction that few writers adhere to so rigidly. In fact, most seeing is a combination of describing (moving the reader through space) and narration (moving the reader through time). Notice the combination of the two in the following as Alexander H. Leighton helps us see his jeep ride through Hiroshima.

We approached Hiroshima a little after daybreak on a winter day, driving in a jeep below a leaden sky and in the face of a cold, wet wind. On either side of the road, black flat fields were turning green under winter wheat. Here and there peasants worked, swinging spades or grubbing in mud and water with blue hands. Some in black split-toed shoes left tracks like cloven hoofs. To the north, looming close over the level land, mountains thrust heavy summits of pine darkly against the overcast. To the south and far away, the bay lay in dull brightness under fitful rain.

"Hiroshima," said the driver, a GI from a Kansas farm, who had been through the city many times, "don't look no different from any other bombed town. You soon get used to it. You'll see little old mud walls right in the middle of town that wasn't knocked down. They been exaggerating about that bomb."

Within a few miles the fields along the road were replaced by houses and shops that looked worn and dull yet intact. . . . Half a mile farther on we passed the bus, small, battered, gray, standing half obliterated by the cloud of smoke that came from the charcoal burner at the back while the driver stood working at its machinery.

Children of all ages waved, laughed, and shouted at us as had the children in other parts of Japan . . . .

Like the children of Hamelin to the piper, they came rushing, at the sound of our approach, from doorways and alleyways and from behind houses, to line up by the road and cheer. One little fellow of about six threw himself into the air, his little body twisting and feet kicking in a fit of glee.

The adults gazed at us with solemn eyes or looked straight ahead.

—"That Day at Hiroshima"

In this passage Leighton moves us through time and space, advances the action, and stops the action—in short, combines narration and description to help us see. John Steinbeck does the same thing as he describes and narrates the enduring odyssey of a land turtle. We see that the turtle's fatigued features coincide with his resigned movement through the teeming grass.

The sun lay on the grass and warmed it, and in the shade under the grass the insects moved, ants and ant lions to set traps for them, grasshoppers to jump into the air and flick their yellow wings for a second, sow bugs like little armadillos, plodding restlessly on many tender feet. And over the grass at the roadside a land turtle crawled, turning aside for nothing, dragging his high-domed shell over the grass. His hard legs and yellow-nailed feet threshed slowly through the grass, not really walking, but boosting and dragging his shell along. The barley beards slid off his shell, and the clover burrs fell on him and rolled to the ground. His horny beak was partly open, and his fierce, humorous eyes, under brows like fingernails, stared straight ahead.

—*The Grapes of Wrath*

As I hope you can see now, when you describe you are often narrating as well, and when you narrate you are often describing. So while the distinction is an important one to make, it can be misleading in that it ignores that the two are actually parts of the same thing—seeing. Therefore, when I suggest, as I will do, that you narrate an event or describe a scene in order to sharpen your writing skills, I do not want to imply that the two kinds of writing are exclusive of each other. Instead, I prefer that you use the words more broadly, knowing that description can include narration and vice versa—or perhaps even latch on to a word that encompasses them both—seeing.

HOW TO WRITE SEEING

I suggest that you try your hand at writing seeing because the experience will make you more sensitive to the visual power of words, the way seeing enhances prose, at times clarifies it and enriches it. Moreover, I predict that if you take a look at any major expository magazine, most of the opening paragraphs will be either descriptive or narrative or both—two very good ways to introduce expository material. But what do you narrate or describe for practice? And how do you go about it? What are the most efficient and effective ways to communicate what you see?

I try to answer these questions for my students by asking them to think back a moment to the primitive time of scouts and explorers—people whose ability to record and communicate what they saw was as valuable as their bravery. They were valuable because in their mind, as if it were a sacred pouch, they could store and bring back the sensory detail of life and nature far beyond the safe radius of the tribal territory. They could describe other creatures, places, and events so vividly that the members of their tribe were magically transported into that mysterious jungle or onto the dangerous sea whose might and sound and fury they themselves could experience within the safety of their own mind. It was not unusual, then, for the teller of these tales to become an important member of the tribe. Not only could he report what he had seen, but he could also, through the magic of his language, entertain with stories of his own invention, initiating, in the course of it all, the narrative tradition that continues to this day.

What separated the great storyteller from the mediocre? What were the storyteller's secrets? They are the same now as they were then.

Use concrete words
Create mental pictures by using simile or metaphor
Capture dominant atmosphere
Control point of view

Concrete Detail and Mental Pictures

Good storytellers know how to translate what their senses report to them into concrete words. Imagine an elephant hunt. Let's assume it's the first time many in the tribe had ever heard of such a brave act as the killing of the undisputed giant of their world. Assume you have been waiting expectantly at home for the thrill of vicariously sharing this experience which the storyteller will recreate for you. Imagine your disappointment if the storyteller said simply: "The elephant was speared. He fell down. It took a long time to kill him. He breathed steadily for several minutes before he died." It's not a very satisfactory account, is it? What's missing? The "what's missing" is the visual. In that mental purse of his, the storyteller has not brought back the videotape of the elephant's death. Take a look at another elephant killer describing *his* elephant's death. Here, we see much more.

When I pulled the trigger I did not hear the bang or feel the kick—one never does when a shot goes home—but I heard the devilish roar of glee that went up from the crowd. In that instant, in too short a time, one would have thought, even for the bullet to get there, a mysterious, terrible change had come over the elephant. He neither stirred nor fell, but every line of his body had altered. He looked suddenly stricken, shrunken, immensely old, as though the frightful impact of the bullet had paralyzed him without knocking him down. At last, after what seemed a long time—it might have been five seconds, I dare say—he sagged flabbily to his knees. His mouth slobbered. An enormous senility seemed to have settled upon him. One could have imagined him thousands of years old. I fired again into the same spot. At the second shot he did not collapse but climbed with desperate slowness to his feet and stood weakly upright, with legs sagging, head drooping. I fired a third time. That was the shot that did for him. You could see the agony of it jolt his whole body and knock the last remnant of strength from his legs. But in falling he seemed for a moment to rise, for as his hind legs collapsed beneath him he seemed to tower upward like a huge rock toppling, his trunk reaching skyward like a tree. He trumpeted, for the first and only time. And then down he came, his belly toward me, with a crash that seemed to shake the ground even where I lay.

I got up. The Burmans were already racing past me across the mud. It was obvious that the elephant would never rise again, but he was not dead. He was breathing very rhythmically with long rattling gasps, his great mound of a side painfully rising and falling. His mouth was wide open—I could see far down into caverns of pale pink throat. I waited a long time for him to die, but his breathing did not weaken. Finally I fired my two remaining shots into the spot where I thought his heart must be. The thick blood welled out of him like red velvet, but still he did not die. His body did not even jerk when the shots hit him, the tortured breathing continued without a pause. He was dying, very slowly and in great agony, but in some world remote from me where not even a bullet could damage him further. I felt that I had got to put an end to that dreadful noise. It seemed dreadful to see the great beast lying there, powerless to move and yet powerless to die, and not even to be able to finish him. I sent back for my small rifle and poured shot after shot into his heart and down his throat. They seemed to make no impression. The tortured gasps continued as steadily as the ticking of a clock.

—George Orwell, "Shooting an Elephant"

This is quite different, isn't it? We not only learn about the elephant's death, we see it. In forceful detail we see him sag flabbily to his knees, we see his mouth slobbering, we see him topple like a rock, we feel the earth shake, we hear his tortured gasps of breath as we stare down into the pale, pink cavern of his throat, and we step back from his blood flowing out like red velvet. This storyteller uses *concrete detail* (no general descriptions) that he will combine with *mental pictures* that he creates by comparing what he sees to other things with which we are familiar: the trunk reaching skyward *like* a tree, the throat looking *like* a pale pink cavern, the blood flowing *like* red velvet, the tortured gasps continuing *as consistently as* the ticking of a clock. These mental pictures are more effective and more accurate than, "He fell down, his trunk went up, the blood flowed, he breathed steadily." So the first two secrets of the successful storyteller are (1) to use concrete detail and (2) to create mental pictures by comparison. As Joseph Conrad believed, the storyteller's task "is, by the power of the written word, to make you hear, to make you feel—it is before all, to make you see."

With this notion of using concrete detail and creating mental pictures by comparison still stirring in your mind, let's quickly move from land to sea. Here is Melville "seeing" the greatest giant of the earth.

> The White Whale tossed himself salmon-like to Heaven. So suddenly seen in the blue pain of the sea, and relieved against the still bluer margin of the sky, the spray that he raised, for the moment, intolerably glittered and glared like a glacier; and stood there gradually fading and fading away from its first sparkling intensity, to the dim mistiness of an advancing shower in a vale. . . . Suddenly the waters around them slowly swelled in broad circles; then quickly unheaved, as if sideways sliding from a submerged berg of ice, swiftly rising to the surface. A low rumbling sound was heard; a subterraneous hum; and then all held their breaths; as bedraggled with trailing ropes, and harpoons, and lances, a vast form shot lengthwise, but obliquely from the sea. Shrouded in a thin drooping veil of mist, it hovered for a moment in the rainbowed air; and then fell swamping back into the deep. Crushed thirty feet upwards, the waters flashed for an instant like heaps of fountains, then brokenly sank in a shower of flakes, leaving the circling surface creamed like new milk round the marble trunk of the whale.
>
> —*Moby Dick*

Once again we share experience through the storyteller's eyes as we see the whale leaping "salmon-like" and see the sea-spray glittering and glaring *like* a glacier; we see the water upheaved *as if* sliding from a submerged iceberg and we hear the low rumbling followed by the subterraneous hum, and then instantly we see the shroud of mist, the rainbowed air and heaps of fountains and disturbed water circling *like* milk around the marble trunk of the whale. Melville carefully flashes mental pictures into our minds—the writer's version of moving pictures. Normal Mailer does the same thing in his description of another kind of whale.

> Apollo-Saturn leaped into ignition, and two horns of orange fire burst like genies from the base of the rocket. . . . Flames flew in cataract against the cusp of the flame shield, and then sluiced along the paved ground down two opposite channels in the concrete, two underground rivers of flame which poured into the air on either

side a hundred feet away, then flew a hundred feet further. Two
mighty torches of flame like the wings of a yellow bird of fire flew
over a field, covered a field with brilliant yellow bloomings of
flame, and in the midst of it, white as a ghost, white as the white
of Melville's Moby Dick, this slim angelic mysterious ship of stages
rose without sound out of its incarnation of flame and began to as-
cend slowly into the sky, slowly as Melville's Leviathan might
swim, slowly as we might swim upward in a dream looking for the
air. And still no sound.

—*Of a Fire on the Moon*

In Mailer's description we see, but do not hear. He concen-
trates on just one sense. It is as though we are senseless except
for sight—as it must have been for a brief moment for Annie
Dillard:

The night I stayed too late I was hunched on the log staring spell-
bound at spreading, reflected stains of lilac on the water. A cloud
in the sky suddenly lighted as if turned on by a switch; its reflection
just as suddenly materialized on the water upstream, flat and floating, so that I couldn't see the creek bottom, or life in the water
under the cloud. Downstream, away from the cloud on the water,
water turtles smooth as beans were gliding down with the current
in a series of easy, weightless push-offs, as men bound on the moon.

—*Pilgrim at Tinker Creek*

Hearing

But seeing is not all the storyteller can do for his reader. We
have seen the pale pink caverns of the elephant's mouth, the
whale leaping salmon-like, fire bursting genie-like from the
base of the rocket, and those dark, smooth-as-beans turtles
pushing across the water as if bounding on the moon, but we
can also hear, and the good storyteller doesn't ignore that
sense. Listen to the following:

Then it came, like a crickling of wood twigs over the ridge, came
with the sharp and furious bark of a million drops of oil crackling
suddenly into combustion, a cacophony of barks louder and louder
as Apollo-Saturn fifteen seconds ahead of its own sound cleared the
lift tower to a cheer which could have been a cry of anguish from

that near-audience watching; then came the ear-splitting bark of a thousand machine guns firing at once, and Aquarius shook through its feet at the fury of this combat assault, and heard the thunderous murmur of Niagaras of flame roaring conceivably louder than the loudest thunders he had ever heard and the earth began to shake and would not stop, it quivered through his feet standing on the wood of the bleachers, an apocalyptic fury of sound equal to some conception of the sound of your death in the roar of a drowning hour, a nightmare of sound.

—Norman Mailer, *Of a Fire on the Moon*

When other birds are still, the screech owls take up the strain, like mourning women their ancient u-lu-lu. Wise midnight hags! It is not honest and blunt tu-whit tu-who of the poets, but, without jestling, a most solemn graveyard ditty, the mutual consolations of suicide lovers remembering the pangs and the delights of supernal love in the infernal groves. Yet I love to hear their wailing, their doleful responses, trilled along the woodside; reminding me sometimes of music and singing birds; as if it were the dark and tearful side of music, the regrets and sighs that would fain be sung. They are the spirits, the low spirits and melancholy forebodings, of fallen souls that once in human shape night-walked the earth and did the deeds of darkness, now expiating their sins with their wailing hymns of threnodies in the scenery of their transgressions. . . . *Oh-o-o-o-o that I never had been bor-r-r-r-n!* sighs one on this side of the pond, and circles with the restlessness of despair to some new perch on the gray oaks. Then—that I never been bor-r-r-r-r-n! echoes another on the farther side with tremulous sincerity, and—bor-r-r-r-n! comes faintly from far in the Lincoln woods.

—Henry David Thoreau, *Walden*

Both Mailer and Thoreau not only explain what the sound was like, but they actually reproduce it through the sound of their own words: the "crickling" of twigs, the "bark" of oil "crackling" and the Oh-o-o-o-o and bor-r-r-r-n of the owls. We call this device onomatopoeia, the use of words that imitate the sound of their meaning: Bacon "sizzles," cats "hiss," dogs "bow-wow," bees "buzz," frogs "croak," birds "flutter." And as Tennyson knew, sound can echo sense: "The moan of doves in immemorial elms,/And the murmuring of innumerable bees." The effective spinner-of-tales, then, knows that he cannot only help us see what he sees, but he can, with concrete detail and onomatopoeia, reproduce what he hears. And he often does both at once. Here is D. H. Lawrence:

> The lake was quite black, like a great pit. The wind suddenly blew with violence, with a strange ripping sound in the mango trees, as if some membrane in the air were being ripped. The white-flowered oleanders in the garden below leaned over quite flat, their white flowers ghostly, going right down to the earth, in the pale beam of the lamp—like a street lamp—that shone on the wall at the front entrance.
>
> —*The Plumed Serpent*

I mention this use of onomatopoeia to underscore my point that "seeing" refers to comprehending through all the senses. The good writer appeals to all our senses even though he knows sight will usually be the most dominant.

Color

Of course, we do not see in only black and white, and all storytellers know they must not only learn the numerous words for color, but they must also study in great detail the way light influences and alters the color before them. Color is especially important to writers of travelbooks, who with their language alone provide a kind of slide show for the would-be sojourner. Here is John Addington Symonds transporting his nineteenth-century English readers to the valleys, mountains, and glaciers that bridge Switzerland and Italy.

> Looking up the valley of the Morteratsch that morning, the glaciers were distinguishable in hues of green and sapphire through their veil of snow; and the highest peaks soared in a transparency of *amethystine* light beneath a blue sky traced with filaments of windy cloud. Some storm must have disturbed the atmosphere in Italy, for fan-shaped mists frothed out around the sun, and curled themselves above the mountains in fine feathery wreaths, melting imperceptibly into air. . . . A glacier hangs in air above the frozen lakes, with all its green-blue ice-cliffs glistening in intensest light. Pitz Palu shoots aloft like sculptured marble, delicately veined with soft aërial shadows of translucent blue. At the summit of the pass all

Italy seems to burst upon the eyes in those steep serried ranges, with their craggy crests, violet-hued in noon-day sunshine, as though a bloom of plum or grape had been shed over them, enamelling their jagged precipices.

—*Italian Byways*

Dominant Atmosphere

As you can literally see, then, two of the storyteller's secrets are the selection of very concrete detail and the use of analogies to create mental pictures. But these are not his only devices. Expert storytellers know that long, but accurate descriptions can put the listener or reader to sleep. Total accuracy isn't always the objective anyway. More often than not the purpose is not to describe an entire scene, but rather the *dominant atmosphere* of the scene. Thus, a writer will think of an adjective or two that dominates what is before him and select details that support that adjective and exclude details that do not. Here is Nathaniel Hawthorne capturing the dominant atmosphere before him—an unrelenting dampness:

All day long, and for a week together, the rain was drip-dripping and splash-splash-splashing from the eaves, and bubbling and foaming into the tubs beneath the spouts. The old, unpainted shingles of the house and out-buildings were black with moisture; and the mosses of ancient growth upon the walls looked green and fresh, as if they were the newest things and afterthoughts of Time. The usually mirrored surface of the river was blurred by an infinity of raindrops; the whole landscape had a completely water-soaked appearance, conveying the impression that the earth was wet through like a sponge; while the summit of a wooded hill, about a mile distant, was enveloped in a dense mist, where the demon of the tempest seemed to have his abiding place, and to be plotting still direr inclemencies.

—*Mosses from an Old Manse*

And here is Charles Dickens capturing a suffocating English fog:

Fog everywhere. Fog up the river, where it flows among green aits and meadows; fog down the river, where it rolls defiled among tiers of shipping, and the waterside pollutions of a great—and dirty—city. Fog on the Essex marshes, fog on the Kentish heights. Fog creeping into the cabooses of collier brigs; fog lying out on the yards, and hovering in the rigging of great ships; fog drooping on the gunwales of barges and small boats. Fog in the eyes and throats of ancient Greenwich pensioners, wheezing by the fireside of their wards; fog in the stem and bowl of the afternoon pipe of the wrathful skipper, down in his close cabin; fog cruelly pinching the toes and fingers of his shivering little 'prentice boy on deck. Chance people on the bridges peeping over the parapets into a nether sky of fog, with fog all round them, as if they were up in a balloon, and hanging in the clouds.

—*Bleak House*

As you can "see," the dominant atmosphere of both these scenes is created by selection of detail that supports the dominant adjective "wet" or "foggy." In Hawthorne's case, we hear the drip-dripping and the splash-splashing and see the unpainted shingles black with moisture and the moss on the walls and the river blurred with raindrops and the earth looking like a sponge and the mist at the summit of the hill where the tempest demon seemed to be waiting. Now there could have been a warm glow from a coachman's lantern or a slice of light from a recalcitrant sun, but we do not see them. Hawthorne does away with details that do not contribute to the dominant atmosphere. To underscore this storyteller's secret, let's move away from this dreary fog and dry out a little in the dominant sunny atmosphere of Frank Norris' Guadalajara.

It was high noon, and the rays of the sun, that hung poised directly overhead in an intolerable white glory, fell straight as plummets upon the roofs and streets of Guadalajara. The adobe walls and sparse brick sidewalks of the drowsing town radiated the heat in an oily, quivering shimmer. The leaves of the eucalyptus trees around the Plaza drooped motionless, limp and relaxed under the scorching, searching blaze. The shadows of these trees had shrunk to their smallest circumference, contracting close about the trunks. The shade had dwindled to the breadth of a mere line. The sun was everywhere. The heat exhaling from brick and plaster and metal met the heat that steadily descended blanket-wise and smothering from the pale, scorched sky. Only the lizards— . . . they lived in chinks of the crumbling adobe and in interstices of the sidewalk—remained without, motionless, as if stuffed, their eyes closed

to mere slits, basking, stupefied with heat. At long intervals the prolonged drone of an insect developed out of the silence, vibrated
a moment in a soothing, somnolent, long note, then trailed slowly
into the quiet again.

—*The Octopus*

Movement

In this passage from *The Octopus,* you can see Norris' sensitivity to detail: the sun's rays, the oily, quivering heat, the
drooped leaves, the mere line of shade, the scorched sky, the
slit-eyed lizards. Everything is still and motionless and all the
detail points directly at that atmosphere.

Yet the good storyteller must also be sensitive to movement,
and the best writers know that just as the sounds of words can
imitate their meaning, so can the length and rhythm of sentences coincide with the movement they describe. In the following description of a tram, D. H. Lawrence uses long, cumu-
lative sentences while the tram moves, but shorter, restful
sentences when the tram stops.

There is in the Midlands a single-line tramway system which boldly
leaves the country town and plunges off into the black, industrial
countryside, up hill and down dale, through the long, ugly villages
of workmen's houses, over canals and railways, past churches
perched high and nobly over the smoke and shadows, through
stark, grimy, cold little market-places, tilting away in a rush past
cinemas and shops down to the hollow where the collieries are,
then up again, past a little rural church, under the ash trees, on in
a rush to the terminus, the last little ugly place of industry, the cold
little town that shivers on the edge of the wild, gloomy country
beyond. There the green and creamy colored tram-cars seem to
pause and purr with curious satisfaction. But in a few minutes—the
clock on the turret of the Co-operative Wholesale Society's Shops
gives the time—away it starts once more on the adventure. Again
there are the reckless swoops downhill, bouncing the loops: again
the chilly wait in the hill-top market-place: again the breathless
slithering round the precipitous drop under the church: again the
patient halts at the loops, waiting for the outcoming car: so on and
on, for two long hours till at last the city looms beyond the fat
gas-works, the narrow factories draw near, we are in the sordid
streets of the great town, once we sidle to a standstill at our termi-

nus, abashed by the great crimson and cream-coloured city cars, but still perky, jaunty, somewhat dare-devil, green as jaunty springs of parsley out of a black colliery garden.

—"Tickets, Please"

Point of View

This sensitivity to movement leads us directly to *point of view*— another important secret of the storyteller. Like the movie director setting up his camera, the writer must decide from what angle the scene, if you will pardon the rhyme, will be seen. Will we be on the hill looking down at the calvary fort or will we be on a desert dune looking straight ahead at the fort gates? The movie director as well as the writer has to frame his scene—he must at all times control the point of view. Compare the points of view in the following two pieces. In the first we are below the rocket. In the second we are above the whale.

> The fire was white as a torch and long as the rocket itself, a tail of fire, a face, yes now the rocket looked like a thin and pointed witch's hat, and the flames from its base were the blazing eyes of the witch. Forked like saw teeth was the base of the flame which quivered through the lens of the binoculars. Upwards. As the rocket keened over and went up and out to sea, one could no longer watch its stage, only the flame from its base. Now it seemed to rise like a ball of fire, like a new sun mounting the sky, a flame elevating itself.
>
> —Norman Mailer, *Of a Fire on the Moon*

> But suddenly as he peared down and down into its depths, he profoundly saw a white living spot no bigger than a white weasel, with wonderful celerity, uprising, and magnifying as it rose, till it turned, and then there were plainly revealed two long crooked rows of white, glistening teeth, floating up from the undiscoverable bottom. It was Moby Dick's open mouth and scrolled jaw; his vast, shadowed bulk still blending with the blue of the sea. The glittering mouth yawned beneath the boat like an open-doored marble tomb.
>
> —Herman Melville, *Moby Dick*

Maintaining your point of view helps you narrow the field of vision (we don't see the horizon in Melville's sea nor the fences around Mailer's rocket, though we know they are there) and presents the reader with a framed picture—a very useful device to keep your "seeing" in focus. Any time you describe or narrate, keep in mind from what angle you are witnessing the scene before you. Keep your eye steady—it will keep your seeing under control.

There are times, of course, when one point of view is too confining and limiting. Occasionally we need the camera, or the eye, to zoom in or back up and "pan" the scene. The secret is always to know what effect you want to create. In the following passage, Tom Wolfe's eye moves as if a gliding bird above the stadium of a stockcar race, radioing and televisioning back to us, and then he suddenly swoops down to the people below for a quick glimpse and just as quickly soars back up to his lofty perspective.

> The cars have been piling into the infield by the hundreds, parking in there on the clay and the grass, every which way, angled down and angled up, this way and that, where the ground is uneven, these beautiful blazing brand-new cars with the sun exploding off the windshields and the baked enamel and the glassy lacquer, hundreds, thousands of cars stacked this way and that in the infield with the sun bolting down and no shade, none at all, just a couple of Coca-Cola stands out there. And already the good old boys and girls are out beside the cars. . . . The good old boys are lolly gagging around with their shirts off and straw hats on that have miniature beer cans on the brims and buttons that read "Girls Wanted—No Experience Required." And everybody, good old boys and girls of all ages, are out there with portable charcoal barbecue ovens set up, and folding tubular-steel terrace furniture, deck chairs and things, and Thermos jugs and coolers full of beer—and suddenly it is not the up-country South at all but a concentration of the modern suburbs, all jammed into that one space, from all over America, with blazing cars and instant goodies, all cooking under the bare blaze—inside a strange bowl.
>
> —"The Last American Hero"

We see in this passage from Wolfe the writer's sensitivity to the storyteller's secrets—his sensitivity to detail, to mental pictures, to the dominant atmosphere, to color and light, to movement and point of view. In brief, sensitivity to *seeing*. You will find this sensibility and mental habit in all good writers. Many spend as much time helping you *see* their story as they do telling it.

PRACTICAL APPLICATIONS OF WRITING SEEING

I realize that you may be mentally whispering to yourself about now, "But I could never write like Wolfe, Mailer, or Melville. How can writing like this help me with expository prose?" I'll give you my frequent reply. By writing seeing—whether narration or description—you are not practicing to become a storyteller; you are practicing *seeing* the world more sharply and distinctly. You are developing the habit of creating mental pictures, using concrete detail, controlling your point of view, communicating dominant atmospheres—all of which are applicable to the various kinds of expository prose. Let's take some practical applications. In technical writing you may have to describe a combustion engine or an injection pump or an electron microscope, or a blast-furnace.

> The blast-furnace is a shaft furnace, 100 ft. or more in height, consisting of a cylindrical bottom portion (hearth with hearth bottom), from which rises an upward-widening, conically tapered portion (bosh) surmounted by a taller tapered structure (shaft) which narrows towards the top where it is closed by means of a system of double conical gates (bells).
> —*The Way Things Work*

In business writing, too, you may have to describe in a report a new accounting procedure or explain banking "network" or define such terms as the "bathtub theorem":

> Using the analogy of a bathtub, the total stock of goods (water in tub) is equal to production (faucet flow) less consumption (drain flow). The rate of accumulation is the excess of inflow over outflow.
> —Erwin Esser Nemmers, *Dictionary of Economics and Business*

In scientific writing you may have to help the reader "see" your information:

> At depths of greater than 1500 feet, all the fishes are black, deep violet, or brown, but the prawns wear amazing hues of red, scarlet, and purple. Why, no one can say. Since all the red rays are strained out of the water far above this depth, the scarlet raiment of these creatures can only look black to their neighbors.
>
> The deep sea has its stars, and perhaps here and there an eerie and transient equivalent of moonlight, for the mysterious phenomenon of luminescence is displayed by perhaps half of all the fishes that live in dimly lit or darkened waters, and by many of the lower forms as well. Many fishes carry luminous torches that can be turned on or off at will, presumably helping them find or pursue their prey. Others have rows of lights over their bodies, in patterns that vary from species to species and may be a sort of recognition mark or badge by which the bearer can be known as friend or enemy. The deep-sea squid ejects a spurt of fluid that becomes a luminous cloud, the counterpart of the "ink" of his shallow-water relative.
>
> —Rachel Carson, "The Sunless Sea"

And in some scientific communication we encounter physical phenomena too grand for the human mind to grasp except when explained by seeing. Star dust is so compact, scientists tell us, that a mere teaspoon would weigh 10 billion pounds, and a neutron star is so volatile that a marshmallow dropped upon its surface would create an explosion equal to an atomic bomb.

Writing seeing, then, is not the sole domain of the storyteller. Thumb through any general interest periodical and take note of the number of articles that narrate and describe—two very useful tools for communicating expository material. Whether you are arguing or expressing or simply informing, you will find yourself needing to make your reader "see" what you are communicating. And do not think you lack the ability. Notice how one of my students chose not to write: "In the casino gloom were rows of slot machines with the arms going up and down." Instead he more richly recounts: "In the casino gloom were the slot machines—rows and rows of luminescent monsters, grinding and clanking, fat little sentinels, their out-of-sync arms ratcheting down, then jerking back to a stiff salute." And Lance Morrow, writing for *Time* magazine, did not say that the next global war will be very "brief," but instead writes with poignantly vivid irony: "In the 20th century war was Dopplered up to the opposite extreme. Today the serious part of a global war might last no longer than several passionate kisses." And finally, a student taking us back to his boyhood during a deer hunt:

> The frozen wind whistled through the deer blind, singing a mournful tune as it formed tiny rivers in the crow's-feet at the corner of the hunter's eyes. The grey-fish-belly sky gradually lightened. Fingers of orange groped from the east as a crazy, blazing falling star flashed into the west—the last of the stars blinked into oblivion with the coming of dawn. The hunter's boots—old and cold and crusted with crystals of frost and snow were still—except for the occasional creak of leather, like a tiny telegrapher tapping out an eerie rhythm for the wind.
>
> —Douglas Walla

Your teacher will ask you to write a descriptive paragraph not to make you into a novelist, but to make you familiar with the techniques that can make your prose more vivid. Most of your writing assignments are not ends—they are the means to help you cultivate writing skills that will be useful in any kind of writing, and particularly expository prose.

My suggestion, then, is that you try your hand at communicating what you see. Go to a place you have never been and try to bring back to the reader the dominant atmosphere. Describe a good friend, both physically and psychologically. Narrate an experience, preferably something that will interest your peers. And remember that whether you are basically narrating or basically describing, you are still *writing seeing* and that means you need to use concrete detail, supply mental pictures, never lose sight of your point of view, and try to be as insightful as possible. The result will be a sensitivity to the visual power of prose.

Exercises

The following passages represent the diversity of uses to which writing seeing can be put and the diversity of effects that can be achieved. As you read through each selection, mark the places where the essay is enhanced because of the vividness. Isolate the techniques used in each piece (dominant impression, controlling point of view, concrete detail, imagery, and so on) and comment upon their effectiveness.

1. The Crested Cranes, which come on to the newly rolled and planted maize-land, to steal the maize out of the ground, make up for the robbery by being birds of good omen, announcing the rain; and also by dancing to us. When the tall birds are together in large numbers, it is a fine sight to see them spread their wings and dance. There is much style in the dance, and a little affectation, for why, when they can fly, do they jump up and down as if they were held on to the earth by magnetism? The whole ballet has a sacred look, like some ritual dance; perhaps the cranes are making an attempt to join Heaven and earth like the winged angels walking up and down Jacob's Ladder. With their delicate pale grey colouring, the little black velvet skull-cap and the fan-shaped crown, the cranes have all the air of light, spirited frescoes. When, after the dance, they lift and go away, to keep up the sacred tone of the show they give out, by the wings or the voice, a clear ringing note, as if a group of church bells had taken to the wing and were sailing off. You can hear them a long way away, even after the birds themselves have become invisible in the sky: a chime from the clouds.

—Isak Dinesen, *Out of Africa*

2. Imagine that we stand on an ordinary seaside pier, and watch the waves rolling in and striking against the iron columns of the pier. Large waves pay very little attention to the columns—they divide right and left and reunite after passing

each column, much as a regiment of soldiers would if a tree stood in their road; it is almost as though the columns had not been there. But the short waves and ripples find the columns of the pier a much more formidable obstacle. When the short waves impinge on the columns, they are reflected back and spread as new ripples in all directions. To use the technical term, they are "scattered." The obstacle provided by the iron columns hardly affects the long waves at all, but scatters the short ripples.

We have been watching a sort of working model of the way in which sunlight struggles through the earth's atmosphere. Between us on earth and outer space, the atmosphere interposes innumerable obstacles in the form of molecules of air, tiny droplets of water, and small particles of dust. These are represented by the columns of the pier.

The waves of the sea represent the sunlight. We know that sunlight is a blend of many colors—as we can prove for ourselves by passing it through a prism, or even through a jug of water, or as nature demonstrates to us when she passes it through the raindrops of a summer shower and produces a rainbow. We also know that light consists of waves, and that the different colors of light are produced by waves of different lengths, red light by long waves and blue light by short waves. The mixture of waves which constitutes sunlight has to struggle past the columns of the pier. And these obstacles treat the light waves much as the columns of the pier treat the sea-waves. The long waves which constitute red light are hardly affected but the short waves which constitute blue light are scattered in all directions.

Thus the different constituents of sunlight are treated in different ways as they struggle through the earth's atmosphere. A wave of blue light may be scattered by a dust particle, and turned out of its course. After a time a second dust particle again turns it out of its course, and so on, until finally it enters our eyes by a path as zigzag as that of a flash of lightning. Consequently the blue waves of the sunlight enter our eyes from all directions. And that is why the sky looks blue.

—Sir James Jeans, "Why the Sky Looks Blue"

3. Few people, comparatively, have ever seen the effect on the sea of a powerful gale continued without intermission for three or four days and nights; and to those who have not, I believe it must be unimaginable, not from the mere force or size of surge, but from the complete annihilation of the limit between sea and air. The water from its prolonged agitation is beaten, not into mere creaming foam, but into masses of accumulated yeast, which hang in ropes and wreaths from wave to wave, and, where one curls over to break, form a festoon like a drapery from its edge; these are taken up by the wind, not in dissipating dust, but bodily, in writhing, hanging, coiling masses, which make the air white and thick as with snow, only the flakes are a foot or two long each: the surges themselves are full of foam in their very bodies, underneath, making them white all through, as the water is under a great cataract; and their masses, being thus half water and half air, are torn to pieces by the wind whenever they rise, and carried away in roaring smoke, which chokes and strangles like actual water. Add to this, that when the air has been exhausted of its moisture by long rain, the spray of the sea is caught by it as described above, and covers its surface not merely with the smoke of finely divided water, but with boiling mist; imagine also the low rain-clouds brought down to the very level of the sea, as I have often seen them, whirling and flying in rags and fragments from wave to wave; and finally, conceive the surges themselves in their utmost pitch of power, velocity, vastness, and madness, lifting themselves in precipices and peaks, furrowed with their whirl of ascent, through all this chaos; and you will understand that there is indeed no distinction left between the sea and air; that no object, nor horizon, nor any land-mark or natural evidence of position is left; that the heaven is all spray, and the ocean all cloud, and that you can see no farther in any direction than you could see through a cataract. Suppose the effect of the first sunbeam sent from above to show this annihilation to itself, and you have the sea picture of the Academy, 1842, the Snowstorm, one of the very grandest statements of sea-motion, mist, and light, that has ever

been put on canvas, even by Turner. Of course it was not understood.

—John Ruskin, *Modern Painters*

4. It was in Burma, a sodden morning of the rains. A sickly light, like yellow tinfoil, was slanting over the high walls into the jail yard. We were waiting outside the condemned cells, a row of sheds fronted with double bars, like small animal cages. Each cell measured about ten feet by ten and was quite bare within except for a plank bed and a pot for drinking water. In some of them brown, silent men were squatting at the inner bars, with their blankets draped round them. These were the condemned men, due to be hanged within the next week or two.

One prisoner had been brought out of his cell. He was a Hindu, a puny wisp of a man, with a shaven head and vague liquid eyes. He had a thick, sprouting moustache, absurdly too big for his body, rather like the moustache of a comic man on the films. Six tall Indian warders were guarding him and getting him ready for the gallows. Two of them stood by with rifles and fixed bayonets, while the others handcuffed him, passed a chain through his handcuffs and fixed it to their belts, and lashed his arms tight to his sides. They crowded very close about him, with their hands always on him in a careful, caressing grip, as though all the while feeling him to make sure he was there. It was like men handling a fish which is still alive and may jump back into the water.

—George Orwell, "A Hanging"

5. The golf gallery is the Punchinello of the great sports mob, the clown crowd, and uncontrollable, galloping, galumphing horde, that wanders hysterically over manicured pasture acreage of an afternoon, clucking to itself, trying to keep quiet, making funny noises, sweating, thundering over hills ten thousand strong, and gathering, mousey-still, around a little hole in the ground to see a man push a little ball into the bottom of it with a crooked iron stick. If the ball goes in they raise a great shout and clap their hands and sometimes slap one an-

other on the back, crying "Oh, boy!" and "Beautiful, beautiful, magnificent!" And when the white pellet just sneaks past
the rim of the orifice or twists out of it, or goes up and looks
in and sticks on the edge, a great mass murmur of pity runs
through the group and they sound their "Oh's" like a Greek
chorus greeting the arrival of a new set of catastrophes. Then
it is that they make their absurd clucking noises and shake their
heads, some in unison, some in anti-unison, like mechanical
dolls all set off at once.

The golf gallery is closest of any to the game that is being
played. Every individual in the stampede is familiar with the
implements used and the problems that arise from tee to green.
They are really vicarious players, and the crass outsider who
rattles a toy movie camera at one of the artists just as he is about
to apply a delicate brush of his poker against the side of the
quiescent ball, is given the hissing and glaring-at of his life.
The Jones galleries were something to see, up and away over
the hills before the master had completed the poem of his follow-through, running, crowding, tearing, galloping, hustling—men, women and children, in sunshine or in cloudburst,
their tongues hanging out, their faces red, their sports clothing
dishevelled, elbowing one another in the wild route over the
lea to secure a momentary vantage point from which to bear
witness to the next miracle.

—Paul Gallico, "A Large Number of Persons"

6. During the time of the spring floods the best near view
of the fall is obtained from Fern Ledge on the east side above
the blinding spray at a height of about 400 feet above the base
of the fall. A climb of about 1400 feet from the Valley has to
be made, and there is no trail, but to any one fond of climbing
this will make the ascent all the more delightful. A narrow part
of the ledge extends to the side of the fall and back of it, en-
abling us to approach it as closely as we wish. When the afternoon sunshine is streaming through the throng of comets, ever
wasting, ever renewed, the marvelous fineness, firmness, and
variety of their forms are beautifully revealed.

At the top of the fall they seem to burst forth in irregular spurts from some grand, throbbing mountain heart. Now and then one mighty throb sends forth a mass of solid water into the free air far beyond the others, which rushes alone to the bottom of the fall with long streaming tail, like combed silk, while the others, descending in clusters, gradually mingle and lose their identity. But they all rush past us with amazing velocity and display of power, though apparently drowsy and deliberate in their movements when observed from a distance of a mile or two. The heads of these comet-like masses are composed of nearly solid water, and are dense white in color like pressed snow, from the friction they suffer in rushing through the air, the portion worn off forming the tail, between the white lustrous threads and films of which faint, grayish pencilings appear, while the outer, finer sprays of waterdust, whirling in sunny eddies, are pearly gray throughout.

At the bottom of the fall there is but little distinction of form visible. It is mostly a hissing, flashing, seething, upwhirling mass of sand and spray, through which the light sifts in gray and purple tones, while at times, when the sun strikes at the required angle, the whole wild and apparently lawless, stormy, striving mass is changed to brilliant rainbow hues, manifesting finest harmony.

The middle portion of the fall is the most openly beautiful, lower, the various forms into which the waters are wrought are more closely and voluminously veiled, while higher, towards the head, the current is comparatively simple and undivided. But even at the bottom, in the boiling clouds of spray, there is no confusion, while the rainbow light makes all divine, adding glorious beauty and peace to glorious power.

This noble fall has far the richest, as well as the most powerful, voice of all the falls of the Valley, its tones varying from the sharp hiss and rustle of the wind in the glossy leaves of the live oaks and the soft, sifting, hushing tones of the pines, to the loudest rush and roar of storm winds and thunder among the crags of the summit peaks. The low bass, booming, reverberating tones, heard under favorable circumstances five or six miles away, are formed by the dashing and exploding of heavy masses mixed with air upon two projecting ledges on the face of the cliff, the one on which we are standing and another about 200 feet above it. The torrent of massive comets is continuous at time of high water, while the explosive, booming notes are wildly intermittent, because, unless influenced by the wind, most of the heavier masses shoot out from the face of the precipice, and pass the ledges upon which at other times they are exploded.

Occasionally the whole fall is swayed away from the front of the cliff, then suddenly dashed flat against it, or vibrated from side to side like a pendulum, giving rise to endless variety of forms and sounds.

—John Muir, "Yosemite Falls"

7. Supper was at six and was over by half past. There was still daylight, shining softly and with a tarnish, like the lining of a shell; and the carbon lamps lifted at the corners were on in the light, and the locusts were started, and the fire flies were out, and a few frogs were flopping in the dewy grass, by the time the fathers and the children came out. The children ran out first hell bent and yelling those names by which they were known: then the fathers sank out leisurely in crossed suspenders, their collars removed and their necks looking tall and shy. The mothers stayed back in the kitchen washing and drying, putting things away, recrossing their traceless footsteps like the life-time journeys of bees, measuring out the dry cocoa for breakfast. When they came out they had taken off their aprons and their skirts were dampened and they sat in rockers on their porches quietly.

It is not of the games children played in the evening that I want to speak now, it is of a contemporaneous atmosphere that has little to do with them: that of the fathers of families, each in his space of lawn, his shirt fishlike pale in the unnatural light and his face nearly anonymous, hosing their lawns. The hoses were attached at spigots that stood out of the brick foun-

dations of the houses. The nozzles were variously set but usually so there was a long sweet stream of spray, the nozzle wet
in the hand, the water trickling the right forearm and the
peeled-back cuff, and the water whishing out a long loose and
low-curved cone, and so gentle a sound. First an insane noise
of violence in the nozzle, then the still irregular sound of ad-
justment, then the smoothing into steadiness and a pitch as accurately tuned to the size and style of stream as any violin. So
many qualities of sound out of one hose: so many choral differences out of those several hoses that were in earshot. Out of
any one hose, the almost dead silence of the release, and the
short still arch of the separate big drops, silent as a held breath,
and the only noise the flattering noise on leaves and the
slapped grass at the fall of each big drop. That, and the intense
hiss with the intense stream; that, and that same intensity not
growing less but growing more quiet and delicate with the turn
of the nozzle, up to that extreme tender whisper when the
water was just a wide bell of film. Chiefly, though, the hoses
were set much alike, in a compromise between distance and
tenderness of spray (and quite surely a sense of art behind this
compromise, and a quiet deep joy, too real to recognize itself),
and the sounds therefore were pitched much alike; pointed by
the snorting start of a new hose; decorated by some man play-
ful with the nozzle; left empty, like God by the sparrow's fall,
when any single one of them desists: and all, though near alike
of various pitch; and in this unison. These sweet pale stream-
ings in the light lift out their pallors and their voices all together, mothers hushing their children, the hushing unnaturally
prolonged, the men gentle and silent and each snail-like with-
drawn into the quietude of what he singly is doing, the urina-
tion of huge children stood loosely military against an invisible
wall, and gentle happy and peaceful, tasting the mean good-
ness of their living like the last of their suppers in their mouths;
while the locusts carry on this noise of hoses on their much
higher and sharper key. The noise of the locust is dry, and it
seems not to be rasped or vibrated but urged from him as if

through a small orifice by breath that can never give out. Also
there is never one locust but an illusion of at least a thousand.
The noise of each locust is pitched in some classic locust range
out of which none of them varies more than two full tones:
and yet you seem to hear each locust discrete from all the rest.

—James Agee, "Knoxville: Summer 1915"

WRITING ASSIGNMENTS

Select one of the following essay topics. After reviewing the
principles covered in Writing Seeing, try to make your essay
as vivid as possible. Show as well as tell.

1. Assume you are part of a group welcoming foreign students to the U.S. for the first time. Part of your duty is to write
an essay explaining a social custom that might at first seem
strange to someone who knows little about our culture. A few
suggestions: "Halloween"; "Blind Dating"; "Slumber Parties"; "Pep Rally"; "The *Car.*"

2. Write a vivid account of the most frightening time in
your life.

3. Write an essay with the word 'fad' somewhere in the
title. Explain what fads are. Why do we have them? Why are
they only temporary? Remember to be concrete.

4. Compare the *you* today with the you as a preteen. Be
as specific as possible. Include physical as well as psychological
differences.

5. What is your least favorite spectator sport? Boxing?
Baseball? Football? Golf? Swimming? In explaining why, be
sure to supply mental pictures.

6. Assume you could, with the wave of your hand, make
disappear any invention or device made in the twentieth century. What would it be? What would be the consequence?

7. Assume the role of a sociologist and review and analyze
either a women's or men's magazine. To what do they appeal?
Why are they organized as they are? Describe the cover of each
and explain why you think the publishers decided to use it.

8. Write a story about your pet and you. Use as many clichés and stale images as you see fit. Then rewrite the story replacing the worn-out mental pictures with fresh ones.

9. Assume you have been given an opportunity to write a column for the local newspaper and have been given total freedom to write whatever you wish as long as you keep it interesting and *vivid.* Decide on a title for your column and write your first essay. You may want to read several columnists to see just what concerns they address.

10. Narrate the worst vacation you ever took. By providing mental pictures, take your readers on the trip with you.

6. Writing Reasoning

THE ARCHITECTURE OF THOUGHT

Humans are animals that reason. This phenomenon in conjunction with language separates us, indeed even isolates us, from every other living thing on our planet. Our early ancestors saw this distinction between animals and humans as a natural law, a natural order, and sometimes as a justification for their superiority over all living things. Reason, in a very real sense, gives us our humanness; reason defines us.

Once civilization evolved from tribal life, once jungle magic and mythical religion became an inadequate means of governing societies, especially those composed of varied religious and cultural backgrounds, humans saw the value of reason: no longer just a distinction between them and the lower animals, reason was a useful guide in keeping organized society together. Reason, in fact, became part of ethics and an equal partner with morality as a skeletal framework upon which human beings constructed such inventions as government and law. When in search of justice, civilized humans have gone not to a God whom they cannot see or hear, not to a medicine man with his secret potions, but to a group of *reasonable* men and women, people like Aristotle, who believed judgment about the rightness or wrongness of an act was an ethical exercise. The ancient philosophers considered ethics (and, thus, reason) a keen pragmatic guide for civilized men and women. Reason, after all, can make us better people. If we are reasonable, we will be more ethical and the world's society will be a good place in which to live. Douglas Ehninger says it eloquently in his book *Influence, Belief, and Argument:*

Philosophically there are simple but compelling reasons why argument is to be preferred over alternative methods for influencing belief and behavior.

Because he believes the proper way to influence others is to bring those persons to see for themselves the rightness or justness of the claims he presents, the advocate who chooses argument as his instrument treats his readers or listeners not as things to be manipulated, but as persons to be reasoned with, as responsible, rational beings whose judgment deserves respect and whose integrity must be honored. Modes of persuasive appeal which seek to circumvent or benumb the understanding are disrespectful of the individuals addressed; they degrade the listeners or readers by endeavoring to produce the automatic, instinctive sort of response characteristic of animals, rather than the considered, judgmental sort of response humans alone are capable of making. Argument, in contrast, is respectful of people and those distinctive qualities of reason, understanding, and reflection which mark them off as "human." Instead of addressing the biological individual, it addresses the person as thinker.

Ehninger goes on to say that by respecting the humanity of others, "by treating them as persons rather than as things," we all reinforce our own humanity and thus become more human ourselves. He makes an important contrast:

Humanity is something we gain for ourselves only insofar as we willingly grant it to those about us. The more skilled we become in the use of emotion, prejudice, or suggestions as instruments of persuasion, the farther we depart from the ideals which ought to govern our relations with our fellows.

Compare this view of reason and clear thinking with that of an enemy of reason, the propagandist. Adolf Hitler, writing in *Mein Kampf* on the same subject, demonstrates his complete understanding that one can manipulate an audience by appealing to its emotions and prejudices.

I came early to realize that the proper employment of propaganda is a real art.

If considerations of humaneness and beauty do not count in the battle, neither can they be used as standards to judge propaganda.

All propaganda must be popular in tone, and must keep its intellectual level to the capacity of the least intelligent among those at whom it is directed.

Hitler goes on to say that propaganda can always succeed because most people let "emotions and feelings rather than sober consideration" determine their thought and action. Aristotle would counter that it's the responsibility of the ethical person not to manipulate others with appeals to emotions.

I begin my discussion of argumentation with this contrasting view of Aristotle and Ehninger, on the one hand, and Hitler, on the other, not only to highlight the importance of logic in making us and keeping us "reasonable" creatures, but also to personalize the two means of influencing and persuading the people of the world: *propaganda* vs. *reason.* What follows will alert you to the dangers of the propagandist and guide you through what Will Durant calls the art and science of reason.

It is a science because to a considerable extent the processes of correct thinking can be reduced to rules like physics and geometry, and taught to any normal mind; it is an art because by practice it gives to thought, at last, that unconscious and immediate accuracy which guides the fingers of the pianist over his instrument to effortless harmonies. Nothing is so dull as logic; and nothing is so important.

—*The Story of Philosophy*

Logic, then, is the formal name for the "science" that attempts to reduce "the processes of correct thinking" to rules. The rules of logic enable us to evaluate and test the truth of our beliefs and conclusions about the world. This ability to test beliefs and conclusions is essential when we wish to persuade others of the soundness of our own thoughts and invaluable when we want to scrutinize the thoughts of others to see whether we should be persuaded by their reasoning.

In this section, *writing reasoning,* my intention is to show you, in as simple a way as I can, how to write a clear, logical, ethical argument. Before you can write your thoughts, however, you have to find them. For that reason, I will be talking for quite some time not about writing, but about thinking. An under-standing of the way "reasonable" men and women think will help you to find and organize your own thoughts.

Induction

I said at the outset of this discussion that men like Aristotle considered the science of reason an ethical exercise that would best guide human beings in their relationships with other human beings, and, by extension, a society's relationship with other societies. It was during his time, the fourth century B.C., that most of the rules of reason we still follow today were estab-lished.

A good way to learn these rules is to transport yourself back a few hundred thousand years and consider the way reason it-self evolved. Our ancient ancestors were able to wrestle their way out of a hostile environment and eventually dominate it because of reason. One of the simplest ways they reasoned was inductively, that is, by drawing conclusions from observing the repetition of events. Ever since they could remember, our early forebears observed that the antlers of deer fell off every spring; once they began herding sheep, they noticed that most sheep live only sixteen years. Because of such repetition in events, they could make *generalizations* about the world: deer antlers fall off every spring; sheep die on the average at sixteen years of age. This ability to make generalizations helped them gain control of their world because they could then make pre-dictions and plan their existence in nature, rather than just react to it. Because of induction they learned when to plant, harvest, prepare for a cold winter, migrate, fish, and hunt. Farmers still rely on inductions made centuries ago: plant un-derground crops when the moon is waning; plant above-ground crops when the moon is waxing. Noting this repetition of events in nature not only helped the primitive humans take some control of their destiny, but also made them acutely aware that there are things in the world called *truths.* If there were truths about the seasons and about poisonous plants, then there must be other truths as well. The world, then, is not only manageable, it is understandable because of these certainties. Arriving logically at these certainties eventually became a science. Scientists would rely on the inductive method of thought to confirm the truth that water freezes at thirty-two degrees Fahrenheit, that the sun completes its cycle around the earth approximately every twenty-four hours, that light objects and heavy objects fall at the same rate of speed.

Induction, then, is the method of arriving at a probable truth by relying upon the repetition of the same fact to lead you to a generalization or conclusion—no matter how mundane: every time I've used that soap my hands have broken out. There must be something in the soap that makes my hands break out. Although the inductive method of reasoning is a very useful way to arrive at conclusions, it *can* be abused, as it often is by the propagandist. However, Aristotle and his colleagues have set out some rules by which to judge the accuracy of any induction.

Sufficient Evidence

I've owned my Karmann Ghia less than a week and I'm already having trouble with the starter switch. A friend at work is likewise having trouble with the starter switch in her Karmann Ghia. I conclude that all Karmann Ghias have bad starter switches. In arriving at this conclusion, I am moving inductively—from the observation of specific examples to a generalization—but I'm arriving at a conclusion too hastily. The thousands of other Karmann Ghia owners may never have had trouble with their starter switches. So while induction can be an accurate way of arriving at conclusions, they must not be drawn too hastily. The rule: In all inductive arguments the evidence must be *sufficient* to warrant the conclusion.

Relevant Evidence

I took my Karmann Ghia to Mac's garage. You should have seen the place: a tin roof, a dirty and greasy floor, a loud radio blaring from somewhere in the back, a customer complaining to the manager about the quality of work. I got out of there in a hurry. I knew I couldn't trust them with my car. Some people think they are "reasoning" when they are not. They just "seem" to be reasoning. In this case, the only evidence relevant to the conclusion that I can't trust my car with them is that there is a customer complaining. The loud radio and dirty floor and tin roof are not relevant to the conclusion drawn. Moreover, one person complaining is not a sufficient sampling of customers to conclude that the mechanics do bad work. In inductive arguments, the evidence must be *relevant* to the conclusion.

Random or Representative Sampling in Statistical Inductions

Assume you are in a business economics class of a hundred students. One day the teacher asks how many in the class favor the tax exemption for business lunches. All but two students raise their hands. The teacher concludes that most students at the university are in favor of tax exemptions for business lunches. This is the inductive method, but it's neither fair nor accurate since the selected sample is not representative of the student body as a whole. It excludes the students in art, drama, physics, philosophy, many of whom might oppose the tax exemption for business lunches. So what is the right way to arrive at an accurate conclusion? There are two ways: (1) We can *randomly* select a large enough number of students—say 300 in a school made up of a thousand students—and solicit their opinions. Random sampling prevents any bias from influencing the outcome. (2) We can select a group of students *representative* of the entire population. Let's assume, for example, that the university breaks down the following way: 35 percent business; 15 percent engineering; 20 percent liberal arts; 15 percent physical sciences; 10 percent fine arts; 5 percent other. If you wanted to find out what the students as a whole think about tax-exempt business lunches, but couldn't interview every student, you could select a hundred out of the thousand students at the school, keeping the percentages in this group the same as the percentages of students in the various colleges: 35 percent from business; 15 percent from engineering; 20 percent from liberal arts, and so on. Such a method will lead you to a fairly accurate conclusion about the student body's opinion on tax-exempt business lunches. If statistics are to have any relevance at all, they must be a result of random or representative sampling.

Although induction leads to truths, especially in science, for the most part it simply leads to a high probability. So use induction cautiously. After all, it was not that long ago that people thought frogs fell from the clouds since they appeared out of nowhere every time it rained.

FOR PRACTICE

Examine the inductive reasoning in the following. Does the conclusion "reasonably" follow from the evidence?

1. For years I've received letters from Andrew Green, and in every one, way over fifty letters, I have found at least two misspelled words. Needless to say, Andrew is not a very good writer.

2. At random we selected 20,000 names from the phone book—approximately one sixth of the city population. We asked each person what he or she considered to be the most significant problem confronting the city. Eighty percent said they worried most about rapid growth. We believe that this fairly accurately reflects the view of most of our citizens.

3. My sorority is composed of sixty members. Of those sixty only five believe that we should have a female baseball team. That should be evidence enough that most women on this campus do not want a female baseball team.

4. We have predicted that Joan Whitis will win the election. The city is broken down into five economic categories and three ethnic categories. Five percent of our citizens make over $100,000 a year; twenty percent of our citizens make over $50,000 but less than $100,000; forty percent make over

$30,000 but less than $50,000; twenty-five percent make over $10,000 but less than $30,000; ten percent make below $10,000. Sixty-five percent of our citizens are white; twenty percent of our citizens are black; ten percent of our citizens are Mexican-American; five percent are of another race. By interviewing a thousand voters in each of the city's seven precincts, making the percentages of that thousand correspond directly and proportionately to the city's economic and ethnic makeup as a whole, we discovered that Joan Whitis is getting close to seventy percent of the vote.

5. If you want to get a job after college, you should major in business. Last year there were 300 graduates in business who got jobs immediately upon graduation. In engineering, only 12 graduates got jobs; in fine arts, only 3; in anthropology, only 4; and in English only 7. The business school is the place to be.

Deduction

Induction helped our remote forebears take control of their destiny and make sense out of a bewildering world. Each truth established by observation became a small step on the stairway human beings were building to lift themselves out of the purely animal world. Induction also made possible something else—another way to create steps, another way to arrive at reasonable conclusions about the world: *deduction.* For the first time, they could make reliable generalizations about the natural world; they could begin classifying it. Some things were animals; some were plants; some were minerals. Among those things that were animals, some were insects, some were reptiles, some were mammals. Among the mammals, some were land-dwelling, some were water-dwelling. And the classification would continue until there were 15,000 species of mammals alone. Creatures with x characteristics belong in this species; creatures with y characteristics belong in that species. Humans were, in effect, putting their world into categories—categories that eventually led to biological classification of shared characteristics. Grouping creatures into various

classes can be very useful, for it enables humans to reason deductively—that is, to draw an accurate conclusion from two
general premises.

Assume for example that you, as a biologist, know very well
that "all warm-blooded, egg-laying, winged and feathered ver-
tebrates are birds." Then one day you come across a penguin,
the first one ever seen. Upon examination you discover that
even though it doesn't resemble any bird you've ever seen,
it is a warm-blooded, egg-laying, winged and feathered verte-
brate. You conclude, "This creature must be some kind of
bird." The creature is now less mysterious since you can name
it, which is another way of saying categorize it. Induction led
us to the generalization about birds; deduction led you to the
conclusion that this new-found creature is also a bird.

The Supreme Court justices rely upon this same gener-
al-to-specific method: *All laws that violate the* Constitution *must
be struck down; this law violates the* Constitution; *It must be struck
down.* The detective in a convoluted spy novel does the same
thing. He arrives at the scene of the murder. He recognizes
the suspect whom his less astute colleagues are questioning in
the corner—a Russian spy. He immediately goes to the corner
and ties the hands of the suspect. His reasoning goes like this:

All Russian spies carry cyanide pills they swallow if caught
This man is a Russian spy
He carries cyanide pills he will swallow if caught

If the detective's first premise is true, and if, indeed, the man
before him is a Russian spy, then the third statement *must* be
true. He has moved from a generalization to a specific conclusion. But compare this reasoning with the following: The murder victim has a tatoo of a dragon on his left wrist. The detective knows that all the members of a secret Mafia gang are
required to have a dragon tatoo somewhere on their left wrist.
He concludes that the dead man is a member of the Mafia
gang. His reasoning looks like this:

All members of the secret Mafia gang have dragon tatoos on their
left wrists

This man has a dragon tatoo on his left wrist
This man is a member of the secret Mafia gang

On the surface, this line of reasoning appears to be identical to the one above. But it is significantly different. We can demonstrate this difference with a kind of circle language.

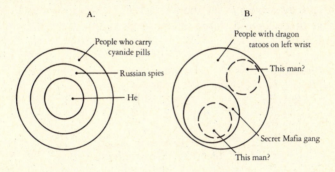

A.

People who carry cyanide pills

Russian spies

He

B.

People with dragon tatoos on left wrist

This man?

Secret Mafia gang

This man?

Categorical Syllogisms

In example A, if it is true that *all Russian spies carry cyanide pills,* and if it is true that *this man is a Russian spy,* then *he* must go within the larger circle and thus *he must carry cyanide pills.* But in example B, even if it is true that *all members of the secret Mafia gang have dragon tatoos on their left wrists,* and even if *This man has a dragon tatoo on his left wrist,* we still can't with absolute certainty place *this man* within the category of *secret Mafia gang.* To avoid such slips in this movement from generalizations to specific conclusions, Aristotle suggested some rules to govern this method of deductive reasoning which rely upon a certain arrangement or form he called the *categorical syllogism*—arriving at truth by showing the relationship of three classes of things by organizing them into two premises and a conclusion. Fortunately it is not necessary to learn the complexities of the rules that Aristotle established to govern the syllogism. With circle language, you can just as confidently see the accuracy or inaccuracy of any deduction. While you do not have to learn the rules of the deductive syllogism, it's helpful to keep in mind a few guidelines:

1. Deduction is a method of argument that moves from generalizations to specific conclusions.

2. When these generalizations and conclusions represent separate and distinct categories, the form of the argument is called a categorical syllogism.

3. A syllogism is a *form* of deductive argument that consists of exactly two premises and a conclusion. All syllogisms must have three and only three categories or classes. Here is a valid syllogism:

Premise 1	All novels are boring	**Generalization**
Premise 2	This book is a novel	↓
Conclusion	Therefore, this book is boring	**Specific conclusion**

Category 1	novels
Category 2	boring things
Category 3	this book

4. The validity, that is, the correctness of the form, of any syllogism can be ascertained by using circle language to show the relationship among the three categories. To translate the above syllogism into circle language, we must look closely at the logical relationship of the categories or classes stated in guideline 3. Looking at premise 1, we can see that category 1, *all novels,* is part of category 2, *boring things.* In circle language this relationship is shown by placing the category *all novels* inside the category *all boring things,* the broadest category mentioned.

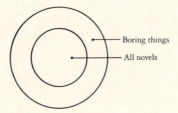

Boring things
All novels

Premise 2 goes on to tell us about the relationship of the third category to the first—namely, that *this book* belongs to the category *all novels*. Translating into circle language, we add a circle to represent *this book* and place it within the circle for *all novels*.

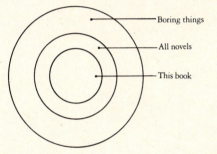

We now have graphic evidence that the conclusion follows from the premises.

The following are three types of valid syllogisms and their circle language translations:

1. Two affirmative premises:

   All cats are finicky
   Jeremiah is a cat
   Jeremiah is finicky

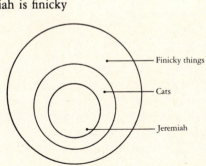

2. Negative premise and affirmative premise:

No legislator is a convicted felon
Stephen Marr is a legislator
Stephen Marr is not a convicted felon

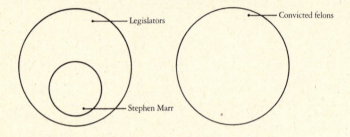

3. Affirmative premise and negative premise:

All diamonds are hard enough to cut glass
This stone is not hard enough to cut glass
This stone is not a diamond

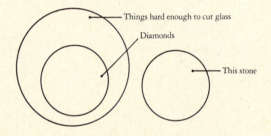

In each of the above examples, you can *see* how the circle language leads to inevitable conclusions. If the premises are true and if the circle language shows that the syllogism is valid, then the conclusion must be true. We use the same circle language to show us when syllogisms are not valid.

All communists read the *Communist Manifesto*
Professor Brewer reads the *Communist Manifesto*
Professor Brewer is a Communist

Although at first glance this may seem to be a valid syllogism, our circle language shows that it is not.

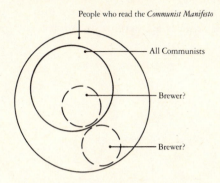

Where do we put Professor Brewer? Although we can put the professor inside the category *People who read the* Communist Manifesto, we cannot with any certainty place him inside the *All Communists* circle. He may or may not be a Communist.

Here are three kinds of invalid syllogisms:

1. Affirmative premise and negative premise:

    All lawyers are college-educated
    Rebecca is not a lawyer
    Rebecca is not college-educated

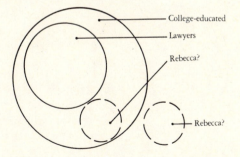

We can put *Rebecca* in more than one place. Thus, the syllogism is invalid.

2. Two negative premises:

   No Lawrence painting has a human figure in it
   This painting has no human figure in it
   This painting is a Lawrence painting

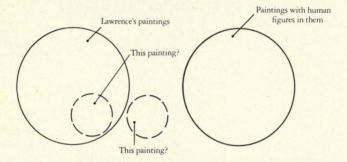

We know *This painting* does not belong in the *paintings that have human figures in them* category, but we can't be sure that it goes within the *Lawrence* category. Thus, it's invalid.

3. Two affirmative premises:

   All professors use big words
   Janet Manry uses big words
   Janet Manry is a professor

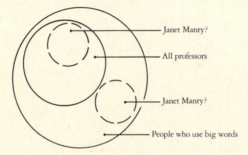

Since we can put Janet Manry in more than one place, the syllogism is invalid.

Validity, Invalidity, and Truth

By drawing circles you can always determine whether your syllogism is valid or invalid. But keep in mind that validity refers to form and not to truth. To illustrate, we can invent nonsense categories and still determine whether the syllogism is valid.

All Fless is Grice
All Slah is Fless
All Slah is Grice   **Valid**

All Fless is Grice
All Slah is Grice
All Slah is Fless   **Invalid**

Try translating these two syllogisms into circle language to test their validity.

Validity in its strictest sense then refers to form and not to truth. Indeed the conclusion to a syllogism may be true and yet the syllogism may still be invalid.

All mammals have vertebrae
All dogs have vertebrae
All dogs are mammals

Even though the conclusion in this example is true, the reasoning process is invalid, and our circle language again shows us why.

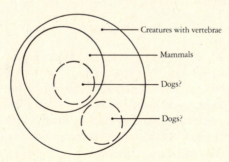

Although we know that all dogs are mammals, we would still be reasoning illogically if we used this form for our argument. For an argument to be reasonable, therefore, the premises must not only be true, they must also be placed in their valid arrangement. When truth and validity are present the conclusion is certain.

A good way to keep the distinction between validity and truth in mind is to remember that a reasonable argument has both good content and good architecture. Good arguments depend not only upon the amount of verifiable evidence you marshal forth, but also upon the arrangement of that material—its architecture.

Hypothetical Syllogisms

Before we explore this deductive form, I want you to think about something a moment. You and a friend are at a movie. Your friend has gone to the lobby for popcorn, leaving an empty seat next to you. A big bruiser with broad shoulders and a pot belly squeezes through the aisle's knees and sits in your friend's seat. You inform him that the seat is taken, but he just huffs and puffs and mutters, "You don't own this seat!" Why did he say that? What does he mean? We know he took the seat because he is a bully, but what was his "reason" for taking the seat—his assumption? If we look at the architecture of his thought we would find something like this:

If you own this seat, then you'd have the right to reserve it
You don't own this seat
Therefore, you don't have the right to reserve it

This "form" of reasoning is also deductive (moving from premise to conclusion, but you are moving from a *hypothetical* premise (If you own this seat), not a categorical one (All communists). Logicians call this form a *hypothetical syllogism,* and just as we can determine the valid or invalid architecture of a categorical syllogism, so can we determine the validity or invalidity of a hypothetical argument.

The first premise of a hypothetical syllogism has two parts, the antecedent and the consequent.

Antecedent	If you own this seat
Consequent	Then you'd have the right to reserve it

In all cases, if you wish the argument to be valid, you must either *affirm the antecedent* (You *do* own this seat) or *deny the consequent* (You *don't* have the right to reserve it) in the second statement. Our insensitive bully's "reason," then, is not logical because the second premise (You don't own this seat) neither affirms the antecedent nor denies the consequent. Rather it denies the antecedent—the "form" of the argument, and thus the argument itself, is invalid.

Let's take a more detailed look at hypothetical arguments. If I can establish the truth of the statement "If I hit the switch, the lights will go off," and then I do hit the switch, the lights *have* to go off. By hitting the switch, I will have affirmed the antecedent.

Affirming the Antecedent	If I hit the switch, then the lights will go off
	I do hit the switch
	The lights do go off

But what if I affirm the consequent?

Affirming the Consequent	If I hit the switch, then the lights will go off
	The lights go off
	I hit the switch

In this case (even if I do establish the truth of the first premise), I cannot conclude with certainty that "I hit the switch." The lights could have gone off for some other reason. By saying "The lights go off" in the second premise, I am affirming the consequent which, if I wish to have a valid architectural form, I cannot do.

What if I deny the antecedent?

Denying the Antecedent   If I hit the switch, then the lights will
go off
I don't hit the switch
The lights will not go off

For the same reason that the bully example didn't work, this
one won't work either. In the above example, I am denying
the antecedent (not affirming it, as I must do for the argument
to be valid), and therefore I can't draw any certain conclusion
from it. Even if I don't hit the switch, the lights may very well
go off for some other reason. And finally, what if I deny the
consequent?

Denying the Consequent   If I hit the switch, the lights will go
off
The lights did not go off
I didn't hit the switch

In this case, if the first premise is true and the lights don't go
off, then we can conclude with certainty that I didn't hit the
switch.

As you can see, a simple rule governs the architectural structure of hypothetical deductions: for a hypothetical syllogism
to be valid, you must either affirm the antecedent or deny the
consequent.

Alternative Syllogisms

Sometimes we draw conclusions that are based on an *ei-
ther/or premise*.

Chocolate is either bad for you or good for you

To advance this statement to a conclusion, we must eliminate
one of the alternatives.

Chocolate is not good for you

The elimination of one of the alternatives now leads inevitably
to an affirmation of the remaining alternative.

Therefore, chocolate is bad for you

This form of reasoning is called the *alternative syllogism,* and it must be used cautiously. For it is true that we can make rational decisions based on an alternative premise (You must sign the traffic ticket or be put in jail; the landfill is either contaminated with nuclear waste or not contaminated with nuclear waste; the syllogism is either valid or invalid), but few things are so black and white. More often than not the alternative syllogism is abused because the user does not and often cannot establish the truth of the alternative premise. "Either you love this country or you hate it." "Either you support our president in everything he does or you are an enemy of the government." "You either like his movies or hate his movies." We will discuss this more when get to fallacies in thought.

Enthymemes and Premises

If you wish to reason with someone, you must develop the habit of discovering what people mean regardless of whether they say it explicitly—the habit of discovering the complete architecture of a thought. When reasoning with you, a friend will often expect you to supply missing elements in his or her thought. Consider, for example, the statement "she can't be a Republican; she's a Democrat." Missing from this statement is the premise "no Democrats are Republicans." Or suppose a friend says, "this law has to be a good law because Congress passed it." Automatically you would conclude that part of the thought is missing and you reconstruct it to include the premise.

Categorical	All laws passed by Congress are good
	Congress passed this law
	This law has to be good

or

Hypothetical	If a law is passed by Congress, it is a good law
	This law was passed by Congress
	It has to be a good law

Either of the above reconstructions provides the *premise missing* from your friend's statements. Arguments with one part—premise or conclusion—missing are called *enthymemes*.

Constructing the Architecture of Thought

As Aristotle noted, construction or reconstruction of a thought in its entirety guides you through reasonable discourse. First, *it helps you isolate those premises accepted by you and your opponent.* Neither of you needs to introduce these into the argument since you both already accept or assume them. For example, an environmental group might argue that an offshore oil well is threatening an endangered species; the oil company might argue that it is not. Neither, however, bothers to argue whether saving endangered species is valuable or worthwhile. Both sides just assume it. The plaintiffs and defendants in a court case do the same thing. Both implicitly accept the premise that the court has the legal right to dispense justice.

Second, *constructing the architecture of your and your opponent's thoughts helps determine where the argument must begin.* Assume, for example, that you are debating with a friend the topic "Should illegal aliens be given a free public education?" You say, "Yes, because illegal aliens pay taxes." Your friend says, "No because illegal aliens are not citizens of this country." The architecture of your two arguments would look like this:

You

Premise	All persons who pay taxes should be given a free public education
Premise	Aliens are persons who pay taxes
Conclusion	Aliens should be given a free public education

Your Friend

Premise	All noncitizens do not have the right to a free public education
Premise	Aliens are noncitizens
Conclusion	Aliens do not have the right to a free public education

In this case you and your friend may be speaking to one another, but you are not arguing with one another until you

begin to consider each other's premises. You believe that anyone who pays taxes should have a right to free education; your
friend believes that only citizens have the right to a free public
education. Before either of you could ever discuss your opinion on the question, you must first support the premise upon
which you base your opinion. Constructing the architecture of
your thoughts helps you discover where you must begin your
argument.

Third, *constructing the architecture of someone else's thought can
expose prejudice and emotion—two enemies of clear thought.* Try to
construct the architecture of thought in the following para-
phrase of a statement made back in the seventies by a sheriff
infamous for arresting male hitchhikers with long hair. Among
those he arrested was a newspaper reporter. The sheriff said
something like this to the reporter's editor who came to in-
quire about his employee's arrest: "Eighty-five percent of the
people in this jail have been longhairs. That indicates to me
that practically all thugs wear long hair. It's kind of a badge.
So, sure, I arrest them all. That's why I arrested your reporter." After analyzing the sheriff's statement, you might construct a deductive syllogism like the following:

All thugs wear long hair
This man wears long hair
He probably is a thug.

If you translate this syllogism into circle language, you will discover that it is invalid: we don't know precisely where to place
the "He."

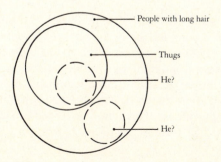

It might be true that all thugs wear long hair and it might also be true that the reporter has long hair, but this doesn't mean that he's a thug.

Constructing the anatomy of one's thought can also expose those who simply rely on emotion, not reason, as a device of persuasion. Assume a woman was caught stealing a $1.60 sandwich at the cafeteria where she worked and was fired by the manager, who charged that she broke a company policy she had pledged to keep regarding free consumption of food by employees. In an emotional editorial, the editor of a local newspaper argues that Mrs. White should be rehired. Here's part of the editor's statement.

> Mrs. White stole the $1.60 sandwich because her two children were hungry. She makes only $300 a month. We don't condone stealing, but there were extenuating circumstances. She was hungry. Her children were hungry. She did what any loving, self-sacrificing mother would do if in her shoes. The immoral act of the management just manifests their callous disregard for human beings. Something so trivial should not cause such pain. If the management has any blood in its veins, it will reinstate Mrs. White immediately.

While we can sympathize or even empathize with Mrs. White and wish that she would not be fired, surely we could not argue her case on the premise established by this editor. Here is the anatomy of the editor's thought.

> If you're hungry, it's okay to steal
> Mrs. White was hungry
> It was okay for Mrs. White to steal

Does the editor really *mean* this? With this premise, the editor would have to condone the stealing of bread from the grocery store by every hungry person in the country. *Emotionally,* the plea sounds good and righteous, but *reasonably* it would permit a wave of "moral" thefts. A more reasonable position might have been to argue that the severity of the punishment was not justified by the offense. This editor, governed by emotion, simply expressed a "feeling" disguised as reason.

Fourth, and last, *constructing the architecture of a thought can help you structure your own argument.* Assume for a moment, you are an attorney. You have been hired by James Smith. The State, in order to honor a past President, is condemning Mr. Smith's farm—land that has been in the family for four generations. Citing the power of eminent domain (the right of a government to take private property for the greater good of the public), the State argues that the farm land and beautiful pecan valley would benefit more people if turned into a state park. How would you argue against the State's takeover of the land?

Your first step would be to construct the State's case. You must know the *architecture* of their thought. After all, they must have had a *reason* for assuming they could condemn someone's farm for the purpose of constructing a state park. Understanding the State's case will help you establish your own. After deliberation you decide the State might do the following:

1. Appeal to emotion—the glory that the President brought to the State, and
2. Construct a logical argument

Since there is no defense against their appeal to emotion, except to point it out to the jurors, you must construct the architecture of the State's argument. A synopsis of it might go like this:

Our society is based upon the social contract theory. While limiting the power of the government to interfere with the rights of the governed, the theory requires in turn that the governed relinquish some of their rights for the good of the whole society. When society was first emerging, the individual, to receive the protection of the tribe, gave up some of his crops or herd, or agreed to serve the community by participating in the defense of the group against its enemies, or both. Even today we all give up some rights in order to receive the benefits that organized society provides—namely, protection or preservation of life itself. The good of the majority, then, not of the minority, is what society must and ultimately does serve. The majority instinct for preservation is served, for example, by drafting men—taking away certain individual rights to freedom in order to protect the whole. The relinquishment of one's rights is not forced upon the individual; it is an accepted part of citizenship. A fundamental premise of our society, then, is that society (or government) can take away certain, specific individual rights for the benefit of the majority. As long as you are a citizen, you must accept this premise, which is essential if society is to function and survive. The power of eminent domain is another example of the right of society to serve the good of the majority. The taking by the public of private land, for instance, is necessary if we wish to build a public road between San Francisco and Los Angeles. If the state was prohibited from condemning private property for this purpose, we might have to drive a hundred miles or more to reach a city only fifty miles away and pay tolls to each property owner whose land we crossed. Mr. Smith, as an American citizen, benefits like everyone else from the power of eminent domain. In the present case, the state honors a President by establishing a park in his name which will be for the recreational use of all citizens. More people will benefit from the park to be developed than from the continued use of this land as a farm.

Let's X-ray this and look at the anatomy.

If you are a member of this society, you give up certain rights to the majority
Mr. Smith, you are a member of this society
You must give up certain rights to the majority

If a use of the power of eminent domain produces a good for the majority (roads, telephone lines), then it is a rightful exercise of the power
This use of eminent domain (taking Mr. Smith's farm) will benefit the majority of citizens
It is a rightful exercise of the power

Well, all that seems reasonable enough. Mr. Smith is in a corner. What do we do? How do we argue his position, which is simply that it's his land and he shouldn't be made to move? We can't argue that he has *rights* to private property because the State will have already addressed that, namely, that each citizen is required from time to time to give up certain rights for the sake of the majority. We must have a different premise. Once we examine the anatomy of the State's thought, we see that their first argument is valid and strong. We can't get around it. But the second seems weaker. Will the State define eminent domain? What do they mean by good or rightful?

These considerations might lead us to conclude, "Yes, the State's first premise is true, but implicit in it is that a member of society gives up rights in order to *protect* society as a whole. A state park isn't protecting anything; its purpose is to provide space for leisure or pleasure. We see that on one point we will have to agree with the State. Indeed, a person does have to give up some rights for the benefit of the majority and, indeed, the power of eminent domain was established for just such a societal need. But eminent domain should be applied only in essential cases, like drafting men to defend our country. Surely a state park is not in this *essential* category. Thus, our premise might be:

> The State has the right of eminent domain to condemn land for the *essential* needs of the majority
>
> A state park is not an essential need of the majority
> The State has no such right in this case

If we set up our argument this way, we will be offering the jury a choice. The outcome of the case will depend upon which premise the jury members accept. If they accept our premise and if they agree a state park is not "essential," then they *have* to accept our conclusion.

It is precisely such a give-and-take between lawyers that is supposed to take place in the courtroom. Indeed, our legal system is based upon an assumption that goes all the way back to Aristotle's acknowledgment of that one phenomenon that separates man from beast—reason. Reason, in legal terms, becomes justice. Yet, people too often seem to regard reason as something you do *to* someone—as if, in proving your point, you are winning or conquering your opponent. Reason is a process, not an end. It is a means *to* truth, not truth. It is an exchange that, as Aristotle believed, civilizes and humanizes mankind.

To summarize, constructing the architecture of an argument helps you to do the following:

Identify those premises accepted by both you and your opponent
Determine where an argument must begin
Expose prejudice and emotion in your opponent's argument
Set up your own argument

In short, finding the architecture of thought brings out the strengths and weaknesses in an argument and eliminates confusion. Have you ever heard someone in the heat of an argument say, "I don't know where you're coming from"? What that person usually means is, "I don't understand your premise." And have you ever stopped someone who's talking feverishly to you and said, "I don't know where you're going"? What you usually mean is, "There doesn't seem to be an architecture to your thought." Logic (the rules governing induction and deduction) removes such confusion in communication. Reason helps you see "where you're coming from" and helps you know "where you're going."

But discovering the architecture of your or another's thought and checking it for validity is just part of the reasoning process. To be truly reasonable you have to take another step.

FOR PRACTICE _____

A. By using circle language, identify the valid and invalid syllogism in the following groups. Remember that you are looking for validity, not truth.

1. No birds can fly
   All parrots are birds
   Parrots can't fly
2. All dentists hurt you
   Your brother hurt you
   Your brother is a dentist
3. All cool people wear designer jeans
   I wear designer jeans
   I am cool

4. All concerned citizens signed the petition
   Steve signed the petition
   Steve is a concerned citizen
5. All cedars are green
   This tree is not green
   This tree is not a cedar
6. All music is soothing
   No dancing is soothing
   No dancing is music
7. No hardware stores sell lettuce
   This store does not sell lettuce
   This store must be a hardware store
8. All chickens have beaks
   This strange thing has a beak
   This strange thing must be a chicken
9. All westerns have sex and violence
   This movie is a western
   This movie will have sex and violence
10. All neece is shuck
    All shuck is tri
    All neece is tri

B. Identify the enthymemes and premises upon which these statements are based.

1. She must be a genius. She teaches physics at the University.
2. I didn't get the diamond ring she wanted because I didn't think it was expensive enough.
3. Stan shouldn't get the job as sportscaster because he has never played any kind of ball.
4. He must be very rich. He drives a Mercedes.
5. "Franco's" is not a high-class restaurant since they don't serve wine.
6. Newspaper advertising for pornographic movies should be banned.

7. The U.S. government should try to protect all endangered species.

8. I don't want to go to that college. It doesn't even have a choral society.

9. He is very sophisticated. He knows all about art.

10. She's a novelist; I bet she can type fast.

C. Identify the architecture of thought in the following arguments. Which are valid and which are invalid?

1. If people want to work they can find work. Neil Carter can't find work, so he must not want to work.

2. No green melons are sweet. This honeydew melon is green. It must not be sweet.

3. Either we increase our defense spending or we become a vulnerable nation. Congress is decreasing our defense spending so we can count on becoming a vulnerable nation.

4. How can you not like him? He's rich and charming.

5. The company offered her a new car and a pay increase so she just had to accept their job offer.

6. If more men than women drink beer, then we should aim our ad campaign at men. Statistics show that men drink more beer than women do.

7. I remember that if she were to move her knight there, she would have checkmated me. She did checkmate me the next move so she must have moved her knight there. I really can't remember.

8. I don't know from what kind of book these pages came, but history books don't have chapters on the growing of bamboo, so it just may be some kind of history book.

9. People below eighteen years of age should be banned from playing video games. Video games harm young people by making them think less.

10. I don't let my children watch TV shows that contain violence. I don't want them to become violent adults.

D. Construct the architecture or architectures of thought upon which the following paragraphs are structured.

1. Our college president tells us that he wants to make our school a "college of the first rank," and few would oppose his goal. But if he is really serious, he must consider the following. If we are to have a college of the first rank, we must provide physical facilities that will create a climate conducive to learning. By conducive to learning, I mean that the scientists must have the latest and finest technical equipment; our engineers must have state-of-the-art laboratories; our artists must have space to sculpt and paint; our historians must have libraries as fine as those at Yale or Harvard. At present, our physicists can't even conduct standard experiments because of lack of equipment and space; our engineering department is stuck with an ancient computer, and every semester it has to turn away students because there simply isn't space. Our artists don't even have their own building in which to gather. At present they meet in the basement of the geology building. Our library is so incomplete that some scholars who otherwise might have come here have gone to other colleges. The chairman of the history department said in his annual report that he is embarrassed to reply when visiting scholars ask him about our library facilities. And I could go on and on. So if our president is serious about making our college a "college of the first rank," then he had better start by finding ways to build the facilities we so desperately need.

2. Our city ordinance makes it pretty clear. "Any and all vehicles that impede the normal flow of traffic are prohibited from using city streets." We have to have this regulation or else we might find semitrailer rigs clogging up every intersection; horse-drawn carriages, interfering with traffic, would diminish the effect of synchronized traffic lights, and go-carts having trouble making it up steep hills might roll back into oncoming cars. The ordinance was passed in order to keep our streets safe and orderly—something impossible if any kind of vehicle were permitted to roam the streets and alleys. And yet, today just such a vehicle is moving through traffic, not only endangering its operator, but also causing congestion at usually quick-moving intersections; it has so little power that al-

ready five accidents have occurred as the vehicle stalled while going up the hill at Main Street. Thirty-two people have been injured, struck by cars they darted in front of. The police chief, the city manager, and the victims of four of these accidents all agree that these small mini-scooters that have become so popular as of late are dangerous for the driver and a constant source of congestion, especially during rush-hour traffic. Just as other vehicles that violate the city ordinance must be banned from the streets, so must these little nuisances that impede traffic flow and endanger lives.

DEFINING YOUR TERMS

Let's return to Mr. Smith v. the State, for a minute. Look at this construction:

> All states have the power of eminent domain
> Texas is a state
> It has the power of eminent domain in Mr. Smith's case

If the State defines eminent domain as the "right to acquire private property to benefit the majority of citizens in any way," and I define eminent domain as "the right to acquire private property to benefit the majority of citizens in essential ways only," then the State and I are not talking about the same thing when we use the term "eminent domain." And until we agree on the proper definition, we can't argue the particular case of Mr. Smith. Take a look at the architectures of thought below:

> If a tree falls in the forest and no one is there to hear it, there is no sound.

> If the police unreasonably search my house, then they have violated the *Constitution*.
> Sergeant O'Henry unreasonably searched my house
> Therefore, he violated my constitutional rights.

In each case you can see that the constructions or forms are valid. But are they perfectly clear? Of course not. We can't argue either of the positions until we know the meanings of the words "sound," or "unreasonable."

To provide clear thought for your listener or reader, you must define the terms of your argument. Neither Descartes nor Voltaire would argue with anyone unless that person first defined his terms. You and I could argue forever about the sound in the forest if by sound you mean "a wave of air vibrating in space" and by sound I mean "the effect of a wave upon the inner ear." Your house is either legally or illegally searched depending on how the Supreme Court justices define "unreasonable."

As an essential element in the process of moving toward truth, defining your terms can be both a reasonable and an ethical act. Reasonable, because your reader or listener can reason with you only after knowing the architecture of your thought and the definition of your terms. Ethical, because you avoid deception, including self-deception, by making sure you mean precisely what you say.

Classification

You will recall that one of the ways our primitive forebears defined their bewildering world was by placing the objects of that world into a hierarchy of "proper" order. They looked around and noticed the *categories* of air, water, earth, fire, and plants and animals, and they separated themselves from other animals by classifying themselves (actually the Swedish botanist Carolus Linnaeus formally did it in the eighteenth century, joining two Latin words, *Homo* and *sapiens*) as an animal who reasons. These reasoning animals eventually organized the living world into species, genera, families, orders, and classes. A house cat, for example, belongs to the species *Felis domesticus,* genus *Felis,* family *Felidae,* order *Carnivora,* class *Mammalia.* When humans began to make music, they (with nature's help) also began to categorize instruments. They could make one kind of tone by blowing across or into a reed, another kind of tone by strumming a string on a bow, and still another tone by beating sticks or pounding stretched leather or gourds. This early classification of tones and instruments led to the organization of an orchestra that we still accept today: a wind section (woodwind and brass), a string section, a percussion section.

If you were to look up the word baobab, the first thing you would expect to be told is to what general class it belongs. And the dictionary complies: "A tree, *Adansonia digitata,* of tropical Africa." Defining a term by putting it on its proper hierarchical shelf so that the reader can see where it belongs in relation to several things is a good place to begin a definition. Calling feminism a *"doctrine* that advocates the same rights for women as those granted men" is different, certainly, from calling it a *"feeling* that women should have the same rights as those granted men." By establishing the category in which a word belongs, you begin the definition. This is precisely what most dictionaries do.

Distinguishing Characteristics

Merely classifying a term is not always sufficient for defining it clearly. Knowing that a baobab is a tree in the *Adansonia digitata* genus doesn't tell us much—certainly nothing about its characteristics. Dictionary makers are aware of this as well, so, after establishing the "class" to which a thing belongs, they often list a few *distinguishing characteristics:* The baobab trees have large trunks, some up to thirty feet in diameter; they have large, pendulous white flowers and a hard-shelled, fleshy fruit called "monkey bread."

Description and Example

Listing the distinguishing characteristics helps narrow the definition of the word baobab, but even these do not help us *see* the object to which the word refers. It's often useful, therefore, to *describe* the object in order to define it. Or even better, place the object before the viewer; many dictionaries do just that when they place those small photographs and drawings in the margins. Description and/or example are useful supplements to any definition.

Comparison and Contrast

Comparing and contrasting two similar objects can help define each more clearly. Comparing and contrasting a baobab tree with an oak helps us see each more distinctly. Comparing and contrasting the appearance and habits of the lion and the tiger can help us understand each more fully. Comparing and contrasting the word "plot" with the word "story" can illuminate each.

> Let us define a plot. We have defined a story as a narrative of events arranged in their time-sequence. A plot is also a narrative of events, the emphasis falling on causality. "The king died and then the queen died" is a story. "The king died, and then the queen died of grief" is a plot. The time-sequence is preserved, but the sense of causality overshadows it. Or again: "The queen died, no one knew why, until it was discovered that it was through grief at the death of the king." This is a plot with a mystery in it, a form capable of high development. It suspends the time-sequence, it moves as far away from the story as its limitations will allow. Consider the death of the queen. If it is in a story we say "and then?" If it is in a plot we ask "why?" That is the fundamental difference between these two aspects of the novel.
>
> —E. M. Forster, "Plot and Story"

Because of the comparison and contrast, the word "plot" and the word "story" now take on a deeper meaning.

Analogy

In the strictest sense comparisons and contrasts are between things in the same genus or class. Analogies, on the other hand, are *comparisons between things in different classes.* If I compare my grandmother's eyes to my grandfather's eyes, I am comparing things in the same class—namely, eyes. If I compare my grandmother's eyes to the blue sea, I am comparing things from different classes—namely, eyes and the sea. Analogy is a particularly useful way to define a phenomenon that can't be literally described. Things like atoms are difficult to define, so scientists, by analogy, tell us that they are units of matter very much like a miniature solar system, the nucleus surrounded by tiny, orbiting electrons. Social scientists use the comparison between ant colonies and human societies to help them define more clearly what they mean by a social structure. In this sense, analogy is both a comparison and a description all at once, and it is often the only way unobservable events can be explained.

Function

An object's *function* is often as important to a good definition as what it is. It does little good to know that a lantern wheel is a "small pinion consisting of circular disks connected by cylindrical bars that serve as teeth," unless we know that it is *used* as a gear in clocks. Similarly, to limit the word *worship* to a set of ceremonies showing reverence to a deity, idol, or sacred object, is not to tell us what worship *does*. Any time you define a term in an argument, remember not to ignore function in your definition.

You can define the major terms in your argument in the following ways: by classifying, listing characteristics, describing or giving an example, comparing and contrasting, inventing analogies, stating function or purpose. You want the terms of your argument to be absolutely clear to your reader, and the more ways you approach it, the more distinct and informative the definition will become. The perfect definition, although difficult to achieve, is one that sets up two interchangeable sets of words connected by the "to be" verb:

Carbon 14 *is* "a naturally radioactive carbon isotope with atomic mass 14 and half-life 5,700 years, used in dating ancient carbon-containing objects."

Without doing any harm to the definition, I can reverse the words:

"A naturally radioactive carbon isotope with atomic mass 14 and half-life 5,700 years, used in dating ancient carbon-containing objects" *is* carbon 14.

But, as you can see, in the following definition I cannot reverse the sets of words:

> Football *is* "a game played with a ball on a rectangular field with goal posts at each end."

If I were to reverse the order of these sets of words, it becomes clear that other games could be substituted for football—soccer or rugby for instance.

Perfect definitions are rarely attainable; but strive, nevertheless, to get as close to perfection as possible by following the methods of definition discussed above.

FOR PRACTICE

Remembering the methods of definition, write an extended definition of the following terms.

1. Happiness
2. An exotic plant or animal most of your classmates have not seen
3. Hobby
4. Pop music
5. Fast food

THE HAUNTS

I like the sound of that word. Some call them places or topics or regions, but I prefer the atmospheric sound of "haunts." Besides, haunt resembles the word "hunt," which is precisely what one does when visiting a haunt. Hunting also takes me back again to our primitive ancestors who "naturally" thought in certain ways. Let me explain.

Remember that reason separates humans from other living things. Part of reason, certainly, is the ordering of the world through induction or deduction. But induction and deduction are structures of thought, and our architecture is incomplete without some material to our thought. Now just as primitive men and women put things into categories and established premises and drew conclusions from repetitive events in nature, so too did they use what rhetorician Edward Corbett calls "tendencies of the mind." That is, in order to make sense out of the world, they may have done such things as the following:

> *Compared and contrasted* their bodies to those of monkeys in order to distinguish themselves from monkeys.
>
> Reasoned that the sun descending in the west *caused* the earth to become dark.
>
> Showed the tribe how to make fire, through *example,* by striking flint rocks.
>
> *Defined* various plants by giving them names and categories.
>
> Studied the workings of a beehive and, after noticing the bees' efficient division of labor, suggested through *analogy* that we organize our society similarly.
>
> Sought expert *testimony* and advice from an old member of the tribe on when to plant or when to migrate.
>
> Reasoned *a fortiori* (Latin for "even more strong") when they thought "if this herb will ease the pain of a leopard bite, then it will also ease your mild headache."
>
> Defended one tribe member's killing of another who was attacking the first because, under the *circumstance,* the first tribe member had no choice.

These tendencies of the mind are the way we reason, the same tendencies you and I call upon every day. They enable us, for instance, to weigh our planet without putting it on a scale and to measure the distance to the nearest star without ever going there. They are what humans use to try to make sense out of a bewildering universe. Aristotle recognized these tendencies of the mind over two thousand years ago and called them the "haunts" (or "topics" from the Latin word "topoi" meaning "place"). They are the places you go when you are hunting for the substance or material of an argument.

As Aristotle realized, there are occasions when you have an opinion but don't have the slightest idea how to argue it. He knew too that if you argue on a topic about which you not only know a great deal but also feel strongly, then you have little trouble finding your argument. In an instance like this you would *naturally* compare and contrast, or define, or illustrate, or give an example, or call upon an expert witness, or any combination of these. But if you don't feel strongly about the subject and you don't know a great deal about it, what do you do? Aristotle would tell you not to waste your time. Go directly to the haunts. That's where you will end up anyway, no matter how long you think; so you might as well go there in the first place. Make a list of the haunts and then run down it to see if any of them will help you argue your point:

Comparison and Contrast
Cause and Effect
Example
Definition
Analogy
Testimony
A fortiori
Circumstance

Let me show you what I mean.

Assume you have just taken your first case as an attorney. You have been hired to defend Zeke Sloan against a charge of indecent exposure. Zeke Sloan was one of those *Homo sapiens* who, in the spring not too long ago, dashed nude across the television screen on the six o'clock news. He "streaked" thousands of TV viewers sitting around their kitchen tables. He's guilty. No doubt. The station has the videotape. But you have to defend him anyway. So what do you do? Aristotle would whisper over your shoulder "go to the haunts." So let's go there.

As you run down the list you notice that certain of the haunts just won't work. You can't give an example—that's what the prosecuting attorney will do. The prosecutor will show the jury the videotape and say, "You see here. This is indecent exposure." Nor can you argue from circumstance. How could we say Zeke Sloan "streaked" America because he had no other choice? What about contrast? Can you contrast "streaking" to anything else? Nothing comes to mind, so you move on. Cause and effect. What was the cause of Zeke Sloan's actions anyway? Why would any normal human being want to streak the six o'clock news? Is there a "reasonable" explanation? Zeke claims it was just part of the spring fad. Spring? That's it. Spring fever. This fad of streaking began in the spring on college campuses. The cold winter, the feeling of being penned up all season, and then a sudden burst of warm weather always affects us humans—we all do crazy things. We have found one haunt that might work. The cause was spring fever; the result was streaking. Exploring that haunt leads us right to comparison. If indeed "streaking" is a spring-fever phenomenon, then what other spring-fever phenomena could we compare it with? What about those in the jury who swallowed gold fish, or sat on flagpoles, or "mooned" the Dairy Queen, or sardined into Volkswagens? Comparison will help the jury understand exactly what Zeke did. We must show them that streaking is no more a crime than sitting on a post office flagpole. And that thought has an architecture.

> All crimes are things that hurt people or society
> Streaking does not hurt people or society
> Streaking is not a crime.

This "line" of reasoning leads us to another one of the haunts—definition. We can define for the jury exactly what "streaking" is and we'll define it as an act that is not a crime. Well, now that we can compare his act with something, now that we can define it, now that we can account for its cause, perhaps we can do something else—contrast it with something. With what? Well, implicit in the prosecutor's definition of "indecent exposure" is that it is offensive to society's moral values, but surely Zeke Sloan's brief appearance on the screen was not the same kind of "offense" as that of a stubble-faced man with a trench coat who "flashes" himself at the Sixth Street bus as it goes by. If that is indecent exposure, then what Zeke did could not be put into that category. The man with the trench coat isn't flashing because of spring fever; his actions are not like those of the goldfish-swallowers and flagpole-sitters; and

Zeke probably didn't shock people as much as he amused them. And that takes us to the haunt of example. Perhaps, we can, after all, use an example. Perhaps we can find some people who watched the Eyewitness News and actually smiled at the incident—and that leads us to testimony. If Mr. Sloan's act was not offensive to someone's moral values and this person is a citizen of the nation, then perhaps the act wasn't indecent exposure (as defined by the prosecutor) after all, and he is charged with a crime he didn't commit. We're getting somewhere. Do you see? We might even find a psychologist who would testify to the importance of spring release in modern society. In fact, we're getting so confident that we might even use an analogy, comparing streaking to the shedding of snake's skin in the spring. "It's just a natural act." At last, we've got a case. We began with nothing, but by exploring Aristotle's "haunts" we found our argument.

Now we might very well lose our case, but we would have argued it the best we could. By going to the haunts we saved ourselves time floundering for a way to argue, and notice that this is a mental "process," not a formula or a rule. By exploring the haunts, you clarify some thoughts, get rid of others, and "move" toward truth from your perspective.

Remember that a paragraph in an essay is a "unit of thought." An argument will usually be composed of several paragraphs, each developed by one of the haunts or by one of the four architectures of thought. Hence, the outline of an essay might look like this:

paragraph 1   Introduction
paragraph 2   Comparison
paragraph 3   Induction
paragraph 4   Cause and effect
paragraph 5   Testimony
paragraph 6   Deduction
paragraph 7   Conclusion

The most efficient way to demonstrate the application of the haunts and the four architectures of thought in an essay is to give you several paragraphs, several units of thought, from a famous and eloquent argument. Imagine for a moment—you are a black man cooped up in jail and charged with parading without a permit. You had come to Birmingham, Alabama, to march peacefully in the streets to protest segregation laws that forced blacks to the back of the bus, forbade them from reading in certain areas of the library and drinking from certain water fountains, even from eating at certain restaurants. You came to Birmingham to expose the unethical and immoral consequences of segregation laws, yet now you find yourself in jail and reading in the newspaper a statement published by eight Birmingham clergymen who say they agree with your ends, but cannot condone your means—the mass demonstrations that always bring violence. You're struck by their ignorance of your perspective and the strength of your argument.

This was just the situation in which Martin Luther King, Jr. found himself. Writing on the margins of the very newspaper he had been reading and then on scraps of paper smuggled to him by a friendly trustee, King resisted an emotional and angry response. Instead, treating the clergymen as humans whose judgment deserves respect, he composed a response in "reasonable terms" to make them see the validity of the cause the marchers espoused. Notice in the following units of thought that King follows Aristotle's ethical approach to argument. He uses almost every valid architecture of thought and every haunt. And by doing so, he constructs an overwhelmingly effective argument. The haunt or architecture used is indicated above each of the following excerpts from King's "Letter from Birmingham Jail."

COMPARISON

I am in Birmingham because injustice is here. Just as the prophets of the eighth century B.C. left their villages and carried their "thus saith the Lord" far beyond the boundaries of their home towns, and just as the Apostle Paul left his village of Tarsus and carried the gospel of Jesus Christ to the far corners of the Greco-Roman world, so am I compelled to carry the gospel of freedom beyond my own home town. Like Paul, I must constantly respond to the Macedonian call for aid.

CIRCUMSTANCE

But your statement, I am sorry to say, fails to express a similar concern for the conditions that brought about the demonstrations. I am sure that none of you would want to rest content with the superficial kind of social analysis that deals merely with effects and does not grapple with underlying causes. It is unfortunate that demonstrations are taking place in Birmingham, but it is even more unfortunate that the city's white power structure left the Negro community with no alternative.

INDUCTION

But when you have seen vicious mobs lynch your mothers and fathers at will and drown your sisters and brothers at whim; when you have seen hate-filled policemen curse, kick, and even kill your black brothers and sisters; when you see the vast majority of your twenty million Negro brothers smothering in an airtight cage of poverty in the midst of an affluent society; when you suddenly find your tongue twisted and your speech stammering as you seek to explain to your six-year-old daughter why she can't go to the public amusement park that has just been advertised on television, and see tears welling up in her eyes when she is told that Funtown is closed to colored children, and see ominous clouds of inferiority beginning to form in her little mental sky, and see her beginning to distort her personality by developing an unconscious bitterness toward white people; when you have to concoct an answer for a five-year-old son who is asking, "Daddy, why do white people treat colored people so mean?"; when you take a cross-country drive and find it necessary to sleep night after night in the uncomfortable corners of your automobile because no motel will accept you; when you are humiliated day in and day out by nagging signs reading "white" and "colored"; when your first name becomes "nigger," your middle name becomes "boy" (however old you are) and your last name becomes "John," and your wife and mother are never given the respected title "Mrs."; when you are harried by day and haunted by night by the fact that you are a Negro, living constantly at tiptoe stance, never quite knowing what to expect next, and are plagued with inner fears and outer resentments; when you are forever fighting a degenerating sense of "nobodiness"—then you will understand why we find it difficult to wait.

DEFINITION/ALTERNATIVE SYLLOGISM/TESTIMONY

One may well ask: "How can you advocate breaking some laws and obeying others?" The answer lies in the fact that there are two types of laws: just and unjust. I would be the first to advocate obeying just laws. One has not only a legal but a moral responsibility to obey just laws. Conversely, one has a moral responsibility to disobey unjust laws. I would agree with St. Augustine that "an unjust law is no law at all."

TESTIMONY/CATEGORICAL SYLLOGISM

How does one determine whether a law is just or unjust? A just law is a man-made code that squares with the moral law or the law of God. An unjust law is a code that is out of harmony with the moral law. To put it in the terms of St. Thomas Aquinas: An unjust law is a human law that is not rooted in eternal law and natural law. Any law that uplifts human personality is just. Any law that degrades human personality is unjust. All segregation statutes are unjust because segregation distorts the soul and damages the personality.

EXAMPLE/ILLUSTRATION

Let me give another explanation. A law is unjust if it is inflicted on a minority that, as a result of being denied the right to vote, had no part in enacting or devising the law. Who can say that the legislature of Alabama which set up that state's segregation laws was democratically elected? Throughout Alabama all sorts of devious methods are used to prevent Negroes from becoming registered voters, and there are some counties in which, even though Negroes constitute a majority of the population, not a single Negro is registered. Can any law enacted under such circumstances be considered democratically structured?

COMPARISON

Of course, there is nothing new about this kind of civil disobedience. It was evidenced sublimely in the refusal of Shadrach, Meshach, and Abednego to obey the laws of Nebuchadnezzar, on the ground that a higher moral law was at stake. It was practiced superbly by the early Christians, who were willing to face hungry lions and the excruciating pain of chopping blocks rather than submit to certain unjust laws of the Roman Empire. To a degree, academic freedom is a reality today because Socrates practiced civil disobedience. In our own nation, the Boston Tea Party represented a massive act of civil disobedience.

We should never forget that everything Adolf Hitler did in Germany was "legal" and everything the Hungarian freedom fighters did in Hungary was "illegal." It was "illegal" to aid and comfort a Jew in Hitler's Germany.

ANALOGY

We who engage in nonviolent direct action are not the creators of tension. We merely bring to the surface the hidden tension that is already alive. We bring it out in the open, where it can be seen and dealt with. Like a boil that can never be cured so long as it is covered up but must be opened with all its ugliness to the natural medicines of air and light, injustice must be exposed, with all the tension its exposure creates, to the light of human conscience and the air of national opinion, before it can be cured.

CAUSE AND EFFECT/HYPOTHETICAL SYLLOGISM

If this philosophy had not emerged, by now many streets of the South would, I am convinced, be flowing with blood. And I am further convinced that if our white brothers dismiss as "rabble-rousers" and "outside agitators" those of us who employ nonviolent direct action, and if they refuse to support our nonviolent efforts, millions of Negroes will, out of frustration and despair, seek solace and security in black-nationalist ideologies—a development that would inevitably lead to a frightening racial nightmare.

ANALOGY

Let us all hope that the dark clouds of racial prejudice will soon pass away and the deep fog of misunderstanding will be lifted from our fear-drenched communities, and in some not too distant tomorrow the radiant stars of love and brotherhood will shine over our great nation with all their scintillating beauty.

By interweaving the architectures of thought and the haunts, King was able to find and then refine his argument and respond clearly and logically to the clergymen's criticism of the march on Birmingham. This essay demonstrates his understanding of the necessity of form or structure in the composition of an argument, his understanding of the relationship of the parts of thought to the movement of thought.

FOR PRACTICE

Suggest ways you might support the following generalizations and conclusions by going to Aristotle's haunts and by constructing the architecture of your argument (induction or deduction). Make an outline of your essay.

1. Einstein is the most important scientist in the twentieth century.
2. Tulip bulbs have the most peculiar history of any plant.
3. I am just a product of my environment.
4. The school is a more significant influence upon children than the family is.
5. Television advertising appeals to insecurity in men and women.

MATERIAL FALLACIES

By now you should be aware of the natural ways we think. In a broad sense, reason is simply organizing reality by a process of comparing, contrasting, defining, classifying, following inductive evidence, seeking wisdom from those who have preceded us, and noticing the causes and effects in the world that always make us ask *why?* In short, our thinking follows certain architectures and/or comes from certain haunts. But just because we "reason" in this manner doesn't always mean that the conclusions are truthful. Indeed, that is the danger of thinking men and women—they can easily deceive themselves.

If you recall my discussion of the architecture of thought, you will remember that we can determine whether any architecture is valid either by drawing circles or applying rules. We call any resulting invalid architectural *forms* logical fallacies or *formal* fallacies: what you say might be true, but the form in which you say it does not necessarily make your conclusion true. *Material* or *informal* fallacies, on the other hand, are fallacies in thought that derive directly out of the "content" or "material" of your thought. Logical or formal fallacies are structural; informal fallacies are material. Most material fallacies arise simply because arguers abuse the haunt where they go to discover their thoughts.

Hasty Generalization

Induction is movement from a series of specific observations to a conclusion or generalization. Its haunt is example. We know that induction can, at times, lead us to something close to truth. If every elk I've had the opportunity to meet has had two ivory teeth, then I can conclude that the next elk I meet will have two ivory teeth as well. All my inductive experience points to the high probability of that conclusion. But people often distort induction by drawing a conclusion too quickly.

> I'm not going to Harvard. I knew two sisters from there and they were both snobs.
> She's a terrible actress. I saw her in *The Beast.*
> I'm not going to like her husband. He's in a fraternity.

Drawing conclusions from too few samples often leads to an inaccurate conclusion, yet many people do it all the time. This fallacious 'reasoning' leads to hasty judgments about people who are a certain color or wear certain clothes or drive a certain kind of car or worship a certain God. From the two fascists or two plumbers or two athletes we meet, we already know about them all. Or do we? While it is true that induction can lead us to truth, it is also true that hasty induction can lead us to untruth. Thus, when writing an argument or weighing that of another, be careful of *hasty generalizations.* Remember too that the first premise of many categorical deductions (All rich people are snobs) is often supported inductively, and, if that induction is a hasty one, then the entire argument will fall apart. Aristotle's concern was not with winning an argument; his concern was with the search for truth by the *process* of argument. Thus, "to argue" sometimes means to admit you don't have an argument after all, to acknowledge that the evidence on which you base your generalization consists of too few examples to point with any probability to the truth of your conclusion.

Post Hoc

You sometimes see a similarly careless mind at work when you consider the way we naturally observe the cause and effect of events that happen around us. Primitive humans may have reasoned, "The snow on our thatched roof caused it to collapse." In this case the conclusion was probably reasonable. So are some others: "Frustration with segregation laws in Alabama leads to the nonviolent marches in the streets"; "If I move my queen there, he will have to move his knight over there"; "The bombing of Pearl Harbor sparked the U.S. to get involved in World War II." But many people see cause and effect relationships that are not reasonable at all. These are called *post hoc* fallacies:

> After the President's first six months in office there was an increase in violent crime in the streets.
> The President's election caused this.
>
> Dancing always leads to promiscuity.

I think you get my point. Be aware of the uses of cause and effect. When you go hunting in your cause and effect haunt to find an argument, be sure you don't bring a fallacious one back.

Faulty Analogy

Simple comparison is a likening of two things in the same genus (her nose is like his nose). Analogy is a comparison of two things of different genuses (his nose is like an Idaho potato). Analogies are useful in helping your reader "see" your thought. Recall how Martin Luther King, Jr., in his "Letter from a Birmingham Jail" compared injustice to a boil.

> Like a boil that can never be cured so long as it is covered up but must be opened with all its ugliness to the natural medicines of air and light, injustice must be exposed, with all the tension its exposure creates, to the light of human conscience and the air of national opinion, before it can be cured.

Good analogy clarifies, and that is its value. Remember from the section on metaphor (p. 118) how John Stuart Mill argued that making citizens into conformists is like turning the Niagara River into a Dutch canal. But analogy can attempt too much if carried too far. In an editorial from the *Amarillo Daily News,* an editor argued that since football is a game of strategy and since Gerald Ford played football, the United States need not worry about the allegations of Ford's unfamiliarity with foreign affairs. By that logic, Joe Namath should be secretary of defense. The game of football and the conduct of foreign affairs may have in common the need to plan and execute strategic moves, but that is where the comparison—a superficial one at that—ends. To build an argument on an analogy of this kind is unwise because, if you carry on with the comparison, you will eventually see that, though the two things may be alike in some respects, they are not alike in many others. Unwarranted extension of the analogy will cause it to fall apart. Limit your use of analogies to clarifying certain points in your argument; don't try to base your entire argument on one.

Either/Or Arguments

One reason to be wary of either/or arguments is that few things in life fall conveniently into only either this or that category, as pointed out in the discussion of alternative syllogisms. The alternative syllogism often oversimplifies the available alternatives. "Either it will rain or the sun will shine" ignores the possible alternative of a cloudy day on which no rain falls. Another reason for the weakness of the alternative syllogism is that it also ignores the possibility that both alternatives could be true at the same time. On occasion rain falls while the sun shines.

So while there are certain alternative propositions that are true (either you are dead or you are alive; either you pay your taxes on time or you pay a penalty), most propositions are rarely so black and white, good and evil, them and us. As you have probably already recognized, this is a favorite fallacy of propagandists because by greatly simplifying issues they eliminate the need to explain their complexity. Oversimplification in such cases can discourage open consideration of all available alternatives.

> Either we beat the Soviet Union at the arms race or America will perish.

Testimony

It is indeed reasonable to ask an authority to support your argument. If you lived 3,000 years ago you might have tried to convince the tribe it was time to move to the mountains. You might bring in the oldest member of the tribe who could testify that just about this time of year every twenty years and just after a rain like this last one, a great flood has filled the valley. Today, you might ask a nuclear physicist to testify that the nuclear power plant in your city is safe. But a pro football quarterback urging you to vote for Candidate X or a movie star telling you as he smiles that Computer Z is better than Computer R is not necessarily a source of expert opinion. Authorities must be just that—authorities on the subject about which you are writing.

Ways We Shouldn't Think But Do

In all the instances above, the fallacy of thought arises out of the natural way we think. We naturally consider the cause and effect of events around us, but if we're not careful we will commit the fallacy of *post hoc.* By realizing this, you learn to be cautious with your argument. But mankind also thinks in certain ways that don't seem natural at all. At least, the ways are not on Aristotle's list of haunts.

Red Herring

To see this evasive technique, all you have to do is watch the weekly interview programs on television. Invariably the guests on "Meet the Press" or "Issues and Answers" will never answer the question they are asked. Instead they introduce other information in order to avoid the question.

Question	Secretary Smith, do you mean that if the Soviet Union puts tanks into Germany, we'll send in our air force from Turkey?
Answer	Well, let me say that we don't expect the Russians to do such a thing. They know we have a defense treaty with the West Germans and they know that the United States has long acknowledged the importance of a secure Europe. I think all this talk about Russia and West Germany is just rumor in the press. Our two largest east-coast newspapers are particularly bad at putting conjecture into print. As you know, I've long advocated more responsible journalism among our country's newspapers.

Don't let anyone who is arguing (in writing or speech) take a red herring (as hunters do) and drag it across the scent of the argument (the rabbit) in order to lead you (the hound) in another direction. Such a technique is manipulation.

You're Another or *Bandwagon*

I have never known why this fallacy is so effective, yet every teenager probably has used it at least once. "Mother, why can't I dye my hair green and pierce my nose and drive my car in reverse? All the other kids are doing it." Of course, the parental reply is always, "You're not the other kids, and their doing it doesn't make it right." Many adults, and especially politicians, also use this fallacy.

Why harp about the way we Americans treated the Indians and blacks? Look at what the Crusaders did to the Moslems.

Advertisers frequently raise this fallacy to the level of bandwagon appeal: Be a Pepper! Millions of Americans are! Buy this car! Everyone else has!

Fallacy of Composition

This is an easy one. Just remember that Harvard may produce bright graduates and the Super Bowl champions may be the best team in football, but just because someone went to Harvard or played on the Super Bowl championship team doesn't necessarily mean that he is the brightest or the best. Don't let the truth or aura of a group be passed on to any specific member of the group.

Begging the Question

I saved the most common fallacy for last. If you will look to the "Letters to the Editor" section of any city newspaper, you will find several instances of this slip in thought: "Obscene movies like that should not be permitted in our town"; "A ridiculous law like that should be rewritten"; "I wouldn't dream of allowing my son or daughter to attend a university where the morals of the young people are permitted to be so low." In each of these statements, the writer begs us to question him because he is assuming in his statement what needs to be proved. He begs the questions, "What is an obscene movie?"; "Why is the law ridiculous?"; "What are low morals?" Begging the question is a fallacy in thought in which the writer or speaker assumes in his statement what needs to proved before we can decide if his statement is reasonable. Before we can consider the reasonableness of, "That tyrannical teacher should be fired," we must first know what the writer means by "tyrannical." We must not let him just assume it.

FOR PRACTICE

Identify the material fallacies in the following statements.

1. Disgusting books like *Lady Chatterley's Lover* should be burned.
2. Are you still the snob you were when you were a teenager?

3. Either a university has good teachers or it has bad teachers, and I've had three courses at Drum College and all three teachers were terrible. That college isn't worth attending.

4. I bet Marie knows all about French history. She lived in Paris for two years.

5. Mr. Gilman will make the better office manager because he's a real family man, won the purple heart in World War II, and manages a little league baseball team.

6. Corrupting television shows like "Dallas" should be taken off the air.

7. Every time I've taken an aspirin for my toothache, I've had bad dreams. The aspirin must cause the dreams.

8. If you, Mr. Williams, were to die tomorrow, your wife and twin boys would be left with less than half of what you make now. Think how more secure and happy they will be if they have enough money to keep them at their same standard of living. With this new policy . . .

9. Our nation is indeed a ship of state. And just as a captain must exercise total authority over the crew, so a President must exercise total authority over the other bodies that help keep the ship of state going.

10. He's not very bright. He played football in college.

11. I'm going to get an electric razor like the one pro golfer Jack Burgess uses. He says it is the best.

12. There's no reason we shouldn't cheat just a little on our income tax; everyone else I know does it.

EMOTIONAL APPEALS

Let me begin this section with a quote.

Franz Boas, in his *Mind of Primitive Man,* tells us that primitive man has the same kind of mind that we have, except that he is more likely to be influenced by emotion. Civilization, Boas says, does not improve the mind, but it decreases emotional association with ideas and thus helps us to think more clearly. If we wish to make sense, we must try to eliminate emotion when emotion is irrelevant.

—LIONEL RUBY, *THE ART OF MAKING SENSE*

Emotion takes the mind away from reasonable thought and influences more our animal, instinctive nature than our human, reasoning mind. However, there *is* a place for emotion. I don't want you to assume that in order to be logical or ethical, or even write a good argument, that you must have ice in your veins. To the contrary, it is emotion that often sparks us to search for the reason for our thoughts. But weeping over a silly, sentimental movie or praising a brave soldier or cringing at the savageness of slavery are emotions quite different, for instance, from the hatred toward the Jews Hitler instilled in many Germans' hearts and the hysteria he fomented by lauding the "superior" character of the Aryan race and viciously attacking the foreign enemy he himself invented.

Emotion *can* make a good argument even more persuasive. In Martin Luther King, Jr.'s "Letter from Birmingham Jail," for instance, we find paragraphs of emotion inserted in between those cooly reasoned thoughts.

> I wish you had commended the Negro sit-inners and demonstrators of Birmingham for their sublime courage, their willingness to suffer, and their amazing discipline in the midst of great provocation. One day the South will recognize its real heroes. They will be the James Merediths, with the noble sense of purpose that enables them to face jeering and hostile mobs, and with the agonizing loneliness that characterizes the life of the pioneer. They will be old, oppressed, battered Negro women, symbolized in a seventy-two-year-old woman in Montgomery, Alabama, who rose up with a sense of dignity and with her people decided not to ride segregated buses, and who responded with ungrammatical profundity to one who inquired about her weariness: "My feets is tired, but my soul is at rest." They will be the young high school and college students, the young ministers of the gospel and a host of their elders, courageously and nonviolently sitting in at lunch counters and willingly going to jail for conscience' sake. One day the South will know that when these disinherited children of God sat down at lunch counters, they were in reality standing up for what is best in the American dream and for the most sacred values in our Judaeo-Christian heritage, thereby bringing our nation back to those great wells of democracy which were dug deep by the founding fathers in their formulation of the Constitution and the Declaration of Independence.

The effect of this one paragraph would be diluted, however, if it had been just part of ten similar paragraphs. It gains its force because King has already "reasonably" stated his argument and convinced his audience of the rightness or truth of his position. Thus, controlled emotion has a place in an argument, but it can never substitute for argument. If you wish to evoke a mood, say at a political convention or medal of honor ceremony, then you would, of course, appeal to the emotions. But if you are debating whether we should break a treaty with a long-standing ally, then you must appeal to the reason of the mind and do so respectfully. Some people think argument is deceiving convincingly; but argument is a means of arriving at truth. If you wish to persuade someone of your position, you try to *tell the truth* effectively and convincingly. To merely persuade effectively and convincingly (emotion) is more an effort to manipulate than to reason.

Appeal to Pity

To introduce emotion into an argument in which it has no place is to shift the reader's attention away from the real issue you are debating. In this way, appeal to emotions serves as a kind of *red herring*. Take, for example, the "arguments" given by a defendant in a drunken driving case. "My wife had just left me, my dog died, and I had just lost my job, and I didn't know what to do. I thought about suicide. So I just got drunk and got in the car." Here our attention is slowly pulled away from a consideration of the charge that the defendant broke the law and to his emotional state. According to the law, there is no excuse—however pitiful—for someone to endanger the lives of other citizens.

Appeal to the People

Similarly, if the same defendant says, "I've never done it before. I'm a regular churchgoer. I grew up in a small town just like most people here," then he is leading the audience away from the consideration of his violation of a law and toward a consideration of his character and background which just happens to be very much like that of Middle America. Appeals to pity or to the people's sense of the average American distracts from logical consideration of a question.

Attack on Character

Attacks upon one's character can be a subtle appeal to prejudice and can impose conclusions upon the audience without ever supporting them. Assume, for example, that the prosecuting attorney speaking to the jury at the close of a spy case says the following: "Now ladies and gentlemen of the jury, you have seen this skinny, spineless, closet Communist was registered in the same hotel as the Russian agent on the very night the documents were stolen." These blatant (and in this case, unfounded) attacks upon the defendant's character can excite the prejudice of any Communist hater and distract him from the evidence in the case. "Skinny," "spineless," and "closet Communist" are not grounds to *reason* that the defendant stole the documents.

Appeals to emotions (pity, the people, attacks on character) are diversions from reason. They are a propaganda tactic. Know when you are being manipulated, and avoid doing it yourself.

FOR PRACTICE

Identify the fallacies and emotional appeals in the following passage:

I understand your needs because I am one of you. I was born on a farm not too unlike the beautiful one I passed on the way here today. I know what it's like to work twelve-hour days, to get the crop in just to see it destroyed by rainstorms in the spring. I know what it's like not having the medical attention you need. I remember having to drive all night long through a blizzard to get my dying mother to a hospital. I love the smell of freshly cut hay, and I still quiver when I hear the "Star-Spangled Banner." I don't have a lot of money like my opponent. I don't have his city-slicked tongue; I don't own a new baby blue Cadillac; I don't live in a mansion; I've never been to Europe. But I do know what's best for my country. I've got the God-given common sense that people like you share. My Yankee opponent thinks people like you and me are reactionary. That's what he called me the other day. He doesn't think there is a Communist movement to undermine our government. But the fact is ever since the radical members of the House like him gained control of the Foreign Affairs Committee, the number of registered Communists has risen 35 percent. He, like a little boy not wanting to face reality, buries his head in the sand and doesn't see the cancer growing—the Communist cancer that the Russians planted many years ago. I say either we take a stand on Communism or we don't. And if we take a stand, that means we pass meaningful legislation to prevent the Communist influence in our textbooks, in our news organizations, in our government, and in our universities. All America-loving, right-thinking people see that it's obvious. To tell you the truth, some of the views of my opponent actually frighten me. If we follow his course, then in a few years—sooner than we would like to imagine—many of us might be wearing grey pajamas into the field every day as we labor for our military governor, and the glorious Communist party leaders will nightly raise their vodka glasses over democracy's worm-filled grave.

WRITING THE ARGUMENT: A SUMMARY

I said at the outset of this chapter that I would be talking about "reasoning" for a long while before I ever mentioned *writing* the argument. Well, now I'm here, and if you've kept up with me all this way, then the rest of this will be easy.

A List of Things to Remember

1. There are certain things you just cannot argue. Is chocolate better than strawberry? Is Margaret a better actress than Susan? Priests are happier than secretaries. The violin has a prettier sound than the guitar. Always separate your mere preference or taste from reasoned judgment.

2. After you select an arguable topic, determine if you will need to approach it inductively or deductively or both. Review the rules that govern induction and deduction.

3. Isolate the enthymemes and premises of your argument so that you will know where you must begin your argument and what premises you do not have to support.

4. Define the terms of your argument as clearly as possible by following one or more of the methods discussed on pp. 256–261.

5. Go to all of Aristotle's haunts and nose around. Here you will find much of the material of your argument.

6. Avoid material fallacies and emotional appeals.

7. With the argument clearly fixed in your mind, make a list of the "units" of thought—usually a paragraph each. Your list might look like this:

Introduction
Comparison
Analogy
Deduction
Cause and Effect
Induction
Conclusion

An argument can be based entirely on one haunt or one architectural structure:

All English novels are boring (example, comparison)
Bleak House is an English novel
It is boring

8. Once your list of thoughts is complete, go through it and arrange them in the most effective order. Generally, you

should begin with the weaker points first and move toward your strong ones. This will slowly build your case.

9. Write as simply and clearly as you can. Remember that if there is any possibility for your readers to become confused, they will.

10. Transitions are extremely important in arguments because they, like thread, weave all units of thought together. Review the section on transitions in chapter 2 (p. 45). Usually the right transitional word or phrase will come to you during the process of writing, but if it doesn't, make sure the reader sees how you move from one paragraph to the next. Just because *you* see how you got there is not enough.

11. Don't worry about style or freshness until your second or third draft. Getting the argument out on the paper is the most important thing—don't think you can keep it all in your mind and then write, in an instant, a perfectly organized argument.

12. The conclusion is extremely important in an argument. For it is there where you bring everything together. Remember that when your readers get to the conclusion, they have read everything you've said, but may still lack the crystalized understanding of the argument that its creator possesses. Thus, you will want to very clearly and concisely state your main point and do so in an effective way. By effective way, I mean reward your reader for spending so much time with you. Take a look at the principles of freshness. Can you make the conclusion visual, witty, or rhythmic?

But why Writing Reasoning? How does that help you write expository prose? Here are three quick answers.

Why Write Reasoning?

1. Most of the kind of writing you will be doing in college will require reasoning. Term papers and essay questions on exams will require you to give your *reasons.* Writing thinking will make you sensitive to order and form, to the clear and continuous movement of thought, and *that* will help you organize

and communicate your reasons. Aristotle's haunts will save you time and will not only help you find your ideas, but will give you practice in the most common paragraph strategies. By writing reasoning you will know how to put your ideas into *units of thought.*

2. Writing an argument requires precision and clarity, which, in turn, require you to follow the principles of clarity and grace, thereby reinforcing your understanding of them.

3. Practicing writing reasoning can help you avoid slips in logic. Many essays are difficult to read not because of some problem with punctuation, transition, or wordiness but simply because of poor logic. The problem in the following student pieces is in the thinking, not the writing.

> Since most poetry of the nineteenth century is decadent, Algernon Swinburne's "Erotion" fits into a timely tradition.

Here the student hasn't established that most poetry of the nineteenth century is decadent and, thus, begs the question and diverts the reader's mind away from the writer's main point.

> Even though there was no humor in Hardy's *Jude the Obscure,* it still stands as a masterpiece in literature.

Here the student implies that all literary masterpieces must have humor—an assertion (implied or otherwise) that pulls the reader's mind away from the purpose of the essay.

> Peering out of my sleeping bag, it took a few minutes to orientate myself. My eyes felt glued shut, but the cool, crisp air and dim early morning light soothed my rather abrupt awakening.

This student makes us imagine an "it" peering out of the sleeping bag. And the reader has to pause at the word "but," because we don't understand its logic with the following clause.

> The birds scurried from the tree like a crowd fleeing a theater in which someone yelled 'fire.'

Do birds, like squirrels, scurry?

We dyed the Easter eggs, after having boiled them in water.

There is no reason for this reversal of sequence of events—even though the reader, having paused in his reading, may be searching for one.

Some students, then, write for their own understanding, not their readers'. Since they know what they mean, they do not stop to consider how someone else might question the writer's logic.

The habit of writing logically can help make exact *any* kind of writing; it can also help keep the prose grammatical. After all, grammar is the "logic" of the language.

A FINAL WORD

At the beginning of this book, I told you that to write well you need both outsight and insight, the outsight that the editor's and reader's mind provides and the insight of the writer who has practiced communicating feeling, seeing, and reasoning. The writing principles of Part 1 will help you keep your prose clear, graceful, and fresh. Writing feeling will help you understand tone and rhythm; writing seeing will help you understand the visual power of language; writing reasoning will make you familiar with form, organization, and smooth movement. The result may be a prose style unique to you, but still thoughtful, rhythmic, visual and clear, graceful and fresh. But outsight and insight, while useful distinctions to make in order to teach writing, are not two separate elements of writing, but rather two kinds of "sight" that work in harmony, often so closely that you cannot distinguish them. Thus, you edit as you write and write while you edit. At one moment, consumed with the speed of thought, you are not thinking about writing principles; at another moment, leisurely reviewing what you have written, you are still thinking about your ideas *as* you de-

liberately apply writing principles. This give-and-take cooperation between insight and outsight after a while becomes so natural that the distinction blurs. When this happens you will have
acquired the Writer's Mind.

WRITING ASSIGNMENTS

As in all assignments, writing about something that genuinely
interests you will make the task more pleasant. I encourage you
to select a topic of current concern to you and argue your point
of view. Here are a few suggestions to get you thinking:

1. Should children below age sixteen be allowed to model
sexually suggestive clothing?

2. Should gay people be allowed to adopt children?

3. Is football having a negative effect on the teenage audience?

4. Has sex education had a positive or negative effect upon
high-school students?

5. Is science more important than art to society?

6. Should the ERA become part of our constitution?

7. Should criminals declared insane go to hospitals or pris-
ons?

8. Should prayer be allowed in public schools?

9. Are there any circumstances in which "mercy killing"
should be legal?

10. Should legislators enjoy immunity from prosecution in
all misdemeanor cases?

APPENDIX

On page 44 I urge you to get a handbook in which you'll find the grammar and punctuation of the language thoroughly presented. I repeat that urging here. But for some of you, a handbook full of rules, habits, and exceptions to rules and habits is too intimidating; for others, there are just too many uninteresting things to remember. To unintimidate the intimidated and to interest the uninterested, I have prepared a brief review of what over a decade of teaching has taught me—the most common mistakes in grammar and punctuation and the points in grammar and punctuation that give students the most trouble. If you can master the following benign rules that govern English, you will be well on your way to cleaning up your prose—and perhaps ready for the handbook I recommend that you read.

GRAMMAR

Pronouns and Case

In English, we put our pronouns into three cases: nominative, objective, possessive. I use the nominative if "I" am the subject of a sentence: *I* hit the ball. I use the objective case if "I" am the object of some action: The ball hit *me.* I use the possessive case if "I" own the ball: It is *my* ball. Here are the cases for pronouns.

Nominative	Objective	Possessive
I	me	my, mine
you	you	your, yours
she	her	her, hers
he	him	his
it	it	its
we	us	our, ours
they	them	their, theirs

Most of the time you will recognize a pronoun in the wrong case: "I threw the ball to she." But you might *not* recognize the ones discussed below—the most common mistakes made with pronouns and case.

Objective Case

Over the past few years the number of persons who do not understand the objective case has been increasing. One possible explanation for this increase is that many television and radio news reporters and sportscasters daily reinforce this lack of understanding through their own ungrammatical utterances. I have heard all of the following stated on television or radio, and all are ungrammatical.

1. Come out and see Marty and I at the Village Shopping Center.

2. Between the F.B.I. and he is a curtain of informants.

3. The ambassador brought a bouquet of roses for the President and she.

4. Between you and I, Carmen, I can't guess why the President chose to give an interview at this time.

5. They will bring Bill and I a victory.

There are two kinds of mistakes here. The first and most common one results from failure to remember that prepositions (to, for, by, toward, between) must have objects, and that the objects are always in the objective case. The correct versions of sentences 2, 3, and 4 are as follows:

2. Between the F.B.I. and him is a curtain of informants.

3. The ambassador brought a bouquet of roses for the President and her.

4. Between you and me, Carmen, I can't guess why the President chose to give an interview at this time.

The second mistake results from not putting the object of a verb in the objective case. In sentences 1 and 5 above, the nominative "I" is used as the object of the verbs "see" and "bring." This mistake usually occurs in a long sentence or around a conjunction. For example, even the speaker in sentence 1 above probably wouldn't say, "Come out and see I at the Village Shopping Center." But when words come between verbs and pronouns ("Marty and I"), they seem to draw attention away from the role of the pronoun in the sentence.

Although not pervasive yet, an increase in the following kind of error is also occurring. This example is from the UPI wire service: "Pete Stockton filed suit alleging the F.B.I. violated the civil rights of himself and his boss." "Himself," like herself or itself, is a reflexive pronoun (see my discussion on p. 295) and not the objective case of the pronoun he. The correct version of the sentence would be: "Pete Stockton filed suit alleging the F.B.I. violated the civil rights of him and his boss." Of course, it would sound better if he wrote "The F.B.I. violated his and his boss's civil rights."

Another point about the objective case concerns the word "but," which can be a conjunction (everybody went, but I stayed home) or a preposition (everybody went but me). When used as a preposition (when "but" means "except"), the pronoun that follows it is always in the objective case. Perhaps because they think it sounds more "educated," many people will make statements like the following:

> She told her story to no one but Alex and he.
>
> No senators but Cranstone and he opposed the bill.

When "but" means "except," it is a preposition and the pronouns that follow must take the objective case.

> She told her story to no one but Alex and him.
>
> No senators but Cranstone and him opposed the bill.

Nominative Case

Once again, most of the time you probably properly place your nominative-case pronouns. The most common mistakes are the following:

> It was him who stood outside the court.
>
> The President and her stood on the south balcony.
>
> If I were her, I would not compromise on the amendment.

The nominative case is reserved for either the subject of the sentence or for what grammarians call the *predicate nominative* —what they mean is that no "to be" verb (in any of its tenses—is, was, were, for example) has an object. Instead it links one thing to another, including pronouns, which must always stay in the same case. Always.

Here is the correct use of case:

Subject
The President and she stood on the south balcony.

Predicate nominative
It was he who stood outside the court.

If I were she, I would not compromise on the amendment.

The problem with *who* and *whom* is also a problem of confusing case. "Who" is the nominative case and never receives any action. "Whom" is the objective case and is always the object of a verb or preposition.

Who, he inquired, will take his place?

Whom did they elect?

To whom should we send the report?

My advice to you is to use *who* when you are sure it's the nominative case, *whom* when you are sure it's the objective case (to whom, for whom, by whom) and don't use either if you're ever in doubt.

I offer a final word. *Appositives* are nouns or pronouns that restate or clarify a preceding noun or pronoun: "Only one member of my family—Carol—has red hair." Remember that a pronoun used as an appositive must take the same case as the word to which it refers. For example:

Two Democrats, Burkett and he, voted against the two Republicans—him and me.

Only two journalists won the award—Langston and I.

They gave the award to two journalists—Langston and me.

Adverbs

When, after, and *where* are adverbs. Adverbs modify adjectives (*deeply* hidden secret) or verbs (He arrived *after* she left) or other adverbs (The river flowed *very* swiftly). *When, after,* and *where* often introduce entire clauses that modify a verb or adjective.

> Babies laugh when you tickle their toes. *(The entire clause introduced by "when" modifies "laugh.")*
>
> After the explosion, he darted from the alley. *(The entire phrase introduced by "after" modifies "darted.")*

With this in mind, consider the illogic of the following.

> Censorship is when one group of people tells another what it can't read.

What does *when* modify? Nothing. Censorship isn't a *when* —it is an instance, practice, or a state, but not a *when.* Correctly written, then: "Censorship is the practice of one group telling another what it can't read." To say that "Ignition is when the spark meets the gas" makes no sense. It should be, "Ignition *occurs* when the spark meets the gas." "Her entrance was after the President had made the toast" should be written, "Her entrance *came* after. . . ." or "She entered. . . ." Her entrance isn't an "after." And a last example: not "My happiest moments were when I was with her," but "My happiest moments *came* when I was with her."

Just remember that you should never write "is where," "is when," "is after," or "was where," "was when," or "was after." Perhaps the most common error is, "There is where he works." It should be, "He works there."

"The reason why" is also a recurring misuse of grammar. *Why* is an adverb. It is used to modify adverbs—"I don't know *why* your mother wouldn't let you play football." It is not used as a substitute for "that." We can't say "The reason why I didn't play football was that my mother wouldn't let me." The *why* is unnecessary to meaning and not a proper use of the adverb.

Which/That

Simply put, use *which* to introduce a clause or phrase that isn't necessary to the meaning of your sentence—anything you might just as well enclose inside parentheses.

Lois Turner's art show, which contained mainly self-portraits, was not well received by the critics.

Use *that* to introduce a clause or phrase that *is* necessary to the meaning of the sentence.

Lois Turner's art show that contained mainly self-portraits was not well received by the critics.

In the second version we know that Lois Turner had more than one art show, and the writer is singling out the one that included the self-portraits.

Relative Pronouns

Don't confuse *where* (an adverb) with *that* (a relative pronoun).

I saw on television where my favorite actor is retiring from acting.

I saw on television that my favorite actor is retiring from acting.

Where must always modify an adjective, verb, or other adverb.

Dangling Modifiers

Any time you introduce a sentence with a modifying phrase or clause, make certain there is something for it to modify. For example, if I say, "Flying through the thick trees, the hunter missed the bird," you would call to my attention that I have said that the hunter was flying through the trees. But would you notice the dangling modifier in the following?

After considering the third contract, the decision was made.

"After considering the third contract" is just dangling. Who or what does it modify? Try another:

Having warned you in our last billing, service is now cut off.

Always check those introductory phrases to make sure there is a word for them to modify.

Verbs

Here are the most commonly misused verbs.

Present	Past	Past Participle
arise	arose	arisen
begin	began	begun
blew	blew	blown
break	broke	broken
choose	chose	chosen
eat	ate	eaten
lead	led	led
spring	sprang	sprung
tear	tore	torn
lay (to place)	laid	laid
lie (to recline)	lay	lain
lie (to tell a lie)	lied	lied
sit	sat	sat
set (to place)	set	set

The most common mistake involves the verb lie. Someone who says, "I laid down under the tree and cried," has said that he put duck feathers (down) under the tree and cried. What the speaker meant was, "I lay down under the tree and cried." It may sound foreign, but it's standard English. I lie down today. I lay down yesterday. I will have lain there for three days.

The champ knocked him to the canvas. He lay there for five minutes.

The old manuscripts were lying (reclining) on his desk.

They weren't "laying" because manuscripts don't own hands with which to lay something.

Either/Neither

When you use *either/or* or *neither/nor* with the subject of your sentence, the *second* noun or pronoun determines the verb you will use. The following are not correct.

Neither Laura nor I are a member.   *(am)*

Neither Laura nor he are a member.   *(is)*

Either you or I are leaving.   *(am)*

Everyone/Someone

Everyone, everybody, no one, nobody, someone, and *somebody* are all singular and so are the pronouns that refer to them. The following are incorrect.

Everyone must pull their own weight.   *(his)*

Everyone was yelling with their hands held high in the air. *(his)*

Nobody in the company has sent in their report.   *(his)*

Either and *neither* are singular and take singular verbs.

Reflexive Pronouns

They hurt theirselves by signing the contract.

He told John and myself to postpone the trip until Monday.

Neither one of these sentences is grammatically correct. "Theirself" is not a word. "Myself" is a reflexive pronoun. That means that it *reflects,* like a mirror, back upon the subject. "Myself" in the above sentence reflects "he," and "he" is not the reflection of myself. Use herself, himself, myself, themselves, itself when the actor and the receiver of the action are the same:

She dressed herself.

They hurt themselves.

It worked against itself.

You do not say: Some friends and myself strolled through the garden.

You may also use the reflexive pronoun as an intensifier or magnifier when a simple *he* or *she* or *I* or *they* is not emphatic enough.

I myself solved the puzzle.

Baseball itself is killing baseball.

She will speak to no one but the Queen herself.

PUNCTUATION

The Comma

1. Use a comma between two complete sentences that are connected by a conjunction (and, but, or, etc.)

I like contemporary music, but my sister prefers Chopin.   *(two sentences)*

I did everything to find them but set a fire.   *(one sentence)*

There is an exception. The "rule" requires us to place a comma between two sentences connected by a conjunction. Thus, I must write:

She is the oldest teacher, and I have taught the longest.

But when the subject of both sentences is the same (although not restated in the second sentence), omit the comma:

She is the oldest teacher and has taught here fifty years.

2. Use a comma to isolate a parenthetical element (phrases or clauses not necessary to the meaning of the sentence).

Four nations, along with seven major universities, are studying the island.

The money, as a matter of fact, is still in the secret account.

John Stanford, who played major league baseball, joined our firm yesterday.

John Stanford who played major league baseball joined our firm yesterday.

Note that in the first version the point that Stanford played baseball is just an extra bit of information. In the second version we know that there must be two John Stanfords—one who played baseball and one who did not.

3. Use a comma to isolate transitional words and phrases that occur at the beginning or in the middle of a sentence.

According to the report, the company increased its wages 12 percent.

There still are, however, several more questions I'd like to ask.

Moreover, she didn't speak to me for a week.

4. Use commas to separate adjectives that have been taken out of their normal word-order.

The storm, merciless and fierce, kept pounding the old ship.

5. Use commas to isolate items in a series.

Plato, Aristotle, Marx, and Jung are four writers I try to avoid. *(Yes, always use that last comma.)*

I have come to stay, to learn, to grow, to flourish.

Note: A very common error is this:

I have no choice but to sneak out of the house tonight, I hope my brother is asleep.

Commas do not separate two sentences. For this, you need a semicolon or a period.

Now let me fudge a little. You may place only a comma between two sentences if they are of identical construction, very short, and if, by doing so, you create a special rhythm.

I came, I saw, I conquered.

Easy come, easy go.

Some you win, some you lose.

An important concluding point. All punctuation must have a purpose. You cannot scatter commas around hoping one will hit. If there is a general rule governing punctuation, it is that there should be no unnecessary punctuation. As Hawthorne says, "The greatest possible mint of style is to make the words absolutely disappear into thought."

The Dash

The dash signals a sudden and momentary break from the anticipated train of thought. Like the queen in a chess game, it can perform the function of other "pieces" of punctuation.

1. It can, like commas and parentheses, set off unessential material from the sentence:

The inhabitants of my backyard—the squirrel, the sparrow, the owl—always disappear in December.

The inhabitants of my backyard (the squirrel, the sparrow, the owl) always disappear in December.

The inhabitants of my backyard, the squirrel, the sparrow, the owl, always disappear in December.

2. It can, like the colon, indicate something is to follow:

He maintained one constant goal: not to maintain one constant goal.

He maintained one constant goal—not to maintain one constant goal.

3. It can, like the comma, create pauses you would supply if speaking the words:

> Uncle Wallace couldn't resist pecan pie—especially that baked by Aunt Erna.

The dash is particularly useful for creating "effective pauses—a pause that adds something to the sentence:

> One can acquire everything in solitude—except character.
> —Stendhal

In writing, the dash is a single line. To create this line on the typewriter use two hyphens. Notice that there is no space between what precedes or follows the dash. Use the dash—though sparingly—to clearly establish relationships among the parts of the sentence or to create an effective rhythm:

> One does not know—cannot know—the best that is in one.
> —Friedrich Wilhelm Nietzsche

The Hyphen

The hyphen is actually a spelling device that indicates you are combining two words to create a new one. "Awful" began as "full of awe," then became awe-full, and finally "awful" "Daisy" moved from "day's eye" to "day's-eye" to "daisy." The hyphen is the intermediate step in a new word's evolution. "Teenage," "lifetime," "bookstore," and "football" were all once hyphenated words. As you write, you will discover that more often than you realize you combine words to create a new meaning. If you write "We send people around the world," there is no reason for a hyphen anywhere. But if you write "We took an around-the-world tour," you are creating an adjective that modifies "tour"; since an adjective is *one* word, you indicate as much with the hyphens. "In a well-timed maneuver, his soft-spoken and self-contained sister-in-law poured her drink into his." The hyphens indicate these are to be treated as one word.

The Senate may vote thirty-two to fifty-four. But "a thirty-two-to-fifty-four vote defeated the proposal." "the nineteenth century gave us Darwin, Dickens, and James," but "the nineteenth-century vase was stolen from the museum."

Proper use of the hyphen can clear up ambiguity. In the business world there have been instances of a single hyphen costing a firm thousands of dollars. The *Wall Street Journal* reported that a supervisor for a government, nuclear installation "ordered rods of radioactive material cut into '10 foot long lengths': he got 10 pieces, each a foot long, instead of the 10-foot lengths required."

The Colon

The colon is a symbol for an expression like, "The following," or "for example," or "here comes an illustration." And something must follow. It is usually a little longer pause than a dash. Remember that a colon must always be preceded by an independent clause.

He likes three subjects in school: art, history, physics.

One more goal is about to be accomplished: a degree in math from the university.

The witness gave the following names: Smith, Jones, Harris.

All the elements of a good mystery were there: the butler, the maid, the murder knife still wet with blood.

The Semicolon

Semicolons separate equal parts of a sentence or sentences.

1. They separate words in a series when commas are already in much use.

The finalists are from Bridgeport, Connecticut; Hamilton, Ohio; Killeen, Texas; New York, New York; Chicago, Illinois.

2. They separate two independent (and thus equal) sentences not connected by a conjunction.

Conservatives conform to the habits of their fathers; liberals conform to the habits of their peers.

3. You may use a semicolon to separate two independent sentences that are already separated by a conjunction for the following reasons:
a. You desire to create a longer pause than a comma:

There was no hope; so I cried.

b. The two sentences are either very long or already heavily punctuated with commas.

To her, the trip was boring, monotonous, and filled with drudgery; but the rest of us thought it was exhilarating, stimulating, and fun.

4. The semicolon separates sentences joined by conjunctive adverbs (therefore, thus, consequently, however, moreover, hence, also, nevertheless, likewise, then).

I do, indeed, like you very much; however, I do not ever intend to marry.

Jack studied harder than every other student; thus, he outscored everyone on the exam.

Remember that the semicolon separates equals; it does not function as a colon.

There are three kinds of boys she doesn't like; tall, short, and medium.   *(incorrect)*

It does not (as a comma does) separate unequal parts of the sentence:

In addition; we must plan to leave early.   *(incorrect)*

Parentheses

Parentheses and the dash can perform the same function. Use of parentheses usually indicates that the information enclosed is more of an independent clause than that separated by a dash:

As we opened the door to the winter wind (I had already buttoned my coat), we all turned away from the storm.

The entire romantic movement (if I might be so bold as to remind you) depended upon the industrial revolution's creation of an unromantic society that could be attacked.

The entire romantic movement—its interest in the Gothic and the macabre—began with capitalism creating real horrors.

Of course, there is one more function of the evening—the one we all most want to see.

The Apostrophe

Three brief comments about the apostrophe.

1. Possessive personal pronouns do not use an apostrophe.

Its *(not it's);* theirs *(not their's);* hers *(not her's)*

The most common misuse of the apostrophe occurs with the possessive pronoun "it." Accustomed to showing possession with the apostrophe (Carol's book; John's hat), many writers forget that possessive personal pronouns do not take an apostrophe. Thus, they may write, "The tree has shed *it's* leaves." It should be "its leaves."

2. Use an apostrophe for plurals of numbers, figures, years, decades, letters.*

He rolled two 12's.

---

*You will find some difference of opinion on this rule. Some handbooks recommend omitting the apostrophe in numbers and letters. Your main concern should be to remain consistent in use of the apostrophe.

He gave the banker seven 20's.

The 1900's were a time of literary turmoil.

I've made three A's this semester.

3. Use apostrophes for plurals of words removed from their meaning. Compare the difference in meaning in the following:

You use too many but's in that sentence.
You use too many if's in that paragraph.

Take out the garbage, Johnny, no ands, ifs, or buts.
I don't know if we should sign it, boss. I think there are too many ifs in that contract.

Italics

Usage dictates that you italicize (which is indicated by underscore with the typewriter) foreign words, the titles of books, plays, long poems, newspapers, magazines, the names of ships, planes, trains, and space shuttles.

Other than these, you may use italics whenever you please. Most writers use italics to:

1. Create emphasis—"Human reason needs only to will more strongly than fate, and she *is* fate."

—Thomas Mann

2. Force the reader to stress words and thus use mental inflection to interpret more clearly the meaning of words—"I said the judge was *disinterested* in the case, not uninterested."

Don't be too timid to use italics, especially to emphasize those words you would naturally stress in speech, but don't overdo it. If *too* many *words* are stressed *in* a paragraph, *then* you remove all effect from any *single* italicized word.

Quotation Marks

Use quotation marks for the following reasons:

1. To indicate the words they enclose are not your own.

"To strive and not to yield" has been my approach to life.

2. To enclose the titles of articles, short stories, and short poems. (Titles of book-length poems such as *Paradise Lost* are italicized.)

In an article entitled "Of Will and Women," Ms. Johnson adopts the feminist position.

3. To indicate you are using a word or words in a way different from the original meaning.

He had a wonderful "time" in prison.

Periods and commas always go inside the quotation mark:

After I read the poem "Sailing to Byzantium," I began the exam.

John said that that was something he just could not "do."

Semicolons and colons go outside the quotation mark:

He stressed three points about "Kubla Khan": rhythm, grace, beauty.

I liked King's "Letter from Birmingham Jail"; I wish I could quote it.

•INDEX•

♦ ACKNOWLEDGMENTS ♦

PART ♦ ONE

Chapter 1

Russell Baker, "Little Red Riding Hood Revisited" in *So This Is Depravity.* New York: Congdon and Lattes, Inc., 1980.

Chapter 2

Joseph Conrad, *The Nigger of the Narcissus,* 1897.

"On Human Life" from "Resolutions: Social Sciences; Human Life; Science Education" in *News Report,* July 1981. Reprinted by permission of the National Academy of Sciences.

From *The Tree Where Man Was Born* by Peter Matthiessen and Eliot Porter. Published in the United States by E. P. Dutton. All rights reserved under International and Pan-American Copyright Conventions. Reprinted by permission of the Publisher, E. P. Dutton, Inc.

From "The Jeaning of America and the World" by Carin C. Quinn in *American Heritage,* April/May 1978. Copyright © 1978 by American Heritage Publishing Co., Inc. Reprinted by permission.

Extract from *Stride Toward Freedom* by Martin Luther King, Jr., p. 212. Copyright © 1958 by Martin Luther King, Jr. Reprinted by permission of Harper & Row, Publishers, Inc.

From "The Bird and the Machine" in *The Immense Journey* by Loren Eiseley. Copyright © 1957 by Loren Eiseley. Reprinted by permission of Random House, Inc.

From "How to Drive Fast on Drugs While Getting Your Wing-Wang Squeezed and Not Spill Your Drink" by P. J. O'Rourke in *National Lampoon,* March 1979. Copyright © 1979 by National Lampoon, Inc. Reprinted by permission.

From "The University of Texas, Inc." by Carmen Hill in *The Daily Texan,* August 5, 1981. Reprinted by permission of the author.

William H. Emmons et al., *Geology: Principles and Processes.* New York: McGraw-Hill Book Company, Inc., 1960.

From "A Calm Look at Abortion Arguments" by Roger Bissell. Reprinted, with permission, from the September 1981 issue of *Reason.* Copyright © 1981 by the Reason Foundation, Box 40105, Santa Barbara, CA 93103.

H. V. Morton, *In Search of the Holy Land,* book jacket. New York: Dodd, Mead & Company, Inc., 1934.

Karen Horney, *The Neurotic Personality of Our Time.* New York: W. W. Norton and Company, 1937.

Edward T. Hall, *The Hidden Dimension.* New York: Doubleday & Company, Inc., 1966.

From "Inward Bound" by Ellen Goodman. Copyright © 1981 by The Boston Globe Newspaper Company/Washington Post Writers Group. Reprinted with permission.

From "A View of the Solar System" and "Why the Sky Looks Blue" in *The Stars in Their Courses* by Sir James Jeans. Copyright 1954 by Cambridge University Press. Reprinted by permission.

From "A Dirge for Social Climbers" by Paul Fussell in *The New Republic,* July 19, 1980. Reprinted by permission of The New Republic, © 1980 The New Republic, Inc.

Erwin Panofsky, "Style and Medium in the Moving Pictures." *Bulletin of the Department of Art and Archaeology,* Princeton University, 1934.

Margaret Church, *Time and Reality: Studies in Comtemporary Fiction.* Chapel Hill, North Carolina: University of North Carolina Press, 1963.

James Underwood Crockett, *Bulbs.* Alexandria, Virginia: Time-Life Books, Inc., 1971.

From "A Warning to Smokers" by Dr. Howard Temin in *Wisconsin State Journal,* March 3, 1976. Reprinted by permission of the Wisconsin State Journal.

From "Packaged Sentiment" by Richard Rhodes in *Harper's,* December 1971. Copyright © 1971 by Richard Rhodes. Reprinted by permission of JCA Literary Agency, Inc.

From "Opening" in "Talk of the Town" in *The New Yorker,* January 24, 1983. Copyright © 1983 by The New Yorker Magazine Inc. Reprinted by permission.

From "Unnameable Objects, Unspeakable Crimes" by James Baldwin. Reprinted by permission of Edward J. Acton, Inc.

Margot Fonteyn, *A Dancer's World.* New York: Alfred A. Knopf, 1979.

From "Return of the Native" by Susan Schiefelbein in *Saturday Review,* November 1977. Copyright © 1977 by Saturday Review Magazine Co. Reprinted by permission.

From "Death in the Open" from *The Lives of a Cell* by Lewis Thomas. Copyright © 1973 by The Massachusetts Medical Society. Copyright © 1974 by Lewis Thomas. Reprinted by permission of Viking Penguin Inc.

From "The Reciprocity of Words and Numbers" by Joan Baum in *The Chronicle of Higher Education,* April 3, 1978. Copyright © 1978 by Editorial Projects for Education, Inc. Reprinted by permission of The Chronicle of Higher Education and the author.

From "Vulture Country" by John D. Stewart. Copyright © 1959 by The Atlantic Monthly Company. Reprinted by permission of Paul R. Reynolds, Inc.

Chapter 3

From "Sonnet xxvii" in *Collected Poems* by Edna St. Vincent Millay. Copyright 1923, 1951 by Edna St. Vincent Millay. Reprinted by permission of Norma Millay Ellis.

Robert Browning, "The Lost Leader" in *Dramatic Romances and Lyrics,* 1845.

T. S. Eliot, "Tradition and Individual Talent" in *Selected Essays.* New York: Harcourt Brace & World, 1960, p. 10.

From *Of a Fire on the Moon* by Norman Mailer. Copyright © 1969, 1980 by Norman Mailer. By permission of Little, Brown and Company.

William Faulkner, "On Receiving the Nobel Prize," from *Essays of the Masters,* edited by Charles Neider. New York: Rinehart & Company, Inc., 1956.

From "The Enigmas of De Chirico" by Robert Hughes in *Time,* April 12, 1982. Copyright © 1982 by Time Inc. All rights reserved. Reprinted by permission from *Time.*

General Douglas MacArthur, "Duty, Honor, Country." Address given at the U.S. Military Academy, West Point, May 12, 1962.

Albert Edward Wiggam, *The New Decalogue of Science.* Indianapolis: The Bobbs-Merrill Company, 1923, p. 30.

Jill Jonnes, "The Tale of Tea, A Fragrant Brew Steeped in History." *Smithsonian,* February 1982.

From "Lovers vs. Workers" by Sam Keen in *Quest,* September 1981. Reprinted by permission of the author.

Loren Eiseley, from "One Night's Dying," in *The Night Country.* Copyright © 1971 by Loren Eiseley. Reprinted with the permission of Charles Scribner's Sons.

Gay Talese, "New York Is a City of Things Unnoticed." *Esquire,* 1960.

From "Selections from the Allen Notebooks" in *Without Feathers* by Woody Allen. Copyright © 1973 by Woody Allen. Reprinted by permission of Random House, Inc. and the author.

Virginia Woolf, *The Death of the Moth and Other Essays.* New York: Harcourt Brace Jovanovich, Inc., 1942.

Andrew A. Rooney, excerpts from "Baseball" and "In Praise of New York City" from *A Few Minutes with Andy Rooney.* Copyright © 1981 by Essay Productions, Inc. Reprinted with the permission of Atheneum Publishers.

Luis Marden, "Bamboo, the Giant Grass." *National Geographic,* October 1980.

From *Man and Superman* by George Bernard Shaw. Copyright © 1957 by The Public Trustee as Executor of the Estate of George Bernard Shaw. Reprinted by permission of The Society of Authors on behalf of the Bernard Shaw Estate.

Michael Shodell, "The Curative Light." *Science 82,* April 1982.

C. G. Jung, "The Meaning of Psychology for Modern Man" in *Civilization in Transition,* 2nd edition. Princeton, New Jersey: Princeton University Press, 1970, pp. 144–145.

James Baldwin, *Notes of a Native Son.* Boston: Beacon Press, 1955.

Reprinted from "Politics and the English Language" in *Shooting an Elephant and Other Essays* by George Orwell by permission of Harcourt Brace Jovanovich, Inc., the estate of the late Sonia Brownell Orwell and Martin Secker & Warburg Ltd. Copyright 1946 by Sonia Brownell Orwell; renewed 1974 by Sonia Orwell.

"Types of Introductory Paragraphs" by Reed Sanderlin. Reprinted by permission of the author.

Albert Rosenfield, "Marijuana: Millions of Turned-on Users." *Life,* July 7, 1967.

Robert Penn Warren, *Southern Harvest.* Houghton Mifflin, 1967, p. xi.

Exerpt from Charles Hudson's review of *Recollected Essays* by Wendell Berry, in *The Georgia Review,* Spring 1982. Copyright © 1982 by the University of Georgia. Reprinted by permission.

From "Is Language Sexist? One Small Step for Genkind" by Casey Miller and Kate Swift in *The New York Times Magazine,* April 16, 1972. Copyright © 1972 by The New York Times Company. Reprinted by permission.

From "Flextime: Work When You Want To" by Barry Stein, Allen Cohen and Herman Gadon in *Psychology Today,* June 1976. Copyright © 1976 by American Psychological Association. Reprinted by permission.

From "The Bloody Sport of Film Criticism" by John Simon in *Horizon,* July 1978. Copyright © 1978 by John Simon. Reprinted with permission from Wallace & Sheil Agency.

Jessica Mitford, *The American Way of Death.* New York: Simon & Schuster, 1963.

Daniel Bell, "Liberalism in the Postindustrial Society" in *The Winding Passage.* Cambridge, Massachusetts: Abt Books, 1980, p. 228.

Carl N. Degler, "Indians and Other Americans." *Commentary,* 1972.

Rudolph Chelminski, "Recollections of a Childhood Friend Named Crow-crow." *Smithsonian,* September 1982.

Aldous Huxley, *Brave New World Revisited.* New York: Harper & Row, 1958.

Walter Terence Stace, "Man Against Darkness." *The Atlantic Monthly,* September 1948.

From "A 'Shark' Goes After the Evidence" in *Time,* January 18, 1982. Copyright © 1982 by Time Inc. All rights reserved. Reprinted by permission from *Time.*

From "The Town Dump" in *Wolf Willow* by Wallace Stegner. Reprinted by permission of the author.

Virginia Woolf, "How Should One Read a Book?" in *The Second Common Reader.* New York: Harcourt Brace Jovanovich, 1932.

From "New Superstitions for Old" in *A Way of Seeing* by Margaret Mead and Rhoda Metraux. Copyright © 1966, 1970 by Margaret Mead and Rhoda Metraux. Reprinted by permission of William Morrow & Company.

From "The Potato" in *The Worm Forgives the Plough* by John Stewart Collis. Copyright © 1973 by John Stewart Collis. Reprinted by permission of George Braziller, Inc., One Park Avenue, New York.

Book review of Allen Wier's *Blanco,* by Don Graham in *Western American Literature,* Winter 1980. Reprinted by permission of Don Graham.

Roger Rosenblatt, "Lebanon: A Legacy of Dreams and Guns." *Time,* January 11, 1982.

William Golding, "Party of One—Thinking as a Hobby." *Holiday,* August 1961.

Marya Mannes, *But Will It Sell?* New York: J. B. Lippincott Company, 1964.

From "A Ride Through Spain" in *The Dogs Bark: Public People and Private Places* by Truman Capote. Copyright 1946 by Truman Capote. Reprinted by permission of Random House, Inc.

From "The Nation Emerges from 25 Dark Years with Too Few Frogs" by James P. Sterba in *The Wall Street Journal,* December 7, 1982. Copyright © 1982 by Dow Jones & Company, Inc. Reprinted by permission of The Wall Street Journal. All rights reserved.

From "Medium" by Jonathan Miller in *THE NEW YORKER,* November 16, 1963. Copyright © 1963 by The New Yorker Magazine, Inc. Reprinted by permission.

"Though Unofficial, Spring Comes Early in Spots" by James Kilpatrick. Copyright © 1977 by Universal Press Syndicate. Reprinted with permission. All rights reserved.

PART ◆ TWO

From "Sailing on Sunlight May Give Space Travel a Second Wind" by Eric Drexler in *Smithsonian,* February 1982. Copyright © 1982 by Eric Drexler. Reprinted by permission of The Sterling Lord Agency, Inc.

Barry Lopez, "A Presentation of Whales." *Harper's,* March 1980.

Loren Eiseley, from "Instruments of Darkness," in *The Night Country.* Copyright © 1964, 1966 by Loren Eiseley. Reprinted with the permission of Charles Scribner's Sons.

Bruno Bettelheim, *The Informed Heart.* New York: The Free Press, 1960.

From "The Physiology of the Giraffe" by James V. Warren in *Scientific American,* November 1974. Copyright © 1974 by Scientific American, Inc. Reprinted by permission.

From "The Spider and the Wasp" by Alexander Petrunkevitch in *Scientific American,* August 1952. Copyright 1952 by Scientific American, Inc. Reprinted by permission.

''Match'' and ''Blast Furnace'' from *The Way Things Work: An Illustrated Encyclopedia of Technology.* Copyright © 1967 by George Allen & Unwin, Ltd. Reprinted by permission of Simon & Schuster, a division of Gulf & Western Corporation.

John Muir. *The Mountains of California.* The Century Co., 1894.

From ''In Praise of Gadgeteers'' in *Spindrift* by John J. Rowlands. Copyright © 1960 by W. W. Norton & Company, Inc. Reprinted by permission.

Aldous Huxley, ''Selected Snobberies'' in *Music at Night and Other Essays.* New York: Harper & Row, Publishers, Inc., 1931.

PART ◆ THREE

Chapter 4

T. S. Eliot, ''Introduction to Selected Poems of Marianne Moore.'' New York: Macmillan Company, 1935.

Reprinted by permission of *Times Books* /The New York Times Book Co., Inc. from *The Star Thrower* by Loren Eiseley. Copyright © 1978 by the Estate of Loren C. Eiseley.

From ''Gamalielese'' by H. L. Mencken in *The Baltimore Sun,* March 7, 1921. Reprinted by permission of the Enoch Pratt Free Library in accordance with the terms of the will of H. L. Mencken.

From ''Columbia's Landing Closes a Circle'' by Tom Wolfe in *National Geographic,* October 1981. Reprinted by permission of National Geographic Magazine and International Creative Management.

David Noonan, ''The Ears of the Earth.'' *Esquire,* April 1982, p. 56.

From ''The New Age of Reason'' by John M. Culkin in *Science Digest,* August 1981. First appeared in *Science Digest* © 1981 by The Hearst Corporation. Reprinted by permission of the author.

''Wooley'' by Mark Strand, originally in *The New Yorker,* April 14, 1980. Copyright © 1980 by Mark Strand. Reprinted by permission of The New Yorker.

''Printed Noise'' by George Will. Copyright © 1981 by The Washington Post Company. Reprinted with permission.

From ''Science, a Wellspring of Our Discontent'' by Walter Orr Roberts in *American Scientist,* March 1967. Reprinted by permission.

Chapter 5

Douglas H. Chadwick, ''Our Wildest Wilderness.'' *National Geographic,* December 1979.

Malcolm Lowry, *Under the Volcano.* London: Jonathan Cape, 1947.

Alexander H. Leighton, ''That Day at Hiroshima.'' *Atlantic Monthly,* October 1946.

Excerpts from "A Hanging" and "Shooting an Elephant" in *Shooting an Elephant and Other Essays* by George Orwell are reprinted by permission of Harcourt Brace Jovanovich, Inc., the estate of the late Sonia Brownell Orwell and Martin Secker & Warburg Ltd. Copyright 1950 by Sonia Orwell; renewed 1978 by Sonia Pitt-Rivers.

Extract from *Pilgrim at Tinker Creek* by Annie Dillard, p. 20. Copyright © 1974 by Annie Dillard. Reprinted by permission of Harper & Row, Publishers, Inc.

Charles Dickens, *Bleak House,* 1853.

Frank Norris, *The Octopus,* 1901.

From "Tickets, Please" from *The Complete Short Stories of D. H. Lawrence,* Volume II. Copyright 1922 by Thomas Seltzer, Inc. Copyright renewed 1950 by Frieda Lawrence. Reprinted by permission of Viking Penguin Inc.

Exerpt from "The Last American Hero" from *The Kandy Kolored Tangerine Flake Streamline Baby* by Tom Wolfe. Copyright © 1965 by Thomas K. Wolfe, Jr. Reprinted by permission of Farrar, Straus and Giroux, Inc.

"Bathtub Theorem" from *Dictionary of Economics and Business* by Erwin Esser Nemmers. Copyright © 1978 by Littlefield, Adams & Co. Reprinted by permission.

Rachel Carson, "The Sunless Sea" in *The Sea Around Us.* New York: Oxford University Press, 1950.

Lance Morrow, "Of Time and the Falklands." *Time,* April 19, 1982, p. 88.

Isak Dinesen, *Out of Africa.* New York: Random House, 1938.

From "A Large Number of Persons" by Paul Gallico in *Vanity Fair,* 1931. Copyright 1931 by Conde Nast Publications Inc. Reprinted by permission of Harold Ober Associates Incorporated.

From *The Yosemite* by John Muir. Copyright 1912 by The Century Company. Copyright renewal, 1940 by Wanda Muir Hanna. Reprinted by permission of the publisher, E. P. Dutton, Inc.

"Knoxville: Summer 1915" from *A Death in the Family* by James Agee. Copyright © 1957 by James Agee Trust. Reprinted by permission of the publisher, Grosset & Dunlap.

Chapter 6

Will Durant, *The Story of Philosophy.* New York: Simon & Schuster, 1926.

E. M. Forster, *Aspects of the Novel.* New York: Harcourt Brace Jovanovich, 1927.

Extracts from "Letter from Birmingham Jail, April 16, 1963" in *Why We Can't Wait* by Martin Luther King, Jr., pp. 78, 79, 83–88, 91, 99, and 100. Copyright © 1963 by Martin Luther King, Jr. Reprinted by permission of Harper & Row, Publishers, Inc.

APPENDIX

William R. Blundell, "Confused, Overstuffed Corporate Writing Often Costs Firms Much Time—and Money." *The Wall Street Journal,* August 28, 1980, p. 19.

I am grateful to the following students for lending me their essays: Bob Asmussen, Kathy Blackbird, Joel Bogen, Robert Bush, Eric Craven, Lynda Curik, Mary Farrington, Brian Fest, David Fuller, Bill Groce, Carmen Hill, Susan Jucker, Jeff Kobs, Gerry McKee, Marianne Merritt, Shari Minton, Tony Moos, Peter Nasser, Russell Scott, Steve Shoupp, Scott Statham, Brian Till, Jaci Valtair, Douglas Walla, and Laura Weekley.